FBI'S TEN MOST WANTED

DARY MATERA

HarperTorch
An Imprint of HarperCollinsPublishers

❦

HARPERTORCH
An Imprint of HarperCollins*Publishers*
10 East 53rd Street
New York, New York 10022-5299

First HarperTorch paperback printing: October 2003

HarperCollins®, HarperTorch™, and ❦™ are trademarks of Harper-Collins Publishers Inc.

Printed in the United States of America

Visit HarperTorch on the World Wide Web at www.harpercollins.com

10   9   8   7   6   5   4   3   2   1

In memory of Special Agent Joseph J. Brock, who was gunned down in the line of duty on July 26, 1952 in an attempt to apprehend bank robber Gerhard Arthur Puff, Top Ten Most Wanted Number 30. Puff was captured during the shootout and was executed for Brock's murder two years later.

In memory of Special Agent Leonard W. Hatton, who died while volunteering to help evacuate the burning World Trade Center towers on September 11, 2001. FBI Most Wanted Number 456, terrorist Usama bin Laden, is believed to have masterminded the attacks on the New York landmarks. Bin Laden remains at large.

Contents

. . . .

Contents

Acknowledgments and Announcements

. . . .

Victims of the current or future FBI Top Ten Most Wanted fugitives who would like to submit an open letter about their experiences, and/or directly confront their attacker in subsequent editions of "Most Wanted," can do so by contacting:

Dary Matera
1628 S. Villas Lane
Chandler, Arizona 85248-1804
480-963-7036
dary@darymatera.com
darymatera@cox.net
www.darymatera.com

This offer includes family members of victims as well.

Similarly, any Top Tenners themselves who would like to similarly offer their feelings are welcome to respond as well.

Thanks to:

Chris at *www.bostonmafia.com* for information on Whitey Bulger and the Boston Mob.

Edmond Mahoney of the Hartford Courant for his definitive stories on Victor Gerena.

Frontline, Time, Newsweek and ABC, NBC, CBS, FOX and CNN for their excellent coverage of Osama bin Laden.

The FBI, particularly Ernie Porter and Rex Tomb at headquarters in Washington, Gail Marcinkiewicz in Boston, Ken Neu, Chris Gregorski, Tim Stanislawski, Larua Bosley, Lisa Boll, Nick Rossi, Larry Likar, Bill Nicholson, Tom Anzelmo, Bill Redden, Paul McCabe, Susan Hershcowitz, Frank Scaviti, Todd Dross, William Crowley; and Detective Michael Holguin, PIO Michael Jorden, Marvin Smilon, Herbert Hadad, Pat Clayton, and all the agents and press officers in the field offices around the nation that shared their time.

Special thanks to Sandy Hodson, Greg Rickabaugh, and Frank Matera, along with all the hardworking newspapermen and women, television and radio journalists, and news photographers and cameramen who write history's first draft. Your work is much appreciated and has not been forgotten.

To Nan S. Morffi for her research assistance.

To my editor at William Morrow, Sarah Durand, and my agent, Stedman Mays of Clausen, Tahan and Mays in New York.

Props to John Walsh and the staff of *America's Most Wanted* for their years of service helping track down hundreds of state and federal fugitives. In loving memoriam to John's son Adam Walsh.

And to: Jamie, Kelly, Diedra, PKL, Tom Zoellner, Emily Lyons, the Rev. Ken Hodgeson, the Rev. Greg Cantelmo, MaryAnn, Ben and Greg Adams, Hillary

Celery Roberts, Chassy Violet, Richie Sabol, Reldon Cooper, Priscilla Hernandez, Sister Mary-Dominic Kopitar.

In memoriam to Special Agents Anthony Palmisano, Edwin R. Woodriffe, Jack Coler, Ronald Williams, and Johnnie L. Oliver, who were all killed in the line of duty while pursuing felons who were subsequently placed on the Top Ten Most Wanted list.

Anthony
Palmisano

Edwin
Woodriffe

Jack
Coler

Ronald
Williams

Johnnie
Oliver

Preface

$30 Million in Bounties
Up for Grabs

• •

Never before in the half-century history of the FBI's famous Top Ten fugitive list have the bounties been anything close to this high—$30,065,000. In fact, the price tags on these particular criminals are so lofty that it's possible they're worth more than all the Old West "Wanted: Dead or Alive" outlaws combined.

You don't have to be a professional bounty hunter to collect. Everyone, young or old, is welcome to try. Find one or more of the ten men on the list, notify the FBI, and the money can be yours. It's that simple.

Better act quickly, however, because in all probability you'll never see anything close to this kind of situation again. It's truly a $$$ blip in time.

If searching for ten seems a bit fatiguing, tracking down the top four will still put a healthy $29,750,000 in your pocket. If four is still too much effort, finding a single one, a certain Saudi Arabian bad guy, will reap $27 million. Of course, there would probably be some travel involved with that one.

Throwing the turbaned terrorist out—and for all we know, he's driving a cab in Boise—still leaves a very realistic $3,065,000 on the table. That's available to those insightful enough to spot any of the remaining nine pictured and detailed on the following pages. They're out there somewhere, crossing paths with people every day. One or more could very well be orbiting your world.

For those interested in getting your feet wet by learning some enthralling history of the FBI's Most Wanted list, start by reading the Introduction and Chapter 1. You'll find fascinating information that reveals the evolution of a society as seen through the eyes of our cops and robbers. Others can cut to the literal chase and proceed directly to Chapter 2, where the cash bonanza begins.

There are many ways to become a multimillionaire in America, some traditional, some decidedly not. Being a part-time bounty hunter—or merely an alert citizen—has now become one of them.

Introduction

How and Why the
Most Wanted List Began
. . . .

*For fifty (plus) years the FBI has sought the pub-
lic's assistance in a very special way. Through
the publication of fugitives in various media, beginning with the newspapers and magazines and
now utilizing new technology, such as the Internet, the FBI continues to seek public assistance
in locating wanted fugitives. The FBI's "Ten Most
Wanted Fugitives" celebrates not only a FBI success story, but emphasizes the need for cooperation in the fight against violent crime.*
        —Former FBI director Louis J. Freeh

People can't get enough of top ten lists.

We chart the best-selling pop songs of the week, the
highest grossing movies, the most popular fiction or
nonfiction books, our favorite cars to buy, our favorite
cars to steal, the NBA and college basketball players
who are scoring the most points or grabbing the most
rebounds, the baseball players with the highest batting

averages or home run counts, and the football running backs with the most yards. We break it down further to chart the top ten songs of the year in a dozen different categories, and repeat the year-end process with a zillion other lists. When that's done, the bean counters tally up the decade, quarter-century, half-century, and century figures to produce more lists!

Everything gets top-tenned. Turn the pages of specialty magazines appealing to a tiny niche of aficionados and you'll learn the ten most popular cigars, wines (red, white, bubbly, etc.), chewing gum, breakfast cereals, computer programs, Internet search sites, Internet girly sites, Internet shoelace history sites, Internet (fill in the blank) sites—you name it. A staple of late night comedian David Letterman's quarter-century act has been a satirical top ten list that offers a humorous spin on pop culture and/or famous people in the news, like the "Top Ten Snack Foods President Bush Should Avoid." The fashion designer known as Mr. Blackwell has made a name for himself chronicling the best—and more eagerly awaited—worst-dressed celebrities.

Sometimes, one list even makes another. Letterman's bits have been compiled into a series of books that—you guessed it—made the best-seller list. The *Book of Lists*, which top-tenned virtually everything under our single and seemingly list-proof sun, spent a long time on the ultimate book chart as well. (Somewhere in the vast universe there probably is a top ten list of hottest "sun stars.")

In this ocean of lists, it takes something really special to stand out. As Mr. Blackwell has proven, it doesn't necessarily have to be a positive achievement to catch the public's imagination.

For the past half century one of the most intriguingly popular lists has combined the love of charts with the public's endless fascination with the lives and actions of outlaws. This horror-movie-like interest increases dramatically when applied to a particular type of criminal—a "Most Wanted" felon on the run. By far the most popular list of this kind is the FBI's Ten Most Wanted Fugitives.

Ironically, the FBI's constantly replenished dubbing of the baddest of the bad guys has a structural quirk that makes it unique among all the other lists. Contrary to popular perception, the FBI doesn't produce a true top ten that, say, *America's Most Wanted* television show host John Walsh could count down Casey Kasem style until he reaches Bad Guy Number 1. Over the years, the FBI has resisted the temptation to scale their list in order of importance. There has never been a Number 1 Most Wanted, or a Number 10. They are all equally most wanted. The same was true of the precursor of the FBI's Top Ten Most Wanted, the less formal "Public Enemy" brand the federal government police force placed on such pre-1950s scoundrels as Al Capone and John Dillinger. The media liked to expand the designation to "Public Enemy Number 1," but that was their concept, not the FBI's.

The reason for such restraint is that these aren't boy bands competing with each other and their solo singing girlfriends for a place on the pop music charts. These are dangerous desperadoes on the loose, who pose a grave risk to society. The FBI doesn't want to deemphasize the importance of catching, say, the spouse murderer at the bottom of the list as opposed to the international terrorist at the top.

At no time in history has this policy been put to the

test more than at the present. One name on the current list leaps out among all the others—Osama bin Laden. The America-hating terrorist leader responsible for the shocking 9/11 World Trade Center/Pentagon atrocity was actually already on the list prior to masterminding the stunning assault on the American people, our buildings, and our senses. Bin Laden made the list years before for a series of bombings at American embassies around the world. Interestingly, as of 2003, the official Most Wanted list on the FBI's own Web page doesn't even mention the 9/11 horror, and still refers to him by his pre-9/11 name of "Usama."

Apparently, the Feds figure everyone knows who they mean and what Usama/Osama has done since. In addition, although the standard poster doesn't say why, they have noted that the reward for the turbaned terrorist's capture has soared from the routine $50,000 to an unprecedented $25 million (plus another $2 million kicked in by the Airline Pilots Association and Air Transport Association).

Putting all that aside, the point is that in hunting so reviled a felon—a worldwide Public Enemy who slaughtered thousands of innocent civilians, caused a war, and defiantly threatens to do even more harm on an equally massive scale—the FBI has steadfastly stuck to its guns and resisted the temptation to throw away tradition and name Bin Laden as their first ever Number 1 Most Wanted. Not even masterminding the simultaneous hijacking of four commercial airliners that were steered into the twin towers in New York, the Pentagon, and had it succeeded, most likely the White House or Capitol, has earned the crazed Arab terrorist leader that dishonor.

"The media always wants to name a Number 1, and

sometimes they just go ahead and do it. But we never have. Not even with Bin Laden," explains the FBI's Public Affairs specialist Rex Tomb, one of those responsible for overseeing the list.

The FBI is, if anything, comprised of traditionalists.

This steadfastness is interesting when considering that the list itself wasn't an FBI creation. As is so often the case, it was actually the idea of a media outlet. In 1949 an International News Service (INS) reporter named James Donovan asked the FBI to give him the scoop on the meanest and toughest criminals they were currently tracking. The resulting story, published on February 7, 1949, in the *Washington Daily News* and other papers around the country, created so much attention that media-savvy FBI Director J. Edgar Hoover knew they were on to something. A year later Hoover announced the first ever officially sanctioned FBI Ten Most Wanted Fugitives list. With all the media invited to participate, the reception was even more overwhelming than the original INS story. (INS later became United Press International.) This was partly because, as Hoover knew, it was a "can't lose" concept that the media was sure to jump on to feed the public's imagination. Secondly, being an inaugural offering, there was special care taken to populate that first Most Wanted chart with a particularly fascinating bunch of bad fellows (see Chapter 1).

Either way, the FBI was off and running. Nine of the first twenty Ten Most Wanted Fugitives, including the very first, were captured as a direct result of the publicity garnered by the listing—which is to say, they were spotted by someone who had read a story, saw a photo, and dropped a dime. That trend has held up over the years, as 445 of the 476 fugitives posted as of 2003 were subsequently located and/or captured, including 145 based upon citizen tips.

In addition, instead of being a onetime fad, the list quickly developed a self-perpetuating quality that gives it a life of its own. Each time a member is caught, there's a splash of fresh stories that almost invariably name and picture the remaining felons on the list. That, in turn, leads to more being recognized and captured. Similarly, each time a new crook is added to the fraternity, the same media splash is repeated. That leads to more arrests, more empty positions, and more new additions. The cycle has been endless. It is thus no surprise that the list has become a cultural phenomena.

The first half century has seen the list not only age gracefully, but readily adapt to the changing times, technology, and the explosion of media outlets. It has also developed a long-term history that can be studied, broken down, and analyzed. Notable aspects and tidbits of Top Ten events include:

- Comedians often make light of the fact that while superstar entertainers often need only a single name (Cher, Madonna, Prince), the world's worst criminals appear to prefer a trio of handles, like Lee Harvey Oswald, James Earl Ray, and Andrew Phillip Cunanan. The "uncanny" coincidence is easily explained and in part is a result of the popularity of the FBI's list. Law enforcement agencies include a wanted criminal's middle name in bulletins to distinguish them from thousands of others who may share the same first and last names. The media, wary of libel issues, has wholeheartedly supported the more lengthy designations.

- The first airing of the popular television show *America's Most Wanted* in the late 1980s resulted in the capture of FBI's Most Wanted Fugitive Number 409, rapist/murderer David James Roberts. Since then, *America's Most Wanted* has directly led to the apprehension of fifteen top-tenners, 500-plus other federal fugitives, along with hundreds more of the state variety.

- A total of twenty-four FBI Most Wanted Fugitives were caught as a direct result of *America's Most Wanted, Unsolved Mysteries*, and similar television programs.

- The Internet crime-hunting era was kicked off in May 1996 when an American teenager living in Guatemala was surfing the web and spotted the photo of Leslie Isben Rogge (Number 430), a bank robber who escaped from an Iowa prison six years before. Rogge appeared to be a dead ringer for a local handyman named Bill Young. Turns out, the teen was on the money. Rogge was promptly captured. (For the current list see: www.fbi.gov/mostwant/topten/tenlist.htm)

- The first woman—kidnapping accomplice Ruth Eisemann-Schier—hit the list in the equal-rights, flower-children year of 1968. There have only been six other women since Eisemann-Schier, and two of those beat their charges, while a third was dropped from the list after remaining in hiding for fourteen years. (She didn't surface for another seven years after that.) The three were 1960s era antiwar protesters and radicals.

- Of the seven women, three were placed on the list back-to-back-to-back within seventy-two hours in October 1970. All were antiwar protesters, two were radical feminists, and at least one was a militant feminist lesbian (see Chapter 1).

- To this day, the popular 1970s graffiti slogan, "Free Angela Davis," remains scrawled behind the scoreboard at Boston's historic Fenway Park. Davis, a Black Panther sympathizer, was the third woman to make the list.

- The now destroyed World Trade Center towers proved to be lightning rods for those destined to earn their way to FBI infamy. Prior to Bin Laden and his crew, terrorist Tamzi Ahmed Yousef had a poster created in his dishonor for the first WTC bombing in 1993. Not only was Yousef a sign of worse things to come, he had the duel distinction of being the eleventh fugitive to be designated a "Special Addition," meaning the list already had ten members when he was deemed wanted enough to push it temporarily to a "Top Eleven."

- Top-tenners have been caught in every state except Alaska, Maine, and Delaware. The most have been captured in California—fifty-nine.

- In contrast to fellow latecomer Alaska, two have been tracked to faraway Hawaii. Apparently, McGarrett and *Hawaii Five-O* aside, being on the lam in a closed-in, highly public tropical paradise is preferable to freezing in a far more secluded and expansive Alaskan blizzard.

- Similarly, a disproportionate number have been taken in balmy Florida (thirty-two) and the aforementioned sunny California. Cons no doubt like the warm rays.

- A scant few of the near five hundred have been captured in North Dakota (one), South Dakota (one), Montana (two), Oregon (four), Rhode Island (two), Vermont (one), and Wyoming (three). Cons apparently don't like single-digit windchill factors.

- That theory flip-flops when it comes to our neighboring countries. More top-tenners have been hauled in from Canada (ten) than Mexico (nine). However, those figures could be skewed by tougher extradition laws and less cooperative police agencies in Mexico.

- New York and Chicago are popular designations for fleeing felons despite the harsh winters. The two colossal cities pump their state capture rates to forty and thirty-two, respectively.

- Twenty-one listees simply surrendered, unable to handle the stress of their sudden new popularity.

- Eight surrendered or were arrested during the small window of time after they were chosen, but before their addition to the list was officially announced. The process generally takes two to four weeks to prepare the posters, update the FBI's Web page (www.FBI.gov), arrange the press conference, and produce the media packages. The eight still count in the running totals.

- Fourteen were found dead. Nine were killed during their capture. Forty-eight were snatched as a result of people seeing their pictures on wanted posters. Thirteen were arrested following magazine stories about the Most Wanted list. And two were recognized and turned in by people touring the FBI's building in Washington. The tourists spotted the felon's pictures in the Most Wanted exhibit.

- Thirty-one were grabbed in foreign countries, some as a result of a joint effort with local authorities. (The FBI has forty-four Legal Attachés worldwide to assist with such captures, and works closely with the International Law Enforcement Network known as Interpol. The FBI, however, does not have arrest authority in other countries.)

- In 1965, armed robbers Samuel Jefferson Veney and Earl Veney became the first brothers to appear on the list together. They were also the first to be arrested together. (The FBI, in conjunction with federal narcotics agents, had been tipped that they were working as machine operators at the same Garden City, N.Y. manufacturing plant.)

- Two years later a second pair of bad brothers, twins Charles Edward Ervin and Gordon Dale Ervin, were put on the list after escaping from a Michigan prison. Both were arrested in Canada by the Royal Canadian Mounted Police. However, unlike the Veneys, the Ervins were grabbed separately twenty-three months apart in different cities—Charles in Ontario and

Gordon in Winnipeg. Only three other "family acts" have shared time on the list.

- The most Top Ten Fugitives captured in a single year was a whopping thirty-three. They were corralled, ironically enough, in the hippie heyday of 1968. Back then, the notably ungroovy, clean-cut, dark-suited FBI agents could be spotted "for miles and miles and miles," to borrow from a song by The Who that was popular at the time.

- Despite the ongoing popularity of such citizen input crime-fighting shows as *America's Most Wanted* and *Unsolved Mysteries*, there were no top-tenners captured in 1993.

- Six men, including political assassin James Earl Ray, were placed on the list two separate times.

- Thirteen fugitives, including Ray again, were added to a full, ten-member list as "Special Additions."

- A cop killer named Billie Austin Bryant spent the shortest time as a poster boy—two hours. He was found hiding in a neighbor's attic four blocks from his home after ambushing and killing two Special Agents who were investigating a Maryland bank robber.

- A cop killer named Donald Eugene Webb has spent the longest time on the list—twenty-two years and counting (see Chapter 6). He beat the record of another cop killer, Charles Lee Herron, who dodged the police for eighteen years, four months, and nine days before relentless agents finally tracked him down in Jacksonville, Florida, in 1968.

• The first male/female team of criminals to be placed on the list together didn't occur until 1987, when fringe group revolutionaries Claude Daniel Marks and Donna Jean Willmott were given the honor. Still together seven years later, the Prairie Fire Organizing Committee and Armed Forces for National Liberation (FALN) supporters surrendered as a pair in 1994. (Prairie Fire was a front for the extremist Weather Underground movement of the 1960s and 1970s. FALN—from the Spanish language translation—was a Puerto Rican terrorist group responsible for hundreds of bombings and acts of terrorism.)

• All top-tenners now carry at least a $50,000 reward, which is paid by the FBI. That policy was instituted in September 1997. Prior to 1997, the bounties varied and were generally applied to special cases. The rewards can soar from the minimum of $50,000 depending upon the circumstances.

• Osama bin Laden has been responsible for a continuing series of new reward records as the price on his head has steadily increased from $5 million to $27 million.

• Although the FBI doesn't openly splash it across the posters, Top Ten Fugitives are still wanted "Dead or Alive," just like back in the Old West. However, the agency advises that a citizen enacting deadly force on a fugitive may encounter serious problems with local authorities, depending upon the circumstances. "If somebody went out and whacked someone and brought his body in, we'd have to look carefully at how it came about," cautions Ken Neu, Assistant Chief of Violent Crimes and Major Offenders. "You could have a murder at that point. If it was self-defense, that might be different."

- The situation overseas is more lenient. The FBI has no authority over what happens during the apprehension process in foreign countries, and therefore tends to ask fewer questions when a fugitive is brought in, regardless of his or her condition. Again, officials advise that local laws in those countries could be troublesome. In addition, fugitives, especially wealthy drug dealers, are sometimes protected by area police.

- Clint Eastwood–like professional bounty hunters are neither encouraged nor discouraged from going after top-tenners as part of their job. For whatever reason—probably distance and expense—no one as of yet has made a career of it. In fact, nobody has ever collected on more than one Top Ten Fugitive.

- Outside America, international bounty hunters and warlords have been known to track down specific wanted criminals purely for the financial windfall. Those who were successful, particularly in the terrorist arena, were dutifully paid for their efforts. "We don't recommend that anybody domestically go out hunting for dangerous fugitives," Neu again cautions. "Such uncoordinated efforts could put our agents in jeopardy, or interfere with the investigation. Normally, what we are actively seeking is information, recognition, and assistance." In other words, spot somebody, make a call, and let the FBI do the treacherous heavy lifting. The reward is the same either way.

• The FBI does not keep track of reward money paid out, and therefore has no running total.

• The legal cases against fifteen top-tenners were dropped before they were captured, forcing their removal from the list. Four others were removed to make room for those thought to be more deserving.

• The oldest person to make the list was Charles Bryan Harris, who was sixty-nine and wanted for a pair of murders in 1965.

• The youngest was Students for a Democratic Society radical David Sylvan Fine, who was singled out at age eighteen after he and three others bombed the Army Mathematics Research Center on the University of Wisconsin campus.

• Despite much publicity to the contrary, former teenage scam artist extraordinaire Frank Abagnale, Jr. was not the youngest person ever listed. Actually, Abagnale was never listed. A big budget movie about his life, *Catch Me If You Can*, based upon Abaganale's book of the same name, was nonetheless recently released. It starred *Titanic* hunk Leonardo DiCaprio and Oscar winner Tom Hanks, and was produced by Oscar winner Steven Spielberg. Abagnale posed as an airline pilot, college professor, stockbroker, pediatrician, assistant attorney general, and other professionals in the mid 1960s while still in his teens in order to pass $2.5 million in bad checks.

• Woody Allen made his directorial debut in 1969 with *Take the Money and Run*, a comedy about a small-time crook who dreamed of making the FBI's Ten Most Wanted list.

Time and technology has changed not only police work itself, but the makeup of the FBI's list. As detailed above, the 1950s trailblazers were mostly bank robbers, burglars, car thieves, and prison escapees. The wild and wooly 1960s and early 1970s spiced the Top Ten with revolutionaries and antiwar protesters generally accused of destroying government property, various acts of sabotage, and assorted kidnappings. The crimes were almost quaint by today's "terrorist" standards. The mid-1970s were the "Godfather" years, as the Bureau turned its attention to breaking up various mob groups proliferating around the country, mainly by grabbing mid- to lower-level hoods and getting them to rat out their superiors. It was no coincidence that the FBI stepped up the pressure on the wise guys in the wake of the popularity of such Mafia movies and books as *The Godfather*. Domestic terrorism was a high priority in the 1970s as well, but didn't capture the public's attention as much as the hunt for suited gangsters with names like Colombo, Gambino, Genovese, Bonanno, and Lucchese. The 1980s and 1990s saw the mobsters come and go on the list, as new members replaced the imprisoned or dead old-timers and grew important enough to be targeted. Sharing time with the old-school gangsters were the even more vicious new-school drug kingpins, along with assorted serial killers.

Y2K, unfortunately, has ushered in the plague of international terrorists bringing their warlike activities to the American mainland.

How does one make the FBI's Top Ten? Although some of the well-known choices appear obvious, it's really a complicated process that involves considerable effort. When a spot opens through the capture, death, or, in rare cases, dropped charges against or the downgrading of a listee, the FBI's Criminal Investigative Division (CID) gathers nominations from the fifty-six Field Offices around the world. These nominations, taken from a pool of around eight thousand fugitives, are local in nature, meaning they're a particular thorn in that Field Office's side. The literal rogue's gallery of nominees is not announced on *Good Morning America* or *The Today Show*, remaining an in-house process pored over by a committee of Special Agents from the CID and Office of Public and Congressional Affairs. A single candidate (usually) is weeded from the pack and sent to the Assistant Director of the CID for approval. If the person passes that step, it's on to the Deputy Director of the FBI for final approval. The "winner" is then unveiled on *America's Most Wanted* or *Unsolved Mysteries,* for maximum exposure.

The two-part criteria used is one part obvious and another rather intriguing. Obviously, the potential listee must be a person "considered a particularly dangerous menace to society and/or have a lengthy record of committing serious crimes," according to the official FBI history compiled and written by Donna J. Dove and Jeffrey M. Maynard (see the FBI popular Web site:

www.fbi.gov/mostwant/topten/tenlist.htm). The more intriguing complementary aspect is that the subjects are not always chosen because they are the most well-known or have committed the most sensational crime. Sometimes those factors actually keep a subject off the list. Since the purpose of the grouping is to publicize criminals that aren't so recognizable and might be blending into society, a fugitive's infamy is taken into account. This is why the public will sometimes scratch their heads and wonder why, say, Patty Hearst and her kidnappers aren't there. In that case, the FBI felt there was so much publicity about Ms. Hearst's bizarre adventure into 1960s style radicalism that it wasn't necessary to place her photo, or those of her kidnappers turned accomplices, on post office walls. "It was for that reason that Patty Hearst was not added to the list when she was a fugitive during the 1970s," confirms FBI spokesman Bill Carter.

This policy, however, is by no means a rule of thumb, as the listings of Bin Laden, African-American revolutionary Angela Davis, and serial killer Ted Bundy prove. (Although, as mentioned, "Usama" bin Laden originally made this list when he was far less known.) Thus, the second criteria is that the FBI must believe that the publicity generated by a list appearance could directly help apprehend the person.

"There are a lot of factors, but the big issue is whether the publicity is the right way to go to capture this particular person," violent crimes specialist Neu says. "In some cases, it can be a detriment."

Neu insists that the FBI doesn't take into consideration similar charges against felons already on the list when choosing new ones, and adds that contrary to popular belief, there has never been designated slots for various criminal activities. This is the "official" policy, despite what appears to be clear-cut placement patterns and decades of individually unique listings. Off the record, FBI officials admit when pressed that diversity is often a goal, and specific crimes can be targeted to create or maintain public awareness of that particular felony.

To its credit, the FBI again bows to stubborn traditionalism when it comes to removing rabble from the list. Generally, the only way to get off once you've been selected is to be found, or found dead. Thus, the agency best known by some via the old Efrem Zimbalist, Jr. television series or the more recent *X-Files* is not above swallowing its pride and letting particularly crafty felons reside on their list for decades. That's the case, as mentioned, with current listee and all-time record holder Donald Eugene Webb. The cop killer is heading into his twenty-third year, clinging to his spot as hundreds pictured with him have come and gone (see Chapter 6). Even some agent's suspicion that Webb has long passed away has not moved the brass to delete the ongoing blight to their otherwise illustrious tracking prowess.

The normal length of stay on the list is a mere 316 days. The pressure brought by achieving such an honor, as noted in the many surrender or suicide cases, can be stifling.

In some situations, charges against a listee will hit a legal snag while the person is still on the run, causing the case to be downgraded or dropped. If dropped, the bureau naturally has to pull the person off. If downgraded, they generally use that person's spot for someone more worthy. In addition, the FBI infrequently will rule that a fugitive "no longer meets top ten criteria," a designation sometimes given to political types whose past protest activities and causes don't seem as antisocial any longer. If not for the FBI's considerable history of leaving people listed that have become something of an embarrassment, like Webb, one might view this vaguely worded requirement as a handy loophole. In fact, like the legal snafus mentioned above, this explanation has more to do with the often difficult prosecutorial process than police work. Sometimes, when dealing with a group of criminals involved in the same crime, FBI agents and prosecutors are able to try accomplices and cohorts of a top-tenner while their partner remains on the loose. If the case proves to be weak and full of holes, chances are the charges against the person on the list will not stand up as well. In these instances, it doesn't make sense to spotlight such a felon. The bureau thus concludes that the space taken up by that particular crook could be better used by someone else. Even so, such cases are rare.

Over the years, the FBI has been more prone to beef up the list beyond ten, as opposed to dropping still-at-large suspects. In October 1970 a stagnant list combined with a rash of crimes committed by groups inflated the roster to an all-time high of "Top sixteen." As law enforcement agencies know, catching one member of a criminal band usually hastens the capture of the rest, so listing an entire mob makes sense. (In the 1970 case, it was four antiwar protesters, including a pair of brothers, who bombed an army building at 3:40 A.M. on a college campus.)

In general, one agent is assigned to manage a case on a full-time basis, with others assisting as needed. The amount of work and manpower is often related to the number of tips received, with staffs beefed up after television airings or news stories. All tips are said to be investigated.

More than anything, the FBI list has brought together two 500-pound gorillas that are often at loggerheads with each other—law enforcement and the media.

"Obviously, we've been taking advantage of the media's attraction to publishing the list and the public's fascination with the lives criminals lead," confirms New York agent Joseph Valiquette.

Rex Tomb, the G-man who manages the FBI's popular Web page as well as the list, concurs. "This is one case where the media and law enforcement team up to do a good job," he says. "It focuses national and, in some cases, international attention on these individuals. It gives you a pretty good leg up." But Tomb cautions that "publicity is something that you really have to use strategically. Usually [agents] come to the media when everything else has been explored. You realize it's pretty hot real estate, so you use it for cases that are important."

The list also acts to inspire the troops. "There are some agents who are absolutely possessed with finding these fugitives," notes San Diego FBI spokesman Jan Caldwell. "It's what they live to do."

At the same time, the list often depresses those portrayed. "It's got to be the worst feeling for a fugitive," Tomb understates. "If you were on the lam, as it were, and you see this huge glare of publicity, with maybe the attorney general or the FBI . . . making this announcement, it's not a very good feeling for you."

Some additional facts help bring Tomb's statement to life. Here's what each individual Top Ten Fugitive is up against:

- The FBI has about 28,000 employees; 11,093 special agents and 16,652 support staff members.
- The agency has a $3.6 billion annual budget.
- There are fifty-six Field Offices and more than four hundred "resident agencies" (smaller offices).
- The bureau's area of responsibility covers more than three hundred different federal laws.

"The pressure is constant all the time," stresses San Diego FBI organized crime specialist Vincent Dela-Montaigne. "They're always running. You can't live two lives continuously forever."

Chapter 1

A Blast from the Most Wanted Past

. . . .

Although there's never been a designated Number 1 bad guy on the FBI's Top Ten list, there was a first ever listee. That inglorious honor went to an aging bandit of the roaring twenties era who was still alive and kicking up trouble in 1950. Thomas James Holden was his name, and robbing banks, mail trains, and staging prison breaks was his game. Holden used a fake pass to escape from the famed Leavenworth prison in 1930, then helped some buddies escape a year later. Captured on a Kansas City golf course in 1932 armed only with his woods and irons, he was returned to his cell. (Another player in the fugitive foursome, Frank "Jelly" Nash, was so lousy a shot, he was off hacking in a distant rough and the FBI missed him.) All Holden's subsequent escape efforts were thwarted. Aging and suffering from a bad heart, he was released in 1947.

Two years later, a drinking party in Chicago got a bit out of hand. Before the last gulp of whiskey was thrown down, Holden ended an argument with his wife

Lillian by shooting her and her two brothers, killing all three. A veteran of life on the run, he promptly fled the state, forcing the FBI to get involved. They did in a way Holden never imagined. Eager to round up the last of the 1920s and 1930s era gangs that once blighted the Midwest, the agency selected the old-timer as their first ever Top Ten Fugitive, using him to kick off the list on March 14, 1950. The International News Service naturally jumped on the story it had helped create the previous year. The INS series of Top Ten reports over the next fifteen months were picked up by, among others, the *Portland Oregonian*, the paper of record in the area where Holden just happened to be hiding. He was made by an *Oregonian* subscriber who contacted the Feds. Holden was arrested and sent away for good.

Morley Vernon King, aside from all his other problems, missed making history by a single day, following Holden on the list as the Number 2 man on March 15, 1950. As with Holden, King had issues with his wife.

A teenage runaway from West Virginia, King joined the Navy and ran far and wide, eventually settling in Casablanca, Morocco—the place of Bogie fame. Of all the gin joints in all the world, a particularly saucy lady named Helen—once the Countess Christina de Zoheb via a previous marriage—walked into a place where King was holding court in 1931. They fell in love and got hitched not long afterward. Returning to America in 1934, the well-traveled young couple opened a restaurant in New Orleans. Thirteen years later the pair were still in the food business, operating the dining room of a hotel in San Luis Obispo, California. The honeymoon, however, was apparently long over.

In early July 1947 the skies were gray and Helen King was dead, strangled with her husband's scarf. Not sure what to do with her, King kept her body in a closet for nearly a week as he went about serving the hotel's hungry visitors. When a houseboy complained of the odor, King passed it off as a new brand of shaving lotion—a heavy musk, no doubt. Realizing Ms. King couldn't languish in the closet forever, King found a steamer trunk in the basement, stuffed her inside, lugged the box out back, and stashed it under the hotel's porch. At some point afterward, it dawned on King that his choice of burial places probably wasn't the smartest move he'd ever made. On July 8 he beat it out of town in the dark of night. The following day, the trunk and its gruesome contents were found.

A skilled traveler, King relied upon the itinerate nature of the restaurant business to quietly find work and blend in. Despite being plastered on the FBI's newfangled Most Wanted Fugitives' posters, and being cursed with distinctively large "Dumbo" ears, he escaped capture until late 1951. Acting on a tip, FBI agents found the elusive King shucking oysters in a Philadelphia restaurant. He would limit his culinary skills to prison cafeterias from that point on.

Number 3 on the first ever list was a burglar named William Raymond Nesbit, a man who failed to choose his partners and their girlfriends wisely. After relieving a Sioux Falls, Iowa, jewelry store of $37,000 worth of baubles in 1936, Nesbit and gang hatched another scheme, one that involved the use of the explosive nitroglycerin. Still hanging around Sioux Falls, they drove five miles outside of town to obtain dynamite and gunpowder to make the nitro. In the process of purchasing the materials, an argument ensued among the thieves. They began brawling. The girlfriend of bandit Harold Baker decided to wade into the fury and try to stop the fight. Bad idea. Nesbit clubbed her on the skull with a hammer, and another gang member shot her. To cover their tracks, both Baker and the girl were dragged into the store's powder house. One of the gang lit a fuse, and those who remained took off. Despite her severe injuries, the lady managed to crawl away before the sparks hit the powder. Her boyfriend wasn't so lucky. In a classic case of literal overkill, 3,500 pounds of dynamite and 7,000 pounds of black gunpowder erupted, incinerating Harold Baker and shattering windows in Sioux Falls.

It was not the most ingenious way for a gang of burglars to lay low after a successful robbery. Aside from alerting half the state, Nesbit and crew had also left a very angry, very determined witness. Baker's girlfriend survived the hammering, the shooting, and the massive explosion, and helped the authorities identify the culprits.

From there, the Nesbit story took another strange twist. The burglar turned bomber was caught in Oklahoma City two months later. He was tried, convicted of murder, and sentenced to life in the South Dakota State Penitentiary. Somehow, during the next nine years, he managed to so ingratiate himself with the prison brass that he was given trusty status, basically becoming a free range prison worker and manservant. He was allowed to leave the prison confines to perform various odd jobs, including gardening and acting as a chauffeur. Not surprisingly, in September 1946 he failed to return from one such outing.

In yet another oddity of law enforcement, a prisoner deemed harmless enough to gain trusty privileges was subsequently considered dangerous enough to become the FBI's third ever Most Wanted Fugitive.

The day Nesbit made the list, March 17, 1950, a woman in St. Paul, Minnesota, needed some newspapers to cover her newly scrubbed kitchen floor. Waltzing in for something to eat after school, the woman's son, James Lewis, fourteen, noticed the paper under his feet. Letting his teenage imagination run away with him, Lewis became convinced that the bad guy pictured in the paper was the same odd person who lived in a cave along the Mississippi River. Lewis and his pal, James Radeck, thirteen, had often chatted with the guy as they explored the river, and were even shown around the cave. The two boys spent the next couple of days living out a scene from *The Adventures of Tom Sawyer* as they investigated their suspicions. Convinced they were on the mark, they finally called the police.

Thanks to a mother devoted to cleanliness and two clever young boys, William Raymond Nesbit spent one of the shortest times on the list in FBI history—two days.

Interestingly, it didn't take long for the FBI's next listee to fall through one of the many cracks in the legal system. Henry Randolph Mitchell, a leprechaun of a man who resembled frail *Laugh-In* comedian Henry Gibson, was part of a Mutt and Jeff team that robbed a Williston, Florida, bank in 1948 to support their gambling habit. By then, banks had become part of the Federal Deposit Insurance Corporation, so the FBI didn't have to wait for the robbers to officially beat town before they could get involved. The tall bandit, apparently more conspicuous, was quickly captured. Mitchell, who sported a long criminal record for such things as narcotics and forgery, proved more elusive. He remained off the FBI's radar for eight years, until the charges against him were dropped by a Federal District Court due to a legal technicality. Prosecutors believed too much time had passed to attempt to rebuild the case so they let it slide. Thus, little Henry Mitchell became the first FBI Most Wanted Fugitive to not only escape arrest, but escaped the Most Wanted Fugitive list as well.

Number 5 was a "gentleman criminal" whose life of crime ultimately caught up with him and made him commit the most ungentlemanly of crimes. An accomplished house burglar who had previously served a couple of prison terms, Omar August Pinson was returning to his vehicle after a routine job when he was met by Oregon State Police officer Delmond Rondeau. The officer was suspicious of Pinson's activities, but not alarmed enough to draw his weapon and force Pinson to freeze. Pinson repaid the courtesy by pulling a .32-20 automatic and blasting the cop. Despite the relatively minor nature of his original crime, Pinson had reached the point in his career where killing a police officer was preferred to serving another day locked up. That's usually a dumb decision. Manhunts for cop killers can be intense and unrelenting. The skilled thief who was unwilling to take another burglary rap was captured in less than a day and sentenced to life. He was sent to the Oregon State Penitentiary, supposedly for good, in May 1947.

Almost two years to the day of this presumed last incarceration, the man who was so skilled at quietly sneaking in and out of ornate homes noisily skittered out of the penitentiary in Spartan, Oregon, sawing through his bars and then dodging a hail of gunfire as he climbed the wall. He was accompanied by a fellow prisoner, William Benson. The police and FBI, suffice it to say, were greatly alarmed. The only thing more dangerous than a desperate cop killer on the loose is a desperate cop killer recently escaped from prison with a running partner covering his back. An intensive manhunt across the upper northwest quadrant of the United States followed. For most of the summer the dragnet came up empty. Then, in early September, Pinson's cell mate was nabbed in Columbus, Ohio. Benson had a whale of a story to relate, one that seemingly changed with every telling. He advised FBI agents that Pinson had been hit during the escape and only made it as far as Kellogg, Idaho, before dying from the wounds. Despite being pressed for time, the cell mate gave his buddy a proper burial somewhere east of Kellogg.

Law enforcement agents have long learned to be skeptical of such convenient tales, and were doubly so when it was revealed that this same man told the local police that the pair never made it out of Oregon before a vicious case of gangrene took hold of Pinson earlier in the summer and killed him as they neared Salem. Despite being even more pressed for time at that point, the con still insisted that he gave his buddy a proper burial, only the hole was near Salem instead of Kellogg.

Even after doubling the odds, the recaptured con was having a hard time bringing officers to the precise spot where Pinson's bones supposedly laid at rest. Meanwhile, a man named Joseph Anthony Dorian— apparently choosing three fake names on his own to assist the police—was dragging his bones in and out of people's homes and carting off their valuables. He was so proficient at it that he became the target of a separate manhunt in Washington and Idaho.

Investigators soon determined that Dorian was Pinson. The shovels were put away in Salem and Kellogg—over the loud objections of Benson, who continued to swear that he'd planted his friend.

With things around Washington and Idaho getting a bit too hot, Dorian, whoever he was, headed to the open spaces of Montana, recruited a new gang, changed his name to Sam Cignitti, and began burglarizing anew. A shootout with a lone police officer outside a hardware store resulted in the capture of two of the three new gang members. Cignitti and a fourth man, Elmer Lee Payton, bolted on foot. Six months later Payton was popped in West Virginia. There was no sign of Pinson, or Dorian, or Cignitti. There was a lead, however. A car purchased by a man resembling Pinson had been registered in South Dakota under the name D. C. Audell. Bulletins were dispatched, and Audell was grabbed in sparsely populated Pierre, South Dakota, on August 28, 1950. It was indeed Pinson, alive and well, toting a load of burglary equipment along with a rifle, shotgun, and a pair of pistols.

The upshot? Pinson's geographically confused cell mate had actually been telling what he remembered of the truth. Burning with fever after the original escape, the wounded Pinson had indeed asked his buddy to bury him. Not waiting for Pinson to actually die, the convict complied, doing a rather shoddy job of it. Pinson woke up in a ditch an undetermined time later lightly covered with brush and rocks. He dusted himself off, got his bearings, and went back to the burglary business.

It's doubtful that the Number 6 man on that inaugural list, Lee Emory Downs, would be offered by the California FBI Field Office to the honchos in Washington today as a first-round recommendation. Downs was a skilled safecracker who sometimes ran with a small gang of robbers and burglars. The job that got him his fifteen minutes of fame was the 1948 robbery of a telephone office in San Jose. Two janitors were tied up, but weren't hurt. Downs cracked the safe, and he and his partner made off with a few bills short of $11,000. It was hardly the Great Train Robbery, even by 1940s standards. Nonetheless, the telephone company back then was a national monopoly that was all but sacrosanct, so Downs had tread upon the holy ground wires. He was traced to a trailer park in the auto racing and spring break party Mecca of Daytona Beach, Florida, where he was snatched up without incident. He might have been planning something nastier at the time, however, as his mobile home was packed with eight guns, nine sticks of dynamite, a dozen electric detonating fuses, and a pair of briefcases packed with bullets.

Downs was hit with a hefty sentence, more than twenty years, and served a good two decades before being paroled. Upon his release, he tried to crack the safe of the Colombian consulate in San Francisco, a rather odd choice unless he bought into wild prison stories that Colombian government officials were stuffing their offices with heaps of cash from their country's coffee or drug barons. There was, of course, no evidence to support that.

Lucky Number 7, Orba Elmer Jackson, had a quirky story that reflected the criminal life of those who fought the law in the first half of the twentieth century. A bored Missouri farmer's son looking for excitement, he stole a car and headed out on the highway, looking for adventure. Trouble was, it was 1924, and cars weren't as prevalent as they are today. An eighteen-year-old kid tooling around the barren roads in a

Model T stuck out like a farmer with a pitchfork in his thumb. Jackson never made it out of Missouri before he was arrested, convicted, and sent away to the Missouri State Penitentiary for six years, a harsh sentence for a youthful crime that would one day be all but written off as "joyriding."

Unfortunately, the punishment did little to cool Jackson's wanderlust. After having two years shaved off his sentence for good behavior, the allure of the internal combustion engine seduced him again. A second grand theft auto charge was complicated by the fact that he'd finally made it out of Missouri—and in the process violated a freshly minted federal law known as the Interstate Transportation of Stolen Motor Vehicle Act. The new statute was designed to curb the rash of easily snatched cars while at the same time dealing with highly mobile thieves who were suddenly able to quickly distance themselves from local police jurisdictions. What it meant to Jackson was three years at a particularly nasty federal penitentiary in Leavenworth, Kansas.

After surviving Leavenworth, Jackson attempted to go straight for a while, toiling as a barber and a shoemaker. Fed up with eking out a living, he decided to rob a store in Poplar Bluff, Missouri. For whatever reason, he savagely assaulted the defenseless old man who ran the place. Once again, luck wasn't with Jackson. The nondescript store doubled as a United States post office. That upped the ante tenfold. After being captured, Jackson was slapped with a twenty-five-year term and dispatched back to Leavenworth.

Subscribing to the William Raymond Nesbit school of warden ingratiation, Jackson spent the next eleven years humbly "yes mastering" his way to low-risk status. He earned a transfer to an honor farm. It was the ultimate irony. The boy who couldn't be kept down on the farm had come full circle. Whatever his true intentions for earning that respite from his cell, Jackson lasted only three weeks before he made a break for it.

As with Nesbit, the same prisoner thought to be rehabilitated enough for chainless farm duty was subsequently considered dangerous enough to have his mug pasted on the FBI's brand new Ten Most Wanted list. And again, just like Nesbit, the listing did Jackson in with record speed. Yet another alert *Portland Oregonian* reader recognized the escapee from a wire service story. The FBI swooped in and found Jackson right where the observant reader said he was—working on a chicken farm down the road. Jackson was taken back "home" to Leavenworth and locked up for good, his agriculture career once and for all ended.

The FBI crew that selected the first Top Ten Most Wanted list placed a heavy emphasis on prison escapees. In fact, as with a number of cases mentioned above, the escape was often considered to be the far greater offense than the original crime. Not so with Number 8, Glen Roy Wright. He was a Public Enemy all the way around.

In his heyday in the 1930s, Wright ran with the infamous Karpis-Barker Gang that plagued the Midwest. A veteran of numerous shootouts with the cops, Wright was a nasty, scarecrow-looking character with knife scars on his face who was known to wield a sawed-off shotgun. Twice, he was shot by the police, once in Kansas and the second time in Arkansas. Wary police officers and FBI agents thought they were done with the deadly, chain-smoking menace after he was stashed in the Oklahoma State Penitentiary for life in

1934. The bars held him for fourteen years before he got his hands on a smuggled-in gun and shot his way out in 1948. After being put on the FBI's list, he was spotted in Salina, Kansas, by a concerned citizen who notified the authorities. He was captured without incident and returned to Oklahoma, where he passed away in his cell in 1954.

Number 9, another prison jumper, gained notoriety in part for a crime right out of today's headlines. Bank robber Henry Harland Shelton was, among other things, a carjacker. Shelton and a running buddy acquired a pistol and blasted their way out of the Michigan House of Correction and Branch Prison on September 5, 1949. After scrounging around in the woods for a couple of weeks, they decided to grab some wheels and rejoin civilization. Brandishing knives, they snatched a late shift electrical worker who was just finishing a midnight lunch outside a cafeteria. Instead of letting him go, they forced the poor man to accompany them on a wild, haphazard two-day trek back and forth across four states. The victim finally turned the tables and escaped from the escapees in Kontmorenci, Indiana, while the cons were having breakfast at a gas station. Figuring that they needed a new vehicle, the pair carjacked and dumped an additional three autos to muddy the trail. Deciding that they needed some spending money, they staged a stickup. The contrasting ideas immediately cleared the muddy trail. Shelton's cohort, Sam Lieb, was captured, but Shelton slipped away again. The FBI stuffed a federal kidnapping charge in Shelton's already thick jacket, hit him with the Interstate Transportation of a Stolen Vehicle statute, and put him on the list.

Three months later the Feds received a tip that Shelton had started frequenting a bar in Indianapolis. Obviously, when you're one of the FBI's Most Wanted, it's not too smart to hang your hat at a place where everybody knows your name. A team of FBI agents and Indianapolis police staked out the place, set to grab Shelton as he entered. Sure enough, he arrived as promised. As the officers closed in, Shelton went for a .45 in his belt. Two FBI agents fired, dropping the con to the pavement.

Shelton recovered from his wounds and was sent back to the slammer with an additional fifty years tacked on to his already lengthy sentence.

Last but certainly not least on that first Top Ten was a swarthy New York hothead who was conspicuous by his lack of the requisite middle name. Morris Guralnick liked to hang around burlesque theaters, so much so that he usually worked the concession stand, shoveling popcorn and cutting candy for the patrons. Things went sour for Guralnick in 1948 when he stabbed his ex-girlfriend during a temper tantrum. By the time the police arrived, he had really worked up a lather. He fought the officers like a wild, cornered animal, going so far as to bite a finger clean off one of the cops. Subdued, he was dispatched to the Ulster County Jail in Kingston, New York.

Before even making it to trial, Guralnick joined a band of imprisoned thugs who ripped apart the joint's plumbing to obtain weapons, which they used to brutally beat a pair of guards and make their escape. The four other men were quickly recaptured, but Guralnick proved to be more nimble. He skipped across the country, putting as much space between him and New York as he could, eventually settling in Wisconsin.

It wasn't far enough, not with the FBI's new Top Ten

list floating around. Noting Guralnick's violent temper, not to mention the fury of a certain four-fingered NYPD officer, the FBI didn't hesitate to award the little hothead the last spot on its first ever compilation. His picture was sent far and wide. A story about the list was subsequently published in *Coronet* magazine. A reader attending law school at the University of Wisconsin in Madison recognized Guralnick as the guy working at a clothing store near the campus. The FBI and Wisconsin police closed in. Throwing an internal switch of some kind, the mild-mannered Wisconsin clothier transformed into the raging New York street animal and fought the officers tooth and nail before eventually being overcome. He was carted back to New York and locked in a cage for good.

Quizzically, famed bank robber Willie Francis Sutton didn't make that first cut. Sutton is often confused for an original top-tenner because he was the first alternate added to the list within a week of its inception following the almost immediate capture of Number 3, William Raymond Nesbit. Sutton was nabbed after someone who saw the FBI flyer spotted the wily robber on a New York subway train. Sutton is best known for his historic crack to the media after being asked why he robbed banks: "Because that's where the money is."

The subway rider who fingered Sutton, Arnold Schuster, became something of a celebrity. That was his undoing. Famed mobster Albert Anastasia spotted Schuster basking in a television interview and ordered his henchmen to rub him out. The triggerman, Frederick J. Tenuto, was already Number 14 on the FBI's Ten Most Wanted list. Anastasia then ordered Tenuto hit to sever the trail of evidence back to him. His body was never found, but famed mob informer Joe Valachi eventually confirmed law enforcement suspicions that Anastasia had Tenuto killed.

As the FBI's list motored through the years, there were, of course, many other notable events. Number 17, Courtney Townsend Taylor, was captured in Mobile, Alabama, after a jeweler recognized him from a flyer and sent his clerk to shadow the felon. Responding rapidly to the jeweler's call, the police arrested the accomplished check forger less than a half hour later.

Joseph Paul Cato, Number 20, a bootlegger who murdered his ex-girlfriend, has some strange dates on his record that read like either a typo or a time traveler. Cato was placed on the list June 27, 1951. He was arrested June 21, 1951. Turns out Cato got wind of his pending placement through an "Identification Order" sent to local police. Wanting no part of the citizen scrutiny that was sure to follow, he surrendered before he could officially make the post office team.

Burglar and prison escapee Ernest Tait, Number 23 (and listed again years later at 133), had convinced himself that he was going to go out in a hail of bullets rather than go back to prison. He had a change of heart when he read in the *Miami News* that he'd made the FBI list. While more than willing to shoot it out with the local cops, Tait figured he had no chance against the suited Feds, whom he believed to be expert shots. The point became moot when he was arrested while his Oldsmobile, and his twin .45s, were up on a dealership's grease rack.

Number 33, armed robber Isaie Aldy Beausoleil, dressed as a woman in 1953 to hide his features from the proverbial army of "alert" newspaper readers. That turned out to be his undoing. Fumbling around in a woman's rest room in a Chicago park, he aroused the suspicion of other women using the facilities. They notified the park police, who promptly bagged a very big fish with a stuffed bra.

Anyone who has had to wait an inordinate amount of time at a railroad crossing can relate to the fate of Number 37, burglar, bank robber, and multiple prison escapee Nick George Montos. Hemmed in by a long freight train in front of them, two Chicago FBI special agents decided to kill time by doing a check on a nearby vehicle that seemed to ring a bell. Bingo. It was registered to Montos, a top-tenner. Equally trapped by the train and traffic, Montos was captured without fuss. Like Tait, Montos was also a double banger, making the list again two years later after an escape. He was recognized and captured in Memphis, Tennessee, the same month he was placed on the list for the second time.

Not to be deterred, a seventy-eight-year-old Montos made news again in 1995 when he came out on the wrong end of a mano-a-mano battle with a seventy-three-year-old fireball of an antique store owner he was trying to rob. Although Montos was armed with a .22 and had tied her up, owner Sonia Paine wiggled free, hit a silent alarm, grabbed a baseball bat, and began wailing on the old hood, knocking him down. Ticked, he clubbed her with the gun butt and sprayed her with mace. That only made her angrier. After the police responded, Montos retreated and drew his weapon. Paine went after him with the bat again, distracting him enough to enable the officer to disarm him.

"I don't take any crap from anybody!" Paine growled, bleeding from a cut on her head that required ten stitches. "I beat the hell out of him!"

Paine was going to allow the robbery to happen until Montos cut the line to the phone her son used. That melted her candle. "I'm not surprised by what my mother did," a relieved Stanley Paine told Boston reporters. "She's a very feisty lady. She's not going to let anyone come in and take what's hers. She worked too hard."

The cut, macing, and pistol-whipping from the double FBI top-tenner didn't rattle the "feisty lady" enough to prevent her from attempting a long held American tradition. She told reporters she was sixty-five. Police records showed she was eight years older.

As with Joseph Paul Cato, Number 49 Joseph Levy's listing and arrest dates appear to be in reverse, this time covering different months. FBI agents in Louisville, Kentucky, recognized the swindler who preyed on lonely women from materials sent from Washington prior to the announcement that he'd made the list. He was arrested April 30, 1953, the day before he officially became a Top Ten Most Wanted Fugitive. To impress his female victims, it was discovered that Levy had sent expensive gifts to President Dwight D. Eisenhower and Vice President Richard Nixon, whom he claimed to be buds with.

As the FBI continued to replace captured top-tenners with fresh new faces, the oddities of their arrests and reactions continued as well. George William Krendich, a former Air Force pilot wanted for murdering his pregnant girlfriend, killed himself in North Dakota three months after becoming Number 57. He ran a tube from his exhaust into his car, a popular suicide technique of the time. Cattle rustler Chester Lee Davenport, Number 65, was arrested in Dixon, California, while milking a cow. Chances are strong that won't happen again. Auto thief Nelson Robert Duncan, Number 69, was arrested in mid-burglary of a store after he and his accomplice failed to close a skylight window. Armed robber Clarence Dye, Number 73, was pulled over by Wisconsin police for a routine check. His ex-girlfriend, who happened to be with him, promptly ratted. Number 77, Otto Austin Loel, found life as a Most Wanted to be a downward spiral. Six months after making the list for stabbing his girlfriend to death for allegedly wanting him to perform a "perverted sex act," he was found living in a steamy, putrid dump in Stanford, Florida, sheltered from the blazing sun by a shack made from palmetto leaves.

Bank robber Kenneth Darrell Carpenter, Number 82, casually reached out to punch the radio button of his car to hunt for a better song as he waited at a stop one February day in 1955 in Arlington, Tennessee. The FBI agent who happened to be in the car beside him recognized the letters L-O-V-E tattooed on Carpenter's fingers and remembered the info on his poster. The agent hit his own radio, calling for help. Carpenter was grabbed within the hour.

In 1958, Number 87, Daniel William O'Connor, successfully used an elaborate series of disguises to escape public scrutiny. O'Connor not only dyed his hair red, grew a bushy mustache, and added a prominent tattoo, he gained fifty-eight pounds to further distance himself from the man on the wanted posters. After all that effort to stay hidden, the thief wanted for assaulting a Canadian police officer was busted after stealing a small trailer worth fifteen dollars from a neighbor in El Cajon, California.

Bank robber and prison escapee Frederick Grant Dunn, Number 108, went the opposite route of the big

eating O'Connor. He disguised himself as a skeleton.
A farmer found Dunn's remains by a stream near
Ellsworth, Kansas. The FBI wasn't sure whether he'd
killed himself or someone did it for him. Robber David
Lynn Thurston, Number 110, survived his first month
on the list in 1959 by laying low. He then decided to
stick up a bustling Broadway restaurant during the
heart of theater season. Police ran him down as he
ducked in and out of the well-dressed crowd. Number
115, weight-loss scammer Walter Bernard O'Donnell,
subscribed to the "hide in plain sight" theory. Posing as
a retired U.S. postal inspector, he often spoke to citizen
groups in the late 1950s. One such citizen recognized
him from a newspaper story on the Top Ten and dropped
the dime that ended O'Donnell's burgeoning public
speaking career. He had previously preyed on women by
posing as a doctor and giving them magic diet pills that
actually knocked them out, enabling him to rob their
homes.

Giving new meaning to the old jokes about the in-
tegrity of used car salesmen, auto thief and bank robber Joseph Lloyd Thomas, Number 123, established
himself as exactly that in Pelzer, South Carolina. He
was taken in after a local resident, no doubt unhappy
with being sold a lemon, suspected that Thomas was a
crook.

Down on his luck and feeling pressured by his recent listing, Number 126, Charles Clyatt Rogers,
ponied up in a Minneapolis, Minnesota, soup line in
May 1960 for a bit of nourishment. It wasn't the escaped murderer's day. A cop who collected FBI
wanted posters spotted him and gave him lunch at the
local jail while waiting for the Feds.

That same year, bank robber Ray Delano Tate put a

new spin on the concept of cutting out the middleman. Tate, Number 142, surrendered to the middleman! Figuring it was the newspapers that were making his life unbearable by publicizing his crimes and photo, he phoned a *New York Daily Mirror* editor and gave himself up to a reporter and photographer.

Armed robber Kenneth Eugene Cindle, Number 145, was fingered by the Good Samaritan who picked him up hitchhiking in Cochran County, Texas, and gave him a ride to work. Cindle was arrested while driving a tractor on a nearby ranch. Number 153, a hostage-taking bandit named Anthony Vincent Fede, was picked up in Los Angeles a few days before Halloween, 1961, carrying a prop pistol and a phony police badge. He was the first top-tenner to have "gone Hollywood."

A postmaster's nightmare, Number 155 Robert William Schuette changed his address more than forty times to avoid detection. The robber and prison escapee was determined not to leave a paper trail. When he was captured in Chicago, he had a newspaper story in his pocket detailing his addition to the Most Wanted list.

Arrested for voyeurism in Atlanta, serial killer/rapist Hugh Bion Morse, Number 157, posted a $200 bail in 1961 and walked out of jail right past his wanted posters on the wall. Raised by a sadistic grandmother who scarred his face with a hammer when he was a child, Morse was eventually recognized and captured in St. Paul, Minnesota.

Somebody wanted drug dealer John Gibson Dillon even worse than the FBI. After surviving three years on the list, Number 158 was found fouling the water at the bottom of a well on a farm in Chelsea, Oklahoma. His feet were weighted down with 400 pounds of oil rig drilling equipment.

Apparently not worried about being conspicuous, Number 164, a psychopathic murderer named Watson Young, Jr. was pulled over in Salina, Kansas, in 1962 for tooling around in an ambulance taken from a local funeral home. The embalming school dropout had his FBI identification order wadded in his pocket.

Most Wanted Number 178, Howard Jay Barnard, learned the magic of stuffing cotton in one's mug long before Marlon Brando won an Oscar for doing likewise in *The Godfather*. When arrested after sticking up a motel in 1964, the robber/escapee was found to have cotton in his cheeks as well as his nose. He also sported gold hair, stage makeup, two sets of clothing, rubber bands around his ears, and had smeared glue on his fingers to avoid being printed.

With the posse closing in, Alfred Oponowicz buried himself under a pool of water in a railroad switching yard in 1964 and used a reed to breathe—a technique he no doubt learned from observing the antics of Wiley Coyote and Bugs Bunny as a kid. The FBI wasn't fooled, yanking Number 182 from his wet hiding place near Painesville, Ohio, and sending the murderer/counterfeiter back to jail.

Gay club female impersonator turned murderer Leslie Douglas Ashley, Number 211, was grabbed in 1964 while working for a traveling carnival as "Bobo the Clown." Fellow carnies discovered Ashley's wanted poster in his open suitcase.

Dressed for success on the range, Number 220, Edward "Fast Eddie" Owens Watkins, fancied cowboy duds. Aware of this, FBI agents canvassed stores selling western clothes in the Montana area in 1966 where the bank robber was reported to be moseying around. Sure enough, a salesman recognized him. The FBI rustled him up. Released nine years later, he had to abandon another bank robbery and free seven hostages in mid-attempt when he suffered a heart attack. Escaping prison in 1980, he robbed seven banks in five weeks without further stressing his weak heart, and was eventually captured at a roadblock in Ohio.

Yet another Kennedy from Massachusetts gained fame in 1965 when the FBI placed a bank-robbing prison escapee on their list. James Edward Kennedy, Number 222, wasn't fortunate enough to be related to his famous namesakes. He was arrested two weeks later in Worcester after a brief car chase and shootout with FBI agents.

After being extradited from Japan to Hawaii in 1966, James Robert Ringrose, Number 236, decided to pull out all the stops. The trigger-happy traveler's checks counterfeiter presented the arresting FBI agents with something he'd been carrying for years for just that moment: a "Get Out of Jail Free" card from a Monopoly game.

Setting a trend that all criminals major and petty would be quick to follow—particularly those arrested on reality television shows—drug addicted bank robber Donald Richard Bussmeyer was taken down shirtless in Upland, California. Not only was Number 251 Bussmeyer bare-chested that warm summer day in 1967, but a tattoo emblazoned on his chest ended all doubt whether he was the FBI's man. "Don Bussmeyer Loves Joyce," the ink proclaimed. His wife was with him at the time. Her name was Hallie.

As with John Gibson Dillon, somebody or -bodies weren't going to wait for the FBI to do their dirty work for them when it came to fugitive Number 270, George Benjamin Williams. Nevada prospectors encountered the bank robber's skeleton near an old mine. Three bullet holes marred Williams's bleached skull.

James Earl Ray hit the list for the first of his two stays in April 1968, following the assassination of civil rights leader Martin Luther King. Although most everyone recognizes fugitive Number 277's name and crime, few remember that he was actually captured in London two months later by British police. For all his notoriety, Ray escaped from his Brushy Mountain, Tennessee, prison cell nine years later and was immediately placed on the FBI list again, this time as Number 351. Unlike his prior overseas adventure, Ray didn't get far. Tennessee prison authorities, relying on bloodhounds, found him a few days later hiding under some leaves in a wooded area not far from the prison.

Phillip Morris Jones, Number 280, spotted his poster in a San Mateo, California, post office in 1968 and promptly decided to give himself up. He walked into the local FBI office and surrendered. The only problem was, the bank robber packed a loaded automatic pistol. Such oversights help explain why law enforcement officers immediately frisk anyone they are arresting, even those passively surrendering.

Bowing to the late 1960s Equal Rights Movement, the FBI didn't hesitate to place Georgia kidnapper Ruth Eisemann-Schier on the list in December 1968. Eisemann-Schier, Number 293, was the first woman so honored. She was captured less than three months later in Norman, Oklahoma. Her accomplice, Gary Steven Krist, had been arrested in Florida two months before. Eisemann-Schier and Krist had taken the twenty-year-old daughter of a wealthy Florida man and then buried her alive in a box stocked with an air pump, food, and water. After her family paid a $500,000 ransom, she was pulled out alive eighty-three hours later.

Fugitive 307, Lawrence Robert Plamondon—Minister of Defense for the radical White Panthers—was arrested in 1970 after a passenger in his van tossed a beer can out the window. (A violation of the Panther's strict tenet against pollution of the land.) Pulled over for littering, the Michigan State Police did a routine license plate check that alerted them as to whom they were dealing with. Plamondon and his cohorts, wanted for various bombings of government buildings, gave up without a fight.

Civil rights activist, Black Panther, and Communist Angela Yvonne Davis made the list at Number 309, Female Number 3, in August 1970, despite already being the recipient of reams of publicity. FBI agents connected Davis to the conspiracy behind a bloody shootout in front of a California courthouse that resulted from an attempt to free fellow radical James McClain. Judge Harold Haley, remembered for a famous photograph showing a shotgun taped to his neck, was killed, as were McClain, a second convict, and Jonathan Jackson, the ringleader of the raid. The prosecutor, Gary Thomas, was paralyzed by a shot in his spine. Davis, a close friend of Jackson and his imprisoned brother George Jackson, was arrested two months later in a New York motel. Known for her robust Afro, she was subsequently acquitted of all charges and released, despite the fact that three of the guns used in the deadly shootout had been purchased by her. (She argued that they were taken by Jonathan Jackson without her knowledge.) Davis went on to become a popular speaker, best-selling author, tenured college professor, and even ran for vice president on the Communist Party ticket in 1980—all firsts for a former listee.

The day after Davis's capture, a second well-known female 1960s radical, Bernardine Rae Dohrn, First Lady of the Weather Underground, was upgraded to the list. The leather boots and miniskirted Dohrn, future wife of Weather Underground leader Bill Ayers, was first charged with inciting riots and later for a bombing conspiracy. (The violence-promoting Weather Underground, a more militant offshoot of Students for a Democratic Society, took credit for bombings at the Capitol in 1971 and the Pentagon in 1972, among others. No one was injured.) Dohrn responded to the charges by hitching up her black mini and declaring war on the American government. The G-men were on a bad luck roll, because not only was Number 314 Dohrn never captured, but she joined the handful of listees to have their federal process dismissed while her pretty picture adorned post office walls. The government dropped the charges rather than submit to a court order forcing them to reveal FBI investigative techniques used against various radicals. Dohrn has since become a member of the American Bar Association's governing body, a noted public speaker, as well as the director of Northwestern University's Children and Family Justice Center. Ayers is a college professor as well.

Undeterred, the FBI shook up another hornets' nest when they placed radical feminist antiwar protesters Katherine Ann Power and Susan Edith Saxe on the list three days after Dohrn, swelling the "Top Ten" to an all-time high of "Top Sixteen." The pair were accused of being part of a Boston bank robbery aimed at funding their future activities. A police officer, the father of nine children, was slain by one of their trigger-happy male accomplices during the heist, which netted $26,000. The FBI was met with fierce resistance from those in the "politically active lesbian community" that supported the two women, particularly the outspoken Saxe. The anger lingers to this day. Saxe was eventually captured in 1975 and served seven years. Power managed to stay free for twenty-three years, changing her name and marrying. By year fourteen it was apparent that sixties-style antiwar protesters weren't being aggressively prosecuted by the courts, so Power was dropped from the list. She surrendered seven years later in Boston and served six years. Both Saxe and Power continue to remain active in various social issues today.

Despite the Davis, Dohrn, and Power setbacks, the Feds did win a few. On November 14, 1973, fugitive Number 319, Twymon Ford Myers, decided to shoot it out with FBI agents and New York police officers in the Bronx. Myers, a member of the militant Black Liberation Army, lost, and was killed in the process. He had been wanted for the cold-blooded murder of at least two New York City foot patrolmen. In contrast to that violent takedown, fellow listee Number 326, serial hitchhiker rapist John Edward Copeland, was scooped up a few years later leisurely riding a bicycle to his home in idyllic Dorchester, Massachusetts.

After a brief respite from the sociopolitical quagmire of the times, another listee gained a sympathetic following in 1975 that has done nothing but intensify over the years. Leonard Peltier (Number 335) became the Angela Davis of the Native American civil rights movement when the longtime American Indian Movement activist was placed on the list. Peltier first gained notoriety when he and fellow AIM leader Russell Means staged a seventy-one-day siege at Wounded Knee, South Dakota. A pair of FBI agents were injured during the long, well-publicized event. Two years later Peltier was part of a confusing shootout on the Pine Ridge Indian Reservation in South Dakota that left two FBI agents dead. Captured in Canada and later convicted of the execution-style murder of the two wounded agents, Peltier remains the object of an often intense tug-of-war between those who feel he's a political prisoner unjustly accused, and the FBI, who maintain that Peltier is just another cold-blooded cop killer.

The cases of Davis, Dohrn, Power, and Peltier were among the first that began to tarnish the once heroic image of the FBI. Prior to that streak, FBI agents were adored by the public, unbreakable in court, and highly popular with juries, who hung on their every word. Afterward, defense attorneys felt freer to attack the agents' methods, abuse of power, policies, and mindsets. Often, the agents were painted in court and the media as fascist government goons that were tools of that great oppressor, "the Man." Woefully unhip old school types like J. Edgar Hoover and Richard Nixon were accused of using the FBI and its still-powerful list as nothing more than a weapon against political enemies. Fortunately, the perception didn't last. For every politically motivated Angela Davis and Leonard Peltier, there were a thousand run-of-the-mill murderers, robbers, thieves, prison escapees, child molesters, terrorists, and their ilk that needed to be hunted down and put away for the overall good of society. As the "trust no one over thirty" radicalism of the 1960s and

1970s began to slide into the kinder and gentler disco days, it became business as usual for the guys in the black suits and symbolic white hats. The Most Wanted Fugitive list powered on as a cultural phenomena.

As if to prove that point, just as the FBI was recovering from the triple whammy of unprecedented batterings of their once pristine image, bolder attacks from increasingly aggressive defense attorneys and liberal politicians, and an evolving media that was focusing more on local news as opposed to national fugitive hunts, something quietly happened that put it all back in perspective. Less than three months after making the criminal big-time, and while the Peltier controversy was still raging, double murderer Roy Ellsworth Smith, Number 349, hung himself in Perry Township, Ohio. The pressure that came with the FBI's famous list had not let up an iota.

Eleven days later, James Earl Ray escaped from prison. The same liberal Democrat faction that was criticizing the FBI for the Davis and Peltier cases was now depending upon the agency to recapture the man accused of stilling the voice of one of the greatest civil rights leaders of all time, Martin Luther King. As mentioned above, Ray was placed on the list for the second time, Number 351, and was captured two days later.

After Ray was tossed back inside his Tennessee cell, things settled down to a more "normal" pace—meaning that the thrills, chills and dangers of chasing America's Most Wanted Fugitives continued. So did the seemingly never-ending stream of blunders committed by the hunted, and the odd quirks in the cases.

The commonly named Larry Smith suffered from both in 1977. As with many felons before him, the murderer and prison escapee sought to escape the heat of being a Public Enemy by leaving the country. Some-times that works. Other times it can be a fugitive's un-doing. Smith, Most Wanted Number 353, chose the closest English-speaking country he could find—Canada. Unfortunately, he failed to bone up on some of his new country's more unusual traffic regulations. He was flagged by Toronto's finest for "illegally driving past a street car's open door." Identified as a major American bad guy through his fingerprints, he was presented to the FBI all but covered in ribbons.

Most Wanted 360 was another famous name, but this one didn't come with a legion of leftist supporters. Theodore Robert Bundy, Ted Bundy for short, was a handsome, intelligent serial killer who preyed on dark-haired young women throughout the 1970s while carving a murderous path across America. By 1978 he'd raped and/or murdered more than thirty young women from Seattle to Florida. Finally captured in Pensacola for speeding, he was convicted of multiple counts of homicide in 1979 and was executed ten years later.

Leo Joseph Koury, Number 367, escaped the clutches of the FBI for twelve years, then died of massive cerebral vascular hypertension. The man who made a fortune operating gay bars in Richmond, Virginia, and got in trouble for rubbing out competitors, succumbed to the oppressive stress of being on the list.

David Fountain Kimberly, Jr. sought refuge from the long arm of the law on a tiny island in the Florida Keys. It wasn't tiny enough. Florida FBI agents tracked Number 379 to Matacombe Key in 1982 and brought the attempted murderer back to civilization to pay his debt to society. Ironically, some historians believe Matacombe Key derived its unusual name from the Spanish words *matar hombre*, which means "to kill a man."

Mutula Shakur, stepfather of 1990s rap star Tupac Shakur, was a radical era throwback who followed Kimberly Jr. on the list at position 380 in July 1982. Shakur, an ex–Black Panther turned Black Liberation Army leader, was accused of being the mastermind behind the ambush robbery of a Brinks truck near Nanuet, New York, on October 20, 1981. Shakur's "posse" was a rainbow coalition of former Weatherman Underground, Students for a Democratic Society, Black Panther, and Black Liberation Army members. A Brinks guard and two police officers were slain in the violent heist, which netted $1.6 million. Most of the gang was captured within a week, with the stragglers rounded up months later. Shakur wasn't apprehended until early 1986. He was later convicted of bank robbery and conspiracy. Tupac Shakur's mother, Afeni Shakur, was also a Black Panther. She was charged with conspiring to blow up a string of New York department stores in 1971, but was acquitted while eight months pregnant with Tupac.

Despite his musical and acting success, Tupac Shakur couldn't escape his parents' legacy. The digital underground turned solo star was convicted of sexual abuse after the 1993 gang rape of a teenage fan. Free on a $1.4 million appellate bond, he was gunned down in Las Vegas on September 7, 1996, by members of the California Southside Crips street gang. The hit was reported to be a million dollar contract job performed on behalf of New York rapper Notorious B.I.G. Tupac and B.I.G. had been spearheading a violent California/New York rapper feud for years. Tupac Shakur was twenty-five when he was killed. B.I.G., a creation of rapper/producer Puff Daddy (now going by the name P. Diddy), was assassinated himself six months later in Los Angeles. B.I.G.'s murder, believed to be a payback, has never been solved.

Six years after Ted Bundy's murderous ways were halted, yet another serial killer of massive proportions was discovered to be on the loose in both America and Australia. Christopher Bernard Wilder, a successful Florida construction and electrical contractor, raced cars on the Grand Prix circuit, photographed beautiful women, and lived the life of a playboy. Unbeknownst to those around the tracks and modeling agencies, he was already facing various sex-related charges in Australia when he began a string of kidnappings, rapes, and murders in America. Driving back and forth across the country in early 1984, he left a trail of bodies, snatching, raping, torturing, and killing young women the whole way. Wilder, Top Ten Fugitive Number 385, was eventually shot to death with his own .357 Magnum in a struggle with New Hampshire state troopers. His sudden death in April 1984 left dozens of missing persons cases in America and Australia unresolved, including the fate of two beautiful young models, Rosario "Shari" Gonzalez, twenty, and Elizabeth Kenyon, twenty-three, who vanished in Miami at the start of his two-month death run in early 1984.

Carmine "the Snake" Persico, the boss of New York's legendary Colombo Mafia family, was put on the list as Number 390 in 1985 during a crackdown on organized crime. He was arrested in Wantagh, New York, two weeks later and was subsequently convicted, along with eight other New York Mafia bosses, on an array of racketeering charges.

Multiple murderer David James Roberts's (Number 409) capture in 1988 kicked off a rash of apprehensions following features on the new television program, *America's Most Wanted*. Sixteen of the next twenty-six fugitives who made the list were located as a result of that popular program, the equally popular *Unsolved Mysteries*, or a combination of the two. The programs continue to produce solid tips to this day.

Mexican drug lord Juan Garcia-Abrego, Number 440, was listed in 1995 and captured by Mexican authorities a year later. His arrest and extradition signaled a new wave of cooperation between the two countries.

Fugitives 441 and 442, Abdel Bassett Ali Al-Megrahi and Lamen Khalifa Fhimah, helped kick off the current era of Middle Eastern terrorists on the FBI posters when they made the list in 1995 for the 1988 bombing of Pan Am Flight 103 over Lockerbie, Scotland. Not only did the bomb kill 259 passengers and crew members, but eleven Lockerbie villagers perished on the ground from falling debris. The pair were arrested together in Holland in 1999.

The capture of Thang Thanh Nguyen, Number 446, in 1998 was another demonstration of the FBI's long reach. Nguyen was arrested in the People's Republic of Vietnam and turned over to FBI agents in Thailand. He was wanted for the murder of a New York restaurant owner he was trying to shake down for gold and cash.

A gay serial killer named Andrew Phillip Cunanan created a splash in 1997 when he took spot Number 449 after murdering fashion designer Gianni Versace outside Versace's Miami estate. Cunanan spent only six weeks on the list before killing himself in a North Miami Beach boathouse.

While Cunanan was stirring up trouble on the East Coast, Tijuana drug cartel leader Ramon Eduardo Arellano-Felix, Number 451, was doing likewise in the West. A stereotypically loud, flashy, and deadly drug kingpin, Arellano-Felix was wanted for the assassination of a Catholic cardinal and the deaths of more than a dozen Mexican law enforcement officers, among other things. He was one of five brothers said to be running the ruthless cartel. Arellano-Felix, the organization's enforcer, was killed on February 10, 2002, in a shootout with Mexican authorities in Mazaltan, Mexico.

Harkening back to the old days, the FBI elevated Outlaw Motorcycle Club president Harry Joseph Bowman, 453, to Top Ten status in 1998 for a series of crimes that included racketeering, murder, bombings, and drug trafficking. Bowman was arrested a year later at his home in Sterling Heights, Michigan.

As a result of yet another highly controversial social battle, the Feds put antiabortion activist James Charles Kopp on the list in 1999 for the shooting death of an abortion doctor in western New York. Kopp was arrested in France in 2001.

All of which leads to the current edition of the FBI's Ten Most Wanted Fugitives, probably the most heinous, dangerous, and deadliest group ever assembled.

Chapter 2

Victor Manuel Gerena—
Armed Robber/Revolutionary
· ·
Reward: $50,000 for Gerena, Up to $700,000 for the Money

Unlike virtually every other Top Ten Fugitive, past or present, the FBI pretty much knows exactly where longtime Most Wanted Victor Manuel Gerena is. The high school wrestling star turned Puerto Rican activist is no doubt right where he's been since shortly after he served as the inside man in the disquietingly easy, $7.1 million robbery of a Wells Fargo depot in Connecticut in 1983. Gerena is a mere ninety miles from American soil, hanging out in Cuba under the protective wing of Fidel Castro.

Getting such men away from the cigar chomping dictator can be a bear. Castro, as history has repeatedly shown, likes nothing better than putting matches in the toes of his giant neighbor to the north. For the past twenty years Victor Gerena has been one of those matches.

The situation in Cuba regarding American criminals on the run is as bizarre and nonspecific as everything else about the island nation that remains the last bastion of communism in the Western Hemisphere. Uncle Sam has long been forced to swallow Castro's constant insults, annoyances, unfriendly acts, and the embracing of our Most Wanteds, out of respect for the greater ideal of keeping its paws off independent sovereign nations. The Bay of Pigs fiasco aside, simply overpowering the bearded dictator with America's vastly superior military, an option that would thrill the huge Cuban exile community that has flourished in South Florida, has been ruled out year by year, decade by decade, for nearly a half century. Afraid of angering Castro's communist supporters around the world—a group that has diminished considerably in number and power—the policy has been to use trade embargoes, economic sanctions, and other nonviolent measures and hope Castro's rule collapses from within.

Unfortunately, the fatigues-wearing politico has proven to be resilient. He's clung to power going on five decades now, with no sign of losing his iron grip. The current game plan is to simply wait until the seventy-six-year-old leader dies of old age, another process that's taken exceedingly long. Every now and then, reports that the aging dictator is in ill health builds the hopes of people from Miami to Washington, D.C. Invariably, Castro recovers, calls his nation of severely impoverished and oppressed people together, and launches another one of his maddening, four-hour diatribes against the U.S. to prove that he's still in fighting shape.

The only measure of vengeance Uncle Sam ever gets is the presence of a Marine military base in Guantanamo Bay, Cuba, the result of treaties that predate Castro's rule. Usually when a country goes red and becomes an enemy, such military bases are the first to go.

For reasons that will have historians scratching their heads for centuries to come, America has managed to hang on to this particular thorn in Castro's side.

To demonstrate the startling incongruity of the situation, while Castro was said to be sheltering some of 9/11 terrorist Osama bin Laden's al Qaeda leaders on his side of the island, America was using their corner to imprison Taliban forces captured during the recent war in Afghanistan.

Which means that Puerto Rican terrorist Victor Gerena is now closer than ever to a large-scale American prison facility. Unfortunately, he remains on the protected side of Castro's divided kingdom.

For decades, FBI agents, relatives, and those in and around West Hartford, Connecticut, have wondered what kind of life Gerena is living in Cuba. Castro has been known to be wildly schizophrenic when it comes to harboring the hundred or so American fugitives populating the island. He allows some of them to live in relative comfort, which by Cuban standards could mean little more than occasional running water, intermittent electricity, and enough basic food to survive. Others he tires of, takes their money and possessions, and either tosses them on the street or into one of his wretched prisons. Virtually all are forced to give up any idea of "the good life" in exchange for adhering to the continuing spirit of Castro's "people's revolution"—which basically translates to everyone else suffering in gnawing poverty while Castro lives high on the hog.

Former Black Panther turned cop killer turned airline hijacker William Lee Brent wrote a book about his life in Cuba. He was jailed for twenty-two months, then later "volunteered" to work in the blazing hot sugarcane fields and on a hog farm. He subsequently became an alcoholic.

Chances are, Gerena has suffered a similar fate. According to extensive FBI surveillance, it's apparent that he never saw a dime of his historic score. The money was quickly snatched up by Castro and the Puerto Rican anti-American revolutionary group "Los Macheteros" that he was briefly working with. Gerena probably rues the day he ever set foot on the decaying island where basic necessities have been sparse for decades and salaries for professionals with college educations top out at thirty dollars a month. He probably also rues the day he decided to throw in with the violent and greedy Puerto Rican independence gang that changed his life.

To make matters worse, of all the fugitives Castro has housed over the years, Gerena presents the dictator with a particularly sticky problem. The others committed their crimes on their own, then fled to Cuba. In Gerena's case, evidence is strong that the Cubans had a hand in planning and financing the robbery. (The former Cuban agent who did so, Jorge Masetti, later wrote a book published in France detailing precisely how.) That makes Castro an accomplice in what was then the second biggest heist in American history. Such a revelation, which the normally defiant and boastful Cubans have long denied, would hamstring Castro's efforts to have the stifling trade embargoes lifted. That came close to happening during the liberal Clinton administration. (Castro instead ended up with the famous refugee boy, Elian Gonzalez, as a consolation prize.) Castro is desperate to lift those restraints so he can start conning hundreds of millions of dollars' worth of needed goods and supplies from gullible

American businessmen—"conning" because, embargo or not, the scraggly dictator rarely pays his bills to friendly countries, much less avowed enemies. Exiled Cuban pop superstar Gloria Estefan, a leader among Miami's displaced Cuban community, has long warned eager businessmen with visions of sugarcane fortunes in their eyes about Castro's history of welshing on an astronomical scale.

Therefore, while other felons in Cuba are often allowed to speak to journalists and even write books, Gerena is kept under excruciatingly tight wraps. Not a peep has been heard from him in two decades.

As with so many on the FBI's post-Y2K Most Wanted Fugitives list, Victor Manuel Gerena has one whale of a weird story. Born in the summer of 1958, in Puerto Rico North—i.e., New York—Gerena's mother Gloria moved the typically large family to the growing Puerto Rican enclave of West Hartford, Connecticut, when he was twelve. Gloria Gerena left her husband behind and brought her five sons and daughter to Hartford to seek a better life in a smaller, less dangerous city that was filling with Puerto Ricans seeking work in the surrounding tobacco fields. Mama Gerena was a strong-willed, politically active sprite who fiercely supported the ideal of a free Puerto Rico. She often dragged young Victor to meetings where the controversial issue was hotly debated and talk of a violent, socialist revolution filled the air. (Most Puerto Ricans were and remain overwhelmingly against the idea, fearing their cherished American Commonwealth would sink into another dismal Cuba.)

Relatives say Victor wasn't into the political stuff, and they can't recall if he even had an opinion on the matter. Like most teens, he was into more immediate rewards, like girls and sports. The five-foot, seven-inch, 165-pound, dark-haired youth was bull strong. He played football and excelled at wrestling, eventually being chosen captain of the squad. Wrestling was a big deal at Bulkeley High, set in a tough, south Hartford neighborhood where machismo ruled. The team even had fawning group of pert Mat Maids who coddled and adored the brawny youth. Gerena, a charismatic, sensitive leader who wore nice clothes, also was member of the service-oriented Human Relations Club, acted as a peer counselor, and pulled a stint on the student council. In essence, he was a typical high school BMOC (Big Man on Campus).

He wasn't a dumb jock either. During his junior year he was picked out of the crowd to be part of the Upward Bound program that prepared the area's best students for college by busing them to preparatory classes at Trinity College. In 1976, Victor was awarded a $1,000 scholarship for school and community achievement, character, and financial need, and was handed a prized slot as a legislative intern. The slides were being greased to make sure Victor Gerena would be a BMOC beyond high school as well.

From all accounts, there was no hidden dark side. No eyebrow-raising disciplinary problems tainted his "permanent record," not even the playful boyish pranks that acclaimed high school athletes frequently fall victim to. However, there continued to be the influence of his otherwise good-intentioned mother. A devoted, hardworking single mom who believed strongly in education and discipline, she still had that odd, Puerto Rican Socialist Party side that supported island rabble rouser Filiberto Ojeda Rios and his violent Armed Commandos of Liberation, the precursor to the infamous Los Macheteros (the Machete Wielders). Although the Free Puerto Rico forces had minimal overall support, usually garnering a paltry three to five percent vote whenever the issue was placed on the ballots, its members were loud, devoted, single-minded, and determined. (In stark contrast to the independence movement, Puerto Rico's New Progressive Party, which has a solid political stronghold and many elected senators and representatives, wants the island to become America's fifty-first state.)

Victor continued to either ignore or quietly soak in the rhetoric of his mother and her friends, depending upon whom one believes. What isn't debatable is the influence another older woman had in his life. At the state capital, he captured the attention of Marion Delaney, one of those behind-the-scenes political forces whose modest job title belied her actual power. Chief of the clerk's office for the state House of Representatives, most credited her with running the entire state government. Delaney took a liking to the affable teen and set about polishing him like an apple to fit into high society. She advised him on how to dress for success, a subject he was already interested in, and helped smooth out the rough spots in his youthful language and behavior. Yet, as with his mother's unusual militant politics, there was a dark side to Delaney's nurturing.

Victor had been planning to attend the University of Connecticut, or Trinity, possibly on an academic or athletic scholarship. Instead, Delaney steered him toward Annhurst College, which happened to be her alma mater. Annhurst was a small, isolated, Catholic girls school run by French Canadian nuns, that was begrudgingly opening its doors to men in order to survive. Victor should have thanked Ms. Delaney and stuck to his guns. Instead, he let her work her well-practiced persuasive magic. What appealed to him, no doubt, was Annhurst's student body ratio—two-hundred-plus lonely females and less than twenty-five accommodating guys.

Those figures so tantalized him that he overlooked the glaring negatives on the flip side of the Annhurst coin. The ethnic diversity was minimal. The rural setting, though lovely, was staggeringly boring. The nearest town didn't even offer a disco where students could blow off steam on the weekends. A college without a bar? Annhurst, not to be confused with Amherst College in Massachusetts, obviously offered no athletic teams for men, and had never emphasized them for women. Such a setting, combined with its previous longstanding coeds-only policy, spoke of an institution geared toward intensive academic study. Not even a wealth of females could make up for those deficiencies.

Add in the fact that most of the nuns never wanted boys to foul the environment to begin with, and it's not hard to understand why Gerena's mood sunk and his grades plummeted. Plus, for the first time, he began to get into trouble. The initial offense could be expected—trying to sneak a girl into his dorm room. Understandable as that might be, it was nonetheless an "I told you so" jaw-dropping major crime among the celibate nuns of Annhurst. Gerena's second offense was also predictable. Someone was ducking into the offices and making unauthorized long-distance calls. Someone who was very homesick, no doubt. The records pointed to Gerena. He refused to fess up. A few months later, Annhurst was minus one troublesome male. Gerena dropped out.

Instead of regrouping and transferring to UConn or

Trinity the following semester, the failure hit Gerena hard. With no other college experience to go by, he found Annhurst's academic standards and workload to be daunting. If it was like that everywhere, he reasoned, he wasn't college material. His confidence shattered, he bounced around a number of menial jobs and moved in with a woman he'd previously left behind who still saw the former glory under the fresh coat of tarnish. They quickly had a child. For Victor, it had been a dizzying descent. In record time he'd plunged from can't miss high school star sent away to conquer the world, to the kind of fallen hero that causes the townsfolk to sadly shake their heads behind his back.

Itching to escape such disappointing looks, he switched mates, hooking up with the famously named but not *the* Pamela Anderson, another old friend from his brighter days. They both decided to join the Army, and later married. A second daughter followed. Army life wasn't Victor's thing either. After a string of AWOLs, both his military career and marriage came to abrupt ends.

Victor returned home to the same pitiful looks. After a brief stint as an elementary school special education counselor, he took a job that seemed to epitomize the Horatio Alger story in reverse—he became a part-time security guard. From high school hero to security guard in barely half a decade. Friends said his whole attitude had changed. Gone was the bright smile and crackling charisma of a lady-killing high school jock. In its place were sadness, depression, and a world weariness that made him appear older than his twenty-four years.

Ironically, the same mind-numbing, five-dollar-an-hour, Wells Fargo security job that symbolized his personal descent became his ticket to a second chance at stardom.

Two thousand miles away in Puerto Rico, Los Macheteros were starting to flex their socialist muscles. They attacked a U.S. Navy bus in Sabana Seca that was taking eighteen people to a communications transmitter site on the island's eastern coast. The rebels blocked the bus's path and sprayed it with bullets, killing two seamen and wounding ten others. A communiqué said the ambush was revenge for the hanging of a fellow rebel being held in a Tallahassee jail. (The death had been ruled a suicide.) Los Macheteros followed in January 1981 by using the explosive iremite to destroy eleven Puerto Rican National Guard jets valued at $45 million while they sat on the ground at a military facility in Carolina, Puerto Rico. The nine-minute assault wiped out the 198th Tactical Squadron. The rebels circulated a videotape played repeatedly on the local news that showed them preparing for the attack decked out in military fatigues and army boots. Those destructive acts came on the heels of previous assaults on the Puerto Rican electric company, which caused a whopping $150 million in damages, along with violent campaigns against the island's aqueducts and cement companies. Los Macheteros bombs exploded in New York and Chicago as well, taking out smaller targets. Sometimes the group left behind a machete inscribed with "Los Macheteros" as their calling card.

As with many South American insurgent organizations of the time, they received support, supplies, arms, and training in Castro's Cuba. (Noted international terrorist Carlos the Jackal, a Venezuelan, was a graduate of these Cuban camps.) The weapons and explosives

Los Macheteros used were often of Russian design, getting into their hands by way of Cuba. Los Macheteros "First Comrade in Charge," Filiberto Ojeda, had himself served as a Cuban agent.

The one thing Cuba has never had a lot of, however, is money. Los Macheteros, for all their violent success, were scraping the bottom financially. They needed to turn their attention to funding. Word traveled around the Hartford, New York, and Puerto Rican grapevine that there was a possible independence movement sympathizer in Hartford with a very interesting, albeit menial, job. Los Macheteros dispatched their boy wonder, Juan Segarra Palmer, to handle the recruitment. Palmer, a wiry, dignified man, was everything Victor Gerena wasn't. A child of wealth, instead of attending Blackboard Jungle public schools, he was shipped to ritzy Phillips Academy in Andover, Massachusetts. That paved his way to Harvard. Slick, urban, and passionate, it's not hard to imagine how Palmer seduced Gerena. With little else going on in his life, and made to feel important again, Gerena went along with Segarra's grandiose robbery scheme, one that came complete with a tantalizing code name—"White Eagle"—and was referred to in other documents as nothing more than an "economic operative for the benefit of the revolution." The planning was carried out via long-distance calls made through local pay phones. As the date of the heist approached, Segarra and Ojeda left Puerto Rico and traveled to Hartford to play their secondary roles.

By all accounts, on September 12, 1983, the day of the robbery, Gerena was cucumber cool. Nobody suspected a thing, not his family, coworkers, or even his new fiancée, Ana Soto. In fact, Soto, an aspiring beautician, was eagerly planning to pick up a marriage license that day. The couple was scheduled to be married the coming Friday. The only thing out of the ordinary was that Gerena, in one of the numerous quizzical elements of the plan, had recently obtained an aging, 1973 Buick LeSabre from a local "rent-a-wreck" company. Risking everything on a vehicle that was liable to blow a gasket at any moment was a high-wire act, but may have been done to quell suspicion.

Shortly before noon, Gerena dropped Soto off at City Hall to get the license, then continued on to work. His boss, Security Manager James McKeon, twenty-five, allowed Gerena to park the big car in a loading bay, secluding it from view. Gerena's assignment that day was to pick up bags of cash during a series of stops between Bridgeport and Hartford. He was accompanied by a driver, Timothy R. Girard, twenty-one. McKeon took a second truck north to make similar pickups in Springfield. The runs weren't complete until after 9:00 P.M. Even then the work wasn't over. A ton or more of cash had to be removed, counted, and stored in its proper place.

As the moment approached for Gerena to make his move, the first snag hit. At that time of night, only Gerena and McKeon were scheduled to be around. Instead, Girard lingered. Gerena suddenly had to take the two men down instead of one, including a guy he'd spent the whole day chatting and joking with. Unable to wait any longer, Gerena snuck up behind McKeon as he was doing paperwork, grabbed his gun from his holster, brandished it about, and told the pair that it was a stickup. It's hard to fathom that the heist was so poorly planned and financed that it relied totally upon Gerena being able to snatch his boss's weapon. To give

the otherwise heavily armed and crafty Macheteros the
benefit of the doubt, it was apparently planned that
way to avoid a potential shootout. Whatever the truth,
after successfully taking McKeon's weapon, Gerena
ordered them to the floor. Bringing only a single pair of
handcuffs, he used them on McKeon. He had to improvise with Girard, scrounging up tape and rope. He then
threw coats over their heads and injected both men
with a serum that was supposed to put them to sleep,
with "supposed to" being the optimum words. Possibly
because the dose had to be halved, and equally possibly because Los Macheteros screwed up, the sleeping
juice didn't work. (The FBI would later find no trace of
drugs in the two men's blood.) Either way, it didn't
matter. While the stunned Wells Fargo employees
squirmed on the floor wide-awake, breathing under the
coats, Gerena spent the next ninety minutes stuffing a
half ton of cash into zippered bags of some sort and
packing them into every free inch of space inside the
old car.

Despite the extraordinary length of time, nobody
noticed what was going on. The Wells Fargo depot was
in a business area that had mostly closed for the evening. In addition, the Dallas Cowboys and Washington
Redskins were in the process of a thrilling, 31-30 grid-
iron battle on *Monday Night Football*, and everyone in
town seemed to be glued to their television sets and radios. After stealing as much as he could, Gerena
cranked the car's engine. The corroded battery and
worn cylinders didn't betray him. It fired up and rum-
bled off, the added weight straining the suspension.
The subdued Wells Fargo employees reported that they
heard two beeps before Gerena left the property, no
doubt some kind of signal to his hidden accomplices.

It should be noted that Gerena received no assistance at any point during the robbery. None of the macho Macheteros even helped him hoist the backbreaking, rock-hard loads of cash. No doubt the plan was that if he was caught in mid-robbery—and chances were good, considering the length of time it took—Gerena would carry all the blame on his strong, broad shoulders.

Two additional factors jump out at this point. The first is how incredibly easy it was for a five-dollar-an-hour, unarmed security guard to single-handedly pull off the second-biggest robbery in U.S. history. (Second biggest, in fact, by less than a year, as $11 million was boosted from a Sentry Armored Car warehouse in New York nine months earlier.) Even with all the "sleepless in Hartford" snags, the job went off without a hitch. To be fair, it's understandable that Gerena got the security job. He was a local boy, a high school hero with no criminal record who came from a large and respected area family. It's hard to fault the famous security company from that end. Nor can anyone blame the young security manager and driver. They didn't run the show, and inside jobs are almost impossible to foil once an employee gets the drop. One can question, however, the lack of institutional safeguards and checks and balances in place to prevent such an occurrence. Revolutionary group aside, it has to be tempting for young men making barely above the minimum wage to be surrounded by that much cash.

The second thing that leaps out is why Victor Manuel Gerena didn't floor that old green Buick and take off in the opposite direction of the waiting Macheteros. After all, he had accomplished the robbery entirely by himself. The only possible assistance they provided up to then was the sleeping serum that didn't work. Why should he hand over so rich a reward to a bunch of unseen partners who wouldn't even help him lift the load? The answer is that Victor Gerena wasn't your basic cutthroat thief. In his heart, he wasn't a thief at all. He was a revolutionary! Friends, relatives, and law enforcement agents have long felt he was motivated by the opportunity to win back his mother's respect, while at the same time becoming a hero again to a certain segment of Hartford's community. For some people, those things are worth more than $7 million.

Thus, the dutiful recruit didn't hesitate to bring the pot of gold to his Puerto Rican masters. Somewhere, not far from the now emptied depot, the LeSabre's precious cargo was quickly unloaded into other vehicles, and Victor was whisked by motorcycle to Springfield. Switching vehicles again, he was ferried by auto to Boston.

At this point Gerena was indeed relying on the help, skills, and connections of his grateful fellow revolutionaries. To their credit, instead of just putting a bullet in his head and tossing his body into the closest ditch, they helped him regroup and then head south to Mexico. The Los Macheteros operatives shoved him inside the false closet of a used motor home, and, just in case that wasn't stifling enough, they killed two birds with one stone and squeezed $2 million in there with him. The ruse was more than enough to trick the sleepy Mexican border guards in Laredo.

Once in Mexico, Gerena and the cash were taken to Mexico City, where high-ranking Cuban Embassy officials and espionage agents—including former Cuban agent Jorge Masetti, the guy with the secret literary ambition—provided him with a passport and a one-way ticket on Cubana de Aviacion to his new home. The money would travel in an official Cuban diplomatic pouch, no questions asked. (The remaining $5 million would later be taken to Cuba in a similar manner.)

By all accounts, it was somewhere in Mexico that Gerena learned for the first time that his reward for carrying out the robbery would be a lifetime exile in Cuba. Unfamiliar with world politics, it's possible that the young ex-wrestler had no objection to the plan because he didn't have the faintest concept of the difficulties he would be facing. Cuba, in his mind, was probably another tropical island paradise like Puerto Rico. With his share of the big score, he could live like a king.

Only nobody lives like a king in Cuba except Fidel Castro, especially not a Puerto Rican security guard from Hartford. And the money he was so intimately close to at the depot, inside the Buick, and in the motor home was slated to be gobbled up to the last dime by Castro and Los Macheteros. To add insult to injury, Los Macheteros ruled—over the objection of Juan Segarra Palmer—that Ana Soto, marriage license in hand, was being watched too closely by the FBI and local police to heed Gerena's lonely cries to bring her to him as promised. Soto, who had been briefly arrested after the theft for "hindering prosecution," was devastated by the decision, falling so deeply into despair that she turned to drugs and ended up serving time.

After those staggering developments, Gerena vanished from every known radar screen.

The FBI was able to learn what happened up to that point through a series of wiretaps of the Los Macheteros offices and safe houses from Connecticut to Mexico. What was initially the perfect crime—law enforcement had no clue of the Puerto Rican connection in the early months—began to unravel as Los Macheteros grew high on their newfound wealth and were dying to take credit for the sensationally successful robbery in order to breathe life into their wheezing revolution. A woefully ill-advised attack on a U.S. government building in Hato Rey, Puerto Rico, a month and a half after the Wells Fargo robbery put the FBI on the tail of Los Macheteros. The bombing, done in protest of America's invasion of Grenada to stop Cuba's expansion there, was accomplished with a hand-held antitank rocket launcher and shell that was traced back to Vietnam. The discarded, American-made, bazooka-type weapon known as a "Falcone" had made the long journey from a Da Nang rice paddy to a building that housed an FBI office through the bucket-brigade assistance of North Vietnam, Russia, and Cuba. The affront upon their own space was all the FBI needed to fire up their state-of-the-art listening devices and get serious about bringing down the pesty Puerto Rican militants. The wiretaps and records found in subsequent raids enlightened the FBI as to the details of the Wells Fargo raid and the sad fate of Victor Gerena.

If the FBI hadn't untangled the mystery through skill and hard work, chances are they would have later without wasting a day's effort. Aside from Masetti's book, the otherwise astute Juan Palmer wrote a screenplay about the caper. It wasn't that outlandish an idea. Los Macheteros, after all, were desperately trying to wake up a comfortable Puerto Rican populace that for the most part wanted no part of their silly scheme to cut the ties to America. Most Puerto Ricans like America. Especially the ability to travel to and find work in the wealthy capitalist nation. The four million Puerto Ricans are American citizens who can't vote in U.S. presidential elections but don't have to pay federal income tax—a trade-off most mainland Americans would gladly accept. It's one of the great incongruities of both Puerto Rican and American life that U.S.-educated, anti-American rebels like Juan Palmer were trying to sway and recruit fellow islanders in American cities like Hartford and New York. These were the same Puerto Ricans who had chosen to live, work, buy homes, and raise their families in America rather than stay home in Puerto Rico. A powerful motion picture made in Hollywood, one that starred, say, Eric Estrada as Palmer and Emilio Estevez as Gerena, might do wonders to turn that kind of ingrained "Proud to Be a Puerto Rican American" thinking around.

While it was a good stargazing idea, chasing Tinsel Town was a bad reality. All Palmer's screenplay did was add more confessions to the heaping pile of wiretap transcripts connecting Los Macheteros and Castro to various crimes inside America, including the Wells Fargo robbery.

Prior to Palmer's screenwriting endeavor, the group sent postcards to area newspapers, including the highly interested *Hartford Courant*, to celebrate the first anniversary of the robbery. The cards were signed by Gerena. A follow-up note spoke of Gerena's "perfect state of health" and happiness in joining "the struggle which our people carry out to obtain our liberation." The note added that the money was safe and sound, and included halves of ten-dollar bills later confirmed as being part of the haul.

In truth, the money was in Cuba, where it was anything but safe. Castro skimmed a cool $2 million off the top as payment for his help. Two divided factions of Los Macheteros, at each other's throats over what to do with their new wealth, were said to be sharing the rest, which Castro still controlled in his banks. "Inside the organization, they were just ripping over the money," a law enforcement officer told the *Courant.*

Postcard-signing, fiancé-missing Victor Gerena was sharing in nothing. He didn't even get a cut of the $12,000 worth of toys Los Macheteros soldiers handed out to poor kids in Hartford and Puerto Rico in 1985 to further ingratiate themselves with the still uninterested Puerto Rican community. Photos of Los Macheteros posing as the Three Wise Men were dispatched to the media in an effort to convince their fellow islanders that they were indeed good guys with a righteous cause.

That same year, the FBI pulled together their case against Los Macheteros and earned a grand jury indictment against the main players. All that was left was to round them up, which was done in a series of precision raids in San Juan. Using a crack, two-hundred-member hostage rescue team trained for the 1984 Olympics, they hit the island hard, smoking out thirteen Los Macheteros from thirty homes and businesses. Along with the men, they seized numerous M-16 rifles, a .45 caliber Thompson submachine gun, an Israeli-made Uzi submachine gun that Ojeda used to fire at agents, 145 blasting caps, clocks rigged to be used as detonators, a large roll of fuse, bulletproof vests, camouflage fatigues with hoods, homemade grenades, military manuals, organizational charts, and uniforms intended to disguise rebels as telephone company employees, power workers, U.S. postal carriers, and Puerto Rican police officers. The soldiers were brought back to Hartford, tried, and convicted as common criminals in 1989.

Only the FBI didn't get them all. They didn't get Victor Gerena.

In 2001, Gerena's cousin, a Vietnam veteran named Francisco Jimenez Gerena, traveled from Miami to Cuba to try and find the long-lost Victor. He didn't expect to rescue the fugitive, or even bring him back for judgment. He just wanted to see what happened to the brotherlike relative the entire Gerena family lost touch with two decades before. Francisco Gerena invited *Hartford Courant* reporter Edmund H. Mahony to go along, a decision that may have doomed the effort but allowed Mahony to write a moving account of not only their search, but of life inside today's Cuba. A few years earlier, Mahony had written the definitive tale of the Wells Fargo robbery, Victor Gerena's life, and the rise and fall of Los Macheteros in a studiously researched eight-part series published by the *Courant* in 1999. (The robbery series, Mahony's Cuba story, "Chasing Gerena," and the latest updates can be accessed via the *Courant*'s archives: www.ctnow.com/about/hc-archives.htmlstory.) Most of the facts and details reported here were first uncovered by Mahony in 1999.

Mahony's emotional account of Franciso Jimenez Gerena's gut-wrenching journey has the grinding sense of futility that is all too familiar to anyone who has ever been to the communist island. Repeatedly jerked around by "friendly" Cuban authorities, the two men were promised everything and given nothing. They were even shut off from communicating by telephone with each other at one point, throwing yet another wrench into their search efforts.

"Helpful" Cuban security officials said that they

could deliver a request that Victor Gerena phone his
cousin, "but we can't make him call if he doesn't want
to." It was a highly convenient loophole, considering
Castro has gleefully spent his life making people do
what they don't want to—including remain trapped on
the wretched island when they'd rather be in Miami.
The optimistic excitement of receiving a possible call
was further tempered by the fact that the officer
seemed unconcerned that Francisco Gerena didn't
know the phone number of the place he would be staying at in Bahia Honda, or even if his modest lodging
had a phone. The security officer said not to worry.
They'd find him.

Sure they would.

Aside from the frustrating runaround, the two Americans encountered an ugly form of reverse racism that
didn't speak well of Victor Gerena's life on the island.
Mahony, an Anglo, was welcomed at the Sevilla hotel,
while Francisco Gerena and his Cuban friends were repeatedly hassled and turned away. The Sevilla, it
seems, is only for European tourists and other whites.
Natives and neighboring islanders are not allowed.

Which segues into the issue of Puerto Ricans and
Cubans. Although sister Caribbean islands with similar
histories, the two Spanish nations are separated, among
other things, by the same language, as the popular
British/American saying goes. The Cuban and Puerto
Rican accents and dialogue are as different as a Lon-
doner speaking to someone from Alabama. In America,
Cubans and Puerto Ricans rarely congregate. Although
Miami is the closest major American city to Puerto
Rico and is overwhelmingly Spanish speaking, there is
little Puerto Rican presence in the Cuban-dominated

city. Those from each island who chose to settle farther north selected distinct and distant locations—New York and Hartford for the Puerto Ricans, Union City, New Jersey, for the Cubans.

Regardless, Francisco Gerena was warmly welcomed by the Cuban relatives of a Miami Cuban friend of his, mainly because he was an American from the Cuban Mecca of Miami and had brought a large suitcase full of everyday necessities that are cherished in Cuba, things like flip-flops, soap, razors, toothpaste, toilet tissue, and clothing. The Cubans in Bahia Honda celebrated his visit but could do nothing to help him in his quest other than point out the government spies who were watching his every move.

Growing impatient, Mahony reported that Francisco Gerena returned to the airport to speak to a security officer who had at least been hopeful. A different security officer greeted him tersely and said, "Go back to your hotel and wait. Stop looking for him."

Veteran Cuban travelers say such a passive stance rarely works. The only way to accomplish anything on the island is to stay in the shadows and aggressively pursue one's objective, making friends, spreading around money, and hoping the same Cuban snarls of red tape will work in your favor by paralyzing any attempts to stop you. This, of course, can be extremely risky.

Growing frustrated and impatient, reporter Mahony did finally take a more aggressive stance. Although never officially credentialed as a journalist—that also involved a mind-numbing runaround—he contacted a source in Havana to see if he could help. The man chastised him on the futility of the mission, but did refer him to another Puerto Rican revolutionary on the island, a former anti-American FALN (Puerto Rican Armed Forces of National Liberation) bomb specialist named William Morales. The glib Morales lost his hands and much of his face when a device he was building prematurely detonated in New York.

Hooking up with Morales was a major score. He would surely know about his brother revolutionary Victor Gerena, especially on such a small island where Puerto Ricans are scarce. Despite the fact that Morales himself was an escaped fugitive from American justice, he proved to be easy to find, friendly and chatty. He met the men over dinner and talked about everything under the Cuban sun—everything except Victor Gerena. Earlier, before Morales and his Cuban wife knew the reason for the two Americans' visit, they had questioned Francisco with great curiosity regarding his obviously familiar last name. Once Morales knew their mission, however, he clammed up. Pressed, he finally asked his visitors to please stop asking about Victor.

What the handless Puerto Rican—a man with a face painstakingly rebuilt by American plastic surgeons at the expense of the American taxpayer—did provide was yet another glimpse into life on the lam in Castro's Cuba. As with everyone else, Morales admitted he struggled through the years from the lack of basic necessities, but seemed content enough to be where he was instead of the alternative—an American prison cell serving out a ninety-nine-year sentence. Freedom can be relative.

After that, the pair concluded that locating Gerena, or even receiving that elusive call, was too much to hope for. They left the island knowing no more about the actual post-Hartford life of Victor Gerena than they knew before.

The dispiriting trip could have resulted from typical Cuban soul-wrenching deception—or something much darker. Some whisper that Castro was so afraid of Gerena connecting him to the Wells Fargo plot that he solved the problem the way he's been solving problems for the past half century. When things quieted down, say two to three years after the robbery, he simply summoned Gerena to a meeting—possibly on the premise of giving him an award—and had him executed on the spot à la Joe Pesci in the movie *GoodFellas*. End of Fidel's problema.

The FBI says there is no evidence to support that theory, and they never heard it mentioned on any of the wiretaps. They are proceeding on the belief that Gerena remains alive. In fact, some agents speculate that it's equally likely that Gerena may have pulled off what a million-plus other unhappy Cubans have done over the years—catch a late night boat ride to Florida. If so, he's quietly filtered back into American life under a new identity—so quietly he's astutely resisted the temptation to contact his relatives.

Following the robbery in 1983, Wells Fargo offered a $700,000 reward for Gerena's capture and the return of the stolen money, at the time the highest price ever put on a Ten Most Wanted Fugitive's head. As the years passed and the cash was assumed consumed, the bounty on Gerena dwindled back down to the standard $50,000 the FBI offers. (Wells Fargo will still pay a ten percent reward on any of the money recovered.) Outside of his family, Victor Gerena began to fade into oblivion.

President Clinton changed that for a while in 2000 when he offered clemency and/or early release to members of various Puerto Rican rebel groups, including the imprisoned Los Macheteros. It was one of many such controversial moves Clinton made prior to leaving office. This particular affront to the FBI was said to be a ploy to gain his wife Hillary the Puerto Rican vote in her New York senatorial campaign. The FBI and other law enforcement groups hotly protested the move, and have steadfastly kept Gerena on the list despite the shaved sentences of his former puppeteers.

Victor Manuel Gerena was born June 24, 1958. His hair, which may be thinning and graying, was originally brown. His eyes are green. He's five-seven, stocky, with a dark complexion, and probably weighs about 170 pounds. He has a small scar and mole on his right shoulder. These descriptions are based on the way he appeared twenty years ago and projections of how he might appear today. He has not been seen by anyone outside Cuba since 1983.

The Reward

Chances of the average Joe spotting Gerena and collecting the $50,000 reward, or recovering the money and collecting $700,000—are remote. Gerena is said to be hiding in Cuba, a repressive island nation where foreigners stick out. The $7.1 million from the heist was taken by Fidel Castro and the Puerto Rican revolutionary group Los Macheteros and no doubt has been long spent. (If Gerena has returned to America, he's completely shielded his new identity.)

Chances of a Cuban exile finding Gerena and collecting the $50,000 reward? Good. It wouldn't be too hard for a savvy Cuban to sneak back into Cuba, blend in, spread some money around, and locate the well-known Puerto Rican fugitive. Gerena is probably poor and living among the repressed Cuban people. However, even if that was accomplished, the FBI still wouldn't be able to extradite him. If the $7.1 million was still around, it might have been worthwhile for a small commando unit to try and kidnap Gerena and ferry him to Miami by boat. However, with the guaranteed reward back to the $50,000 minimum, and little hope of finding a dime of the $7.1 million (outside of Castro's pocket), that's hardly worth the trouble.

Chapter 3

James J. "Whitey" Bulger—
Mobster

. . . .

Reward: $1 million

Through the decades, a number of heavyweight mobsters like Carmine "the Snake" Persico and Genovese
family enforcer Carmine DiBiase dotted the Ten Most
Wanted list, but not near as many as one might think.
The reason goes to the heart and purpose of the list itself. Created to publicize lesser known fugitives on the
run, that description rarely fits this special breed of
criminal. The bosses, underbosses, and ranking cap-
tains of America's colorful but deadly Mafia families
tend to be easy to find. That's because they are highly
provincial, preferring to remain at all costs in the territories they rule. The FBI generally knows where they
are—usually right at home. The name of the game in
bringing down mobsters is building a case against the
highly protected and insulated bosses and making it
stick in court.

When indicted, La Cosa Nostra Godfathers invariably turn to their high-priced lawyers to fight the battle
in court rather than leave the comfort of their houses,

favorite restaurants, and nightclub playgrounds. If convicted, they shrug and serve their time, considering it part of "the life" and the price of doing business.

Famed Gambino boss John Gotti, for example, never ran. He successfully fought a string of indictments in court, all while keeping a high public profile. The Dapper Don didn't even head for the hills when the last case looked to be, and was, overwhelming.

A decade before, a massive, interagency task force encompassing eleven separate government divisions convened on Long Island to bring down the lucrative reign of Colombo captain Michael Franzese, known as the "Yuppie Don." Feeling the intensive heat, the more mobile Franzese expanded his billion-dollar gasoline, auto dealerships, music, and motion picture empire to Florida and Los Angeles, but never went underground. When indicted in New York, he simply surrendered in Los Angeles and came back to face the music.

In the same vein, legendary old-timers like Al Capone weren't hard to find when it came time for Eliot Ness and gang to reel them in. It's simply not considered dignified for a mob boss to go on the lam. Away from their kingdoms and estranged from their "family" of loyal soldiers, they become just another vulnerable desperado hiding from the law in unfamiliar places. The easy time mobsters spend in prison is generally preferable to hard time on the road.

Even on a lower level, organized crime soldiers, associates, and wannabes generally don't hit the bricks when sought. They tend to be even more provincial than the higher-ups, and find life away from the city blocks where they command respect and power to be unpleasant. Those who do leave invariably end up coming right back.

All of which explains why the Gottis, Franzeses, Colombos, Genoveses, Gambinos, Bonannos, Luccheses, Profacis, and Capones of the world never graced the FBI's Top Ten despite being some of the most powerful and notorious organized crime figures in American history. When a mobster does hit the list, it's often a lower-level "button-man" assassin, or someone who's wanted more for the information he possesses than the crime he committed.

Which makes it extremely curious as to why Boston Irish mob boss James J. "Whitey" Bulger has gone against the pasta grain and taken flight. Precisely who is Whitey running from? Is the aging Irish hood ducking an indictment on multiple charges of murder and conspiracy, or is he trying to escape the wrath of a legion of fellow mobsters it turns out he ratted out over the years? More intriguing still, is Whitey hiding from a hit squad of rogue FBI agents who don't want the loose-lipped old gangster turned informant anywhere near a witness box? Considering the mob behavior outlined above, there could be more truth in B and C than in A.

What is known is that a cornucopia of improbable, un-mob-like elements seen more in failed Hollywood scripts than on the streets of Boston combined to force Whitey Bulger into hiding. Subsequently, the longtime hood got his Irish mug plastered in a very undignified manner on the FBI's Most Wanted Fugitives list in 1999, spot Number 458, $1 million reward. In the process, Bulger's case has become a can of worms so large it could stock a fishing fleet for an entire season.

It should be noted, right off, that Bulger ran an Irish "clone" faction, known as the Winter Hill Gang, that was based on the militarylike organizational structure of the traditional Italian mob but was loosely knit and wasn't governed by the strict rules and traditions of the sometimes stodgy La Cosa Nostra. Second, Bulger and other Winter Hill members got a bit too cozy with some fast-and-loose FBI agents, serving as informants on other area gangsters while being allowed to run their own criminal operations. Third, Bulger and right-hand man Stephen Flemmi committed some "personal" murders of women that look more like the work of psychopathic serial killers Ted Bundy and Christopher Wilder than a traditional Italian mob boss who has to plant the occasional rival soldier for purely business reasons.

Whitey's story—and it's a whale of a tale—began in the tough Irish neighborhoods of Charlestown and South Boston during the Depression of the 1930s. A notorious street fighter, the light-haired, ultracool Whitey was the Fonz of his day, leading the Mercer Street Gang and earning the envy and adoration of the younger kids who swarmed around like flies and viewed him as a rebel hero. In contrast, Whitey's little brother Billy was a serious, studious child as clean as his brother was dirty. While Whitey was bad to the bone from day one, Billy Bulger was destined to escape the Old Harbor tenements—the first public housing projects constructed in New England—and become an influential State Senate president, and later the president of the University of Massachusetts.

Both Bulger boys commanded respect for different reasons, and few were more in awe than a young kid named John Connolly, a child whose own future path would oddly enough bridge that of the brothers.

The Bulgers had moved into the projects when they opened in 1938, and Whitey quickly began to domi-

nate the tough, low income Irish neighborhood. By the
time Connolly was ambulatory enough to roam around
himself, Whitey Bulger was already a local legend.
Connolly was eight and Whitey nineteen when they
first bumped into each other at the candy store. It was
"like meeting Ted Williams," the youngster recalled.
Bulger, a delinquent with a heart, bought Connolly and
some other kids ice cream cones that day. Not long afterward, Connolly found himself in a scrum with some
bigger boys over the possession of a ball. Whitey appeared Fonzlike out of the blue and chased the bullies
away.

Four years later Connolly's family moved, upgrad-
ing to City Point. He kept in touch with Billy Bulger,
attended Boston College, graduated, then joined the
government police agency and became a Special Agent
for the FBI around the same time the Feds began their
Ten Most Wanted program. Billy Bulger similarly
went the higher education route and graduated to a life
in local politics. Whitey dropped out and robbed
banks. He was busted in 1956 and sentenced to twenty
years. At Alcatraz prison, he volunteered to take acid
(LSD) for government doctors studying the illegal psy-
chedelic hippie drug. In return for "turning on and trip-
ping out," he was able to knock a cool decade off his
sentence, earning parole in 1965.

The nine-year incarceration did little to prevent
Whitey from keeping up with the Billys and Johns. At
the same time his brother was rising up the ranks in
Boston politics, and the little candy store kid John
Connolly was doing likewise at the FBI, Whitey was
becoming a force inside the Winter Hill crime gang
that terrorized South Boston. The Irish mob was then
ruled by an old school pug coincidentally named

Howie Winter—the gang was named for the area it operated in rather than its similarly dubbed boss. Winter and associates made its blood money by getting its claws into hardworking longshoremen via loan sharks, shaking down bookies, selling the typical unneeded protection to area stores and restaurants, hijacking trucks, and fencing stolen goods. They also did the dirty work—i.e., hits—for the bigger, more powerful Italian mob run from Providence, Rhode Island, by legendary New England boss Raymond L.S. Patriarca. The Italians operated in the more upscale areas of North and East Boston and had little desire to scrape for nickels and dimes in the unruly Irish sections. (Patriarca underboss Gennaro Angiulo was caught on an FBI wiretap once reminiscing about how they had to bury twenty Irishmen to take over the prime areas of Boston they desired.)

Howie Winter came to power the old-fashioned way. He was the last captain left standing after a series of brutal turf wars among hot-headed Irish clans left more than sixty mob soldiers dead during the turbulent 1960s. Included among the victims was Somerville gang leader Buddy McLean, Winter's boss. Just under Winter in the new pecking and extorting order were a pair of trigger-happy young turks—James "Whitey" Bulger and Steve "the Rifleman" Flemmi. With Winter's brains and Bulger and Flemmi's muscle, the gang flourished throughout the 1970s until the Feds toppled the leadership by hitting them with an indictment in 1979 for fixing horse races at six East Coast tracks.

Miraculously—or so it seemed at the time—Bulger and Flemmi escaped the police dragnet and assumed their places on the symbolic mob throne inside a garage on Lancaster Street that served as the gang's headquarters. Things continued to go well on Winter Hill, so much so that the Italian Flemmi turned down offers to join his brethren to the north and become an official "made man" in the Patriarca family. (Bulger, being Irish, could not be extended such an honor.) The Italians respected the deadly efficiency of Bulger and Flemmi, and the two mobs operated and even commingled for decades without stepping on each other's toes.

"There's no difference between these guys," a law enforcement officer told the *Boston Globe* at the time. "Some of them got o's before their last name, and some of them got o's at the end."

Bulger's life came full circle in late 1975 when he cut an extraordinary deal in the darkness of Wollaston Beach that would eventually make him one of the most powerful mobsters in America. The offer came from the same little ice-cream-cone-eating kid from the Southie projects, John J. Connolly, who Whitey rescued from the bullies eons before.

Connolly was now a big-shot mob-busting FBI agent of considerable renown. His stock had soared when an informant named Sonny Mercurio gave him the advanced details of where the Italians were holding their latest secret induction ceremony of newly made men. Swinging into action with wiretaps, it was one of the first times the FBI got the now familiar longtime Mafia ritual of fire, blood, and loyalty oaths on tape. Connolly followed that sensational score by reaching out to his old neighborhood hero, Whitey Bulger, making him an offer that was hard to refuse. In return for providing information used to prosecute rival mobsters—mainly members of the dominate Patriarca family—the FBI would look the other way regarding the antics of the less influential Winter Hill Gang. To set the hook, Connolly warned Bulger that a mob war was on the horizon over vending machines, and the Italians were planning to feed the Irishmen up to their police sources. The way Bulger saw it, the Irishmen were finally being given a chance to grab the long end of a deal. They'd be getting the high-powered FBI as partners rather than the less reliable local cops. (Former boss Howie Winter claims there was no such turf war brewing. The FBI fabricated the threat, he says, to push Bulger over the edge.)

Although it involved being a rat, it was a difficult deal for Bulger to reject. The only way he could avoid another long prison sentence was to get his own law enforcement guardians. And not only would he be protected, but he could use the nation's most famous police agency as his own personal goon squad. If anybody got in his way, or rubbed him the wrong way, all he'd have to do was point them out to the Feds and list their most recent crimes. Problem eliminated, clean, simple, and legal. This empowerment appealed to Bulger, a man who couldn't swallow playing second fiddle to anyone, not even bona fide Italian mobsters. He equated it to the Italians "playing checkers" while "we'll play chess," and agreed to his "home boy" Connolly's terms. Newly ordained chess master Whitey Bulger was given the unimaginative code name "Charlie," and officially became the most despised creature in the organized crime universe—a low-down scumbag snitch.

Further greasing Bulger's slide into ratdom was the fact that his best buddy, Flemmi, a former paratrooper in the Korean War, had already agreed to a similar arrangement a few years earlier. The twin informant agreements quickly paid off for both men. The handshake deals were the reason Flemmi and Bulger escaped the devastating horse-race-fixing indictment that chopped the head off the Winter Hill Gang at the dawn of the 1980s and enabled them to leap into the top slots. It wasn't the first time Bulger and Flemmi used their rat power on their own gang brothers, nor would it be the last.

It may have been the proverbial "deal with the devil" from both the FBI and Bulger's perspective, but even its harshest critics had to admit that it served the two organizations well. Bulger and Flemmi had their heavy club and iron-clad protection. In return, the FBI had the moles they needed to eat away at the more threatening Italian mob, eventually bringing it to its knees.

The deal itself was nothing extraordinary on the surface. It was a longstanding FBI policy to "turn" or "flip" gangsters to dismantle a crime family from within, a strategy that has proven to be highly successful throughout the country. The Patriarcas were the kingfishes in Boston, while the Irish gangs were snarling little guppies always battling among themselves, splintering and dying out. The only fly in this particular ointment was that the FBI underestimated the ambition of their new partners. To turn an old cliché, Bulger and Flemmi were given an unlimited leash—and they exceeded it. The pair, already vicious killers, became even more heartless, arrogant, and power hungry than before. In 1981 a wiretap of a Patriarca hangout caught underboss Gennaro Angiulo giving this endorsement of Bulger and Flemmi: "If I called these guys right now they'll kill anybody we tell them to."

Complicating matters was that Bulger and Flemmi's FBI handlers, critics and prosecutors would later charge, danced not only too close to the fire, but in the fire. They began socializing with the pair, dressing like gangsters complete with gold chains and pinky rings, trading expensive gifts on holidays, and becoming, for all practical purposes, a secret amalgamated mob of their own. Connolly went so far as buying a fancy condominium in a unit that also housed the love nests of Bulger and a Winter Hill lieutenant named Kevin Weeks. Fellow FBI agents observing the disquieting transformation began openly referring to Connolly as "Giovanni Connolino."

As he did all along, Connolly offers a persuasive and fiercely stated argument in his defense. He counters that such social interaction and ascetic blending in came with the job of turning and maintaining prized, high-level informants. The less the agents stood out, the more comfortable and trusting the informants became. Bulger and Flemmi not only acted as the eyes and ears of the agency on the streets and in the secret back rooms of organized crime, but promised to warn their new "friends" of any threats or plots made against the lives of investigating FBI agents, a critical trade-off in the G-men's dangerous line of work.

"There was a respect and an admiration there, no question about it," Connolly admitted to reporters, referring to Bulger. "But always looming in the background was the realism of what he did for a living and what I did for a living."

Overlooked, however, was what Connolly's fellow law enforcement officers did for a living. In another sticky situation that could be argued as unavoidable, the FBI naturally couldn't risk letting their law enforcement cousins in on the deal for fear of leaks to rival gangsters. Because of this, Connolly's crew became the embodiment of the starched, arrogant, backstabbing Feds that the local police detectives like Starsky and Hutch loathe on all those popular television shows. Countless man-hours were wasted by Boston state troopers, city detectives, and even federal drug agents who tried to build cases against the Winter Hill Gang leaders only to have them mysteriously disintegrate time after time.

Uglier still, although the agency supposedly stopped short of giving Bulger and Flemmi a license to kill, the bodies nonetheless began to pile up. And not all of it was "business." Most egregious were the twin "Debbie" mutilations and murders that occurred in the early 1980s, but wouldn't be discovered until nearly two decades later. Although flush with power, Steve Flemmi began having routine girlfriend problems that he decided to deal with in a nonroutine gangland style. First, a cute shop girl named Debra Davis incurred his wrath when she decided she'd had enough of his violent, philandering ways in 1981 and announced that she was leaving him. Flemmi had dazzled her with his wise guy charm nine years before when she was only seventeen, plying her with expensive baubles and sports cars, and moving her into his fancy apartment. In a fit of anger, she screamed some idle threats about not only leaving, but exposing her boyfriend, his pal Bulger, and their FBI sugar daddy John Connolly unless he left her alone. That earned her a one-way ticket into a makeshift grave not far from Bulger's home. Prosecutors believe both Bulger and Flemmi had a hand in silencing the young woman, luring her to a "safe" house owned by Flemmi's mother and strangling her there. Davis was buried in a hastily dug hole under a railroad trestle near the Neponset River in Quincy, Massachusetts

Horrific as that was, the case of Debbie Number 2 was even more wrenching. Deborah Hussey was Flemmi's stepdaughter, whom he raised like a harem girl from infancy and turned into a mistress not long after she hit puberty. Thoroughly messed up from the experience, Hussey turned to drugs and prostitution before following in the vocal footsteps of Debbie 1 and threatening to expose the sexual deviancy of her father/lover. She made noises about squealing to, among others, her mother Marion—Flemmi's common-law wife—and her two younger brothers and sister, who were Flemmi's blood children. Taken out and double-teamed à la Debbie 1, the murder hit a snag when Flemmi showed a flash of humanity and balked at killing his daughter/lover. Bulger, displaying no such sympathy, stepped forward and strangled the life out of the twenty-six-year-old. If a further indignity was possible, Father-of-the-Year Steve Flemmi then proceeded to bury his daughter/lover in a mass mob grave near the Southeast Expressway in Dorchester. Debbie 2 was forced to share her eternal resting place with a rat named John McIntyre and a hapless bank robber named Arthur "Bucky" Barrett. Bulger killed Barrett in a common money-grab robbery worthy of a crack addict. McIntyre was planted because he was suspected of squealing on Bulger's gun-running activities to the IRA, the famed Irish rebel army.

Although Flemmi hesitated in killing Debbie 2, he showed no such emotion afterward. He and Bulger cut off her fingers and toes, then hacked out her teeth in an attempt to mask her identity should a pesky dog decide to dig up the triple decker remains one day.

The same informant who led police to the Debbie graves, former Winter Hill lieutenant Kevin "Two Weeks" Weeks, directed investigators to an unmarked grave in nearby Tenean Beach where they unearthed the remains of a long missing Bulger rival named Paul "Paulie" McGonagle. Seven days later, Weeks solved the quarter-century mystery of what happened to Tommy King, a scrappy brawler who had cleaned Bulger's clock in a legendary 1975 bar fight. Ever the sore loser, Bulger made sure King wouldn't live to brag about it.

In between settling old scores and chopping up troublesome girlfriends, Bulger and Flemmi reached all the way to a Tulsa, Oklahoma, country club parking lot to murder Roger Wheeler, owner of the lucrative World Jai Alai gambling auditoriums that entertained bettors in Florida, Connecticut, and Nevada, among other states. The fast-paced imported sport resembles an expanded version of racquetball and entices patrons to bet on Spanish men, mostly from the Basque region of Spain, who fire a hard black ball around with banana-shaped wicker baskets. Bulger and Flemmi were trying to muscle in on the offshoot gaming action, no doubt viewing it as prime plum to skim and fix.

These grisly revelations, at the time, were decades away from being publicly exposed. However, they were widely known among insiders in the mob and law enforcement. In addition, those who preferred to keep their heads in the sand had to deal with the loud cries from the relatives of the two Debbies. The aggrieved families knew exactly who was responsible for what they suspected happened to the young women, and they were infuriated that no one seemed to care.

Police detectives and rival FBI agents outside Connolly's loop who had their own informants began hearing similar tales of murder, drug dealing, and coercion coming out of Winter Hill. Connolly had to constantly ward off his peers, insisting that Bulger and Flemmi were still serving up bigger fish than themselves. As an example, he pointed out another major agency coup. The FBI organized crime fighters were able to bug the Italian mob's headquarters at 98 Prince Street in Boston in 1981 thanks to information from Bulger and Flemmi that enabled the agents to show probable cause and overcome the strict legal protections aimed at limiting wiretaps. It was this kind of ability to overcome the choking snarls of red tape blocking law enforcement efforts that made the Winter Hill pair invaluable crime-fighting tools, despite the increasingly ugly rumors pointing toward a relentless series of murders.

"They were without a doubt the two single most important sources we ever had," Connolly insisted.

Whether that was accurate or not, it was becoming painfully apparent to everyone outside that one elite FBI clique that the Winter Hill gang in general, and Bulger and Flemmi specifically, were becoming as big a pain in Boston's backside as the Italian mobsters they were systematically selling out. The suspicion hovering around the Debbie murders stripped away what remained of the carefully fabricated image of Whitey Bulger as a gentleman bandit who gave turkeys to the homeless and policed his unruly Irish neighborhood. Working around the FBI, the Massachusetts State Police and the U.S. Attorney's Office

built a case so overwhelming against Bulger and
Flemmi in 1995 that not even their FBI zoo keepers
could overcome it. A big part of the reason was that the
duo's main proponent and shield—charismatic superstar agent John Connolly—had retired to a lucrative
security job five years before, clearing the way for the
rival law enforcement officers to swoop in. An indictment was issued hitting Bulger and Flemmi with
thirty-five counts of racketeering and extortion. To add
a bit of irony to the breakthrough indictment, the federal prosecutors threw in the then boss of the Italian
mob as well, Francis "Cadillac Frank" Salemme, tossing a clever wrench into the who'll-rat-who machinery.
The plan was to sweep in and arrest the trio simultane-
ously on January 5.

Unfortunately for the prosecutors and State Police,
Bulger was still tied in to the FBI, both active and retired. When the police mobilized, only the woman-
abusing Flemmi was caught sleeping. Bulger and
Salemme were better prepared. Going against normal
mob boss behavior, both chose to run. Salemme, as expected, wasn't much good at the lam game and was
soon cornered in the Mafia retirement stronghold of
Florida. The circumstances of his arrest remain suspicious to this day.

"Late one Friday afternoon, I received a call from a
Boston agent claiming they had a source who knew
where Salemme was," reveals Bill Redden, former
FBI program manager for La Cosa Nostra. "They
wanted $250,000 within a half hour. I got it approved
and wired half—$125,000—to a designated bank ac-
count, promising to send the rest if the tip turned out
to be legit. They gave us an address in Hallandale,
Florida, just north of Miami Beach. Sure enough,

that's where Cadillac Frank was hiding. We had him in custody that evening, then wired the remaining $125,000. It's my belief today that the 'source' was either Whitey or Flemmi, and that the money was split with FBI agents in Boston. Nobody ever asked questions or investigated."

Bulger has been more adept at hiding out from rats like himself. Tipped from the very onset of the investigation, the aging, then sixty-six-year-old hood—whose long hated nickname "Whitey" had taken on new meaning—made himself scarce around South Boston for most of the previous year, preferring to travel extensively and sail in the warm waters near his new Florida condo. It's now apparent that he spent much of that time planning his long-term escape, including the critical acquisition of a European Union passport issued by his old pals in the Irish Republican Army. Bulger even managed to get his hands on a legal source of income. It was reported in 1991 that he was part of a group that hit a $14 million lottery jackpot. Investigators later determined that Bulger and two partners actually paid the winner—the brother of one of his Winter Hill soldiers—$2 million in cash for a half share of the big score, which was to be paid out in installments over twenty years. Since there were no rules against gangsters winning the lottery or buying a piece of someone else's ticket, lottery officials processed the arrangement and began making the payments, which amounted to $119,000 per year to Bulger.

In another bit of irony, the day the arrest order was given, Bulger was on his way from New York to Boston to bring back a quarrelsome girlfriend who was homesick for her children. Nearing the city, they heard about the arrest of Flemmi on the car's radio. Bulger hung a U-turn and headed back to New York. The next day, the ever bold Bulger completed his intended mission, delivering his girlfriend to a Boston parking lot. Unwilling to go into exile alone, he pulled a fast one on the Feds by swinging by to pick up another girlfriend, Catherine Greig, a bottle blonde, forty-four-year-old dental hygienist. Greig had suddenly been upgraded to "on the lam" girlfriend. Despite the gruesome fate of the Debbies, she apparently jumped at the last second opportunity.

Neither Bulger nor Greig have been tracked down since, despite reports that they've have been spotted in New York, Florida, Louisiana, Wyoming, California, Mississippi, Alabama, Iowa, Chicago, Canada, Ireland, Italy, and even back in South Boston. A reward that has soared to a cool million dollars, and repeated starring appearances on *America's Most Wanted* and *Unsolved Mysteries*, has not shed any light on the current whereabouts of either Bulger or the apparently less quarrelsome Greig. The balding Whitey is said to be sporting a mustache and using various aliases, including Mark Shapeton.

The FBI nearly had him in 1998 when a colorful, streetwise informant named Richie Sabol traced Bulger to a fishing camp on Grand Isle, Louisiana, a beach resort town on a splintered finger peninsula about sixty miles south of New Orleans. Sabol, a slick, fast-talking, New York mob-associate-turned-front-man for numerous Mafia-busting FBI stings, used his wealth of underworld connections to trace the Boston Irishman to the white sand beaches of the Gulf of Mexico and Barataria Bay.

"The FBI asked if I could help them find Whitey,

and I said, 'Sure, I'll make some calls,'" explains Sabol, who is currently in hiding himself, only from the mob's Top Ten Most Wanted list instead of the Feds'. "The reward was $250,000 then, so that wasn't chump change. I got word that the son of a bitch was staying at a house right next to a friend of mine at a fishing joint where New Orleans boss Carlos Marcello used to entertain his pals. Looked like easy money in the Big Easy. When the FBI went to grab him, he was gone. We missed the bastard by one day. I don't know if he was tipped off or what. Maybe the FBI tipped him off? Who the hell knows? That whole Bean Town thing was crazy. You didn't know who was who with them. Who was a cop and who was a crook? Working with the FBI there could get you killed. Since then, the trail's gone bone dry."

Special Agent Redden, now retired, has even stronger suspicions than Sabol. "New Orleans would have reported the investigative efforts to the originating case office in Boston. I think Whitey was once again warned by the Boston agents."

Despite Bulger's well-orchestrated absence and nick-of-time vanishing act, the story didn't end there. Shocking new revelations have popped up seemingly in tune with every mile Bulger has put on his tires, distancing himself from the fallout in Boston. In 1999 a federal investigation into the FBI's handling of Bulger gave the agency a nasty black eye. Ignoring Connolly's arguments of "business as usual," Judge Mark Wolf released a finding that accused a whopping eighteen FBI agents and supervisors of handling informants in an illegal manner. Connolly, naturally, was hit with the bulk of the accusations, including the charge that he monitored the final grand jury investigation and tipped

Bulger not only in time for him to escape, but in time to switch to a less noisy girlfriend prior to his dash. Two months later Connolly himself was arrested and brought to the courthouse in handcuffs, the precise silver jewelry that had not graced Whitey Bulger's wrists for the prior thirty-four years. A four-count indictment officially acknowledged the existence of the joint FBI/Winter Hill Gang, listing Connolly alongside the names of his "good bad guys," Bulger and Flemmi. The trio were charged with racketeering, racketeering conspiracy, conspiracy to obstruct justice, and obstruction of justice.

John Morris, Connolly's former supervisor and head of the Boston Organized Crime Squad, further fueled the headlines when he confessed to a series of payoffs and leaks. Morris testified about secret dinners attended by agents and gangsters, $7,000 in payoffs (a rather paltry sum to buy FBI Special Agents), and the frequent warnings issued to Bulger and Flemmi about pending indictments. Morris's confessions ended up as part of the indictment against Connolly and his pet rats. A subsequent, superseding indictment linked the FBI to a trio of rub-out murders of rival informants whom Connolly was said to have exposed and identified, and tacked on additional racketeering and obstruction of justice charges. The doomed informants were said to be offering information on the various criminal activities of Bulger and Flemmi, including the murder of jai alai tycoon Roger Wheeler.

"The handler of criminals became one himself," announced U.S. Attorney Donald K. Stern.

"Ninety-nine point nine percent of the FBI are decent, hardworking employees," added Charles Prouty,

Special Agent in Charge of the FBI's Boston branch. "This is a bitter pill to all of them."

Connolly has stood firm in the storm, terming the original deal with Bulger "a brilliant business decision" that traded forty-two arrests for two and was anything but secret and illegal. He denies fingering the other informants, and views himself as a political scapegoat. "They're desperate to find someone to hang this all on and they're certainly not going to blame themselves," he told the *Boston Globe*. "They go down the ladder and find the guy who's holding the ladder and blame him. That's what's happening here . . . We got forty-two stone criminals by giving up two stone criminals. What's your return on investment there? Show me a businessman who wouldn't do that . . . I'm innocent of the malicious charges that have been leveled at me in this case."

As he did all along, Connolly continues to have his supporters. FBI agent Nick Gianturco, for instance, told the *Globe,* "He was by far the best informant developer I've ever seen in the bureau."

Others in the FBI disagree. Special Agent Redden, who supervised Mafia investigations nationwide from his office in Washington, D.C., disputes Connolly's "trade-off" logic: "It was the exact opposite of what he says. Whitey was the power in Boston, and the Italians had grown weak from investigations and arrests in the 1970s, culminating with the death of Raymond Patriarca in 1984. His son, Raymond Patriarca, Jr., wasn't strong, and their influence was deteriorating while Whitey's was increasing. Whitey was giving up little fish, while he himself was a serial killer, among other things. Whitey Bulger was an evil man. He was a gangster, a superior gangster, and he was a genius. He should have been the bureau's main focus instead of an informant."

That became painfully apparent in the year 2000 when a one-two punch clobbered both Whitey and the Boston FBI's carefully constructed public relations image. The May publication of a gritty book by *Boston Globe* reporters Dick Lehr and Gerard O'Neill blew the lid off any remaining doubts regarding the sordid Winter Hill Gang/FBI connection. In *Black Mass: The Irish Mob, the FBI and a Devil's Deal*, the fearless *Globe* reporters, who had worked on the book for more than a decade, left no beans unturned. Five months later, in September 2000, the discovery of those mass Debbie graves resulted in Bulger being hammered with yet another indictment, this one accusing him of taking part in eighteen cold-blooded murders. (The imprisoned Flemmi was charged with ten.) The book and public accusations further shattered the decade's-long campaign to paint Bulger as a benevolent godfather who kissed babies, petted cats, didn't kill people or sell drugs. In addition, the families of the Debbies filed civil wrongful death suits against Bulger and Flemmi, seeking to cut off a $30 million share of the gangster's considerable stashes, including Bulger's lottery take.

Flemmi has responded that he was promised immunity against prosecution as a trade-off for thirty dangerous years serving as an FBI mob informant. A district judge bought the argument, preventing prosecutors from using wiretap evidence against both Flemmi and Bulger. Infuriated prosecutors appealed and eventually won a reversal from three appellate judges who ruled that the FBI agents didn't have the authority to offer such blanket immunity. "Any other result would turn the criminal justice system on its head," cautioned U.S. Attorney Donald Stern.

Stripped of his final layer of protection, Flemmi was convicted in 2001 on some of the lesser charges of extortion and money laundering and given a ten year sentence. He still awaits trial on the major counts, including most of the murders.

Flemmi's brother Michael, a thirty-two-year veteran of the Boston police department, was arrested on November 2, 2000, and charged with obstruction of justice, perjury, possession of unregistered weapons, and transfer and possession of machine guns. Prosecutors say Michael Flemmi was moving the guns, as many as eighty, for his brother Stevie the gangster.

That same month, a former State Police lieutenant, his brother-in-law, and the brother-in-law's daughter were indicted in an alleged plot to warn Bulger that the FBI was trying to locate him by tracing various telephone numbers. The woman, an employee of Bell Atlantic, discovered the FBI's activity and then told her dad. Pop informed the cop. The cop then told Winter Hill soldier-turned-informant Kevin Weeks which lines were being tapped. The trio have maintained their innocence.

In April 2001 former Boston FBI agent Robert Fitzpatrick appeared on the investigative news program *60 Minutes* and said he repeatedly warned his bosses that Bulger and Flemmi were killing people and should be cut loose.

On May 28, 2002, John Connolly was convicted of one count of racketeering, two counts of obstruction of justice, and one count of making a false statement to the FBI. He was found innocent of the charges that he leaked information that led to the deaths of the three informants.

"Today's verdict reveals John Connolly for what he became: a Winter Hill Gang operative masquerading as a law enforcement agent," said U.S. Attorney Michael J. Sullivan. After receiving more than two hundred letters on Connolly's behalf, U.S. District Judge Joseph L. Tauro sentenced the retired agent to ten years in prison. Connolly still faces eight civil suits from Bulger and Flemmi's victims, seeking more than $2 billion in damages.

Connolly's former supervisor, John Morris, previously pleaded guilty to accepting money from Bulger and was granted immunity for testifying against Connolly. He was not, however, granted immunity from the wrath of Whitey Bulger.

"I received a call from a shaken John Morris one day saying that Whitey had threatened his life," Special Agent Redden recalls. "He told me Whitey phoned him and said, 'If you know what's good for you, you'll have a retraction printed in the *Boston Globe* saying I was never an informant.' "

No such retraction was ever published.

As for Bulger's Mass Millions lottery share, federal prosecutors, acting on shaky law, seized the remainder of his winnings in 1995. The prosecutors filed a crafty civil suit that claimed Bulger used $700,000 in unreported gang money extorted from bookies, drug dealers, and loan sharks to buy his third of the half share of the $14 million winning ticket. To contest the suit and seizure, Bulger needed to appear. "If he wants to show up in court and fight the forfeiture action, we welcome it," challenged Assistant U.S. Attorney Fred L. Wysak.

Bulger, obviously, never took the bait, choosing to for-feit the remaining $1.9 million rather than be arrested the moment he showed his face.

Despite the Pandora's box that Bulger's capture would open, Boston FBI spokesperson Gail Marcinkievicz emphasizes that the bureau is intent on bringing him in. She brushes off any talk to the contrary as "ab-solutely wrong."

"We want this guy," she says. "At least once a week we fingerprint someone who looks like Whitey. There are lots of seventy-year-old men out there who look like Whitey."

In a final ironic twist, former Winter Hill mob boss Howie Winter, indicted and sent away for life partly due to information provided by Bulger and Flemmi, has refused to cooperate with the FBI in prosecuting his underlings turned rats. "If it was my worst enemy I wouldn't cooperate against them," the old school gang-ster growled to the *Boston Globe*. "I'd rather take a cyanide pill than go trap someone else to save my own ass."

While that, in a strange, mobster way, might seem turn-the-other-cheek noble, Winter added this regard-ing girlfriend-murdering, stepdaughter-mutilating, sex deviant Steve Flemmi: "I thought the world of Stevie Flemmi. He was a man's man."

James J. "Whitey" Bulger was born September 3, 1929. He's about five-eight, 160 pounds, thinning white hair, medium build, blue eyes, Irish, with no known scars or tattoos. He's an avid reader with an interest in history and war. He is known to frequent libraries and historic sites. Bulger is currently on the heart medication Atenolol (50 mg.) and maintains his physical fitness by walking on beaches and in parks with his female companion, Catherine Elizabeth Greig, a fifty-two-year-old blonde. Bulger and Greig love animals and may frequent animal shelters. Bulger has been known to alter his appearance through the use of disguises. He has traveled extensively throughout the United States, Europe, Canada, and Mexico. He uses the names Thomas F. Baxter, Mark Shapeton, Jimmy Bulger, James Joseph Bulger, James J. Bulger, Jr., James Joseph Bulger, Jr., Tom Harris, Tom Marshall, "Whitey."

The Reward

Chances of the average Joe spotting Bulger and collecting the $1 million reward? Excellent. He could be anywhere, and apparently prefers to blend into society rather than hide in seclusion. He'll most likely be accompanied by his girlfriend, who has short blond hair, blue eyes, is about five-six and weighs about 140 pounds. Best bet is a coastal beach area, where the couple would be walking a dog at dawn or dusk. For updates on the search, check out www.bostonmafia.com.

Chapter 4

Eric Robert Rudolph—
Right Wing Revolutionary

· ·

Reward: $1 million

Somewhere in the dark, quiet mountains of western North Carolina, Eric Robert Rudolph must be grinding his teeth over the saga of Richard Jewell. Sure, it may have started out bad for the world's most famous security guard. Real bad. But then, after three months of hell, it got better. Much better.

It all began in the first hour of July 27, 1996, when Jewell, working security for AT&T's Global Olympic Village, spotted a suspicious-looking knapsack abandoned under a park bench near a sound tower in Atlanta's Centennial Olympic Park. Although it was 12:58 A.M., the park was jammed with people grooving to the beat of a late night rock concert that was part of the 1996 Summer Olympics festivities. Jewell alertly cleared the area and notified the federal authorities. An Alcohol, Tobacco and Firearms (ATF) agent crawled up to the pack at 1:08 A.M., eased open a flap, then froze. The oddly altered knapsack contained a powerful homemade bomb. Twelve minutes later, at 1:20

A.M., the bomb exploded. A Georgia woman, Alice Hawthorne, was killed as her fourteen-year-old daughter watched in horror. More than 120 people were injured, some of whom still carry fragments of the nails used as shrapnel in their bodies. A Turkish television cameraman, Melih Uzunyol, succumbed to a heart attack in the subsequent chaos.

Jewell, the obscure everyman with fate thrust upon him, had come through brilliantly in the clutch. Without his fast action, officials believe that as many as a hundred people may have perished. Jewell was a genuine American hero.

For a few short days, that is.

The thirty-three-year-old woke up on the third morning of his coronation to find a screaming front page headline in the *Atlanta Journal-Constitution* naming him as the leading suspect in the bombing. The FBI, the paper breathlessly reported, was investigating him. "FBI suspects hero guard may have planted bomb," the headline read. The story was picked up by the news wires and went out worldwide. Suddenly, Jewell had plunged from hero to villain. Hordes of jabbering media camped out in front of his home. Caravans of FBI agents followed him everywhere he went. The agents swarmed the apartment he shared with his mother and carted off reams of personal belongings, including twenty-two G-rated Walt Disney videotapes and his mom's Tupperware. Follow-up stories painted Jewell in dark tones, claiming he fit the standard profile of a bitter, overzealous wannabe cop so desperate to become a hero that he built and planted a bomb, then "found it" and saved the day. Comedians made hay on national television, terming the hefty security guard the "Una-doofus" and "Una-bubba," in reference to the

Unabomber. They branded his long-suffering mother "Una-mama." Tom Brokaw went on NBC and said, "Look, they probably got enough to arrest him. They probably have got enough to try him . . ."

Actually, they didn't have squat. Not then. Not ever. The reason was that Richard Jewell had absolutely nothing to do with the bombing. He was what he claimed to be all along: a hardworking, salt-of-the-earth, AT&T contract security guard who saved scores of lives by his quick thinking. Yes, the FBI was investigating him, but it's the job of the FBI to investigate everybody in that circumstance. If the Pope had found the bomb, the FBI's investigation would have begun with his Holiness.

After three months of being hounded as if he were Public Enemy Number 1, Richard Jewell was officially cleared by the FBI. The agency and U.S. Attorney lamented the "highly unusual and intense" media coverage that "was neither designed nor desired by the FBI, and in fact interfered with the investigation."

"I lived a nightmare," a relieved Jewell sighed, knowing full well the genie of his true heroics could never be put back into the bottle of public perception.

What exactly went wrong in Jewell's case may take many years to unravel. Did the FBI rely too heavily upon the initial findings of their trained profilers and leak their early suspicions a bit too enthusiastically to the Atlanta reporters? Or, did the Atlanta reporters and editors, eager for a scoop, rush to judgment and make a mountain out of a molehill, nearly ruining someone's life in the process? And, once the *Atlanta Journal-Constitution* jumped into the water, did the lemming-like national media follow blindly behind?

The answers will come, because once he recovered

from the shock, Richard Jewell hired himself some crack libel attorneys, and they've been hammering the media ever since. So far, Atlanta lawyers L. Lin Wood and Wayne Grant have torched NBC, CNN, a community college where Jewell once worked, and other media outlets for more than $2 million and counting. And that doesn't include the undisclosed "six-figure" fee they secured for the movie rights to Jewell's story. The biggest lawsuits—against the *Atlanta Journal-Constitution* and some other major media outlets—are still pending.

So, what does Richard Jewell's misfortune and fortune have to do with Eric Rudolph? The FBI now says it was actually Rudolph, an ultraconservative, radical Christian, antigovernment, antiabortion revolutionary, who planted the explosives in Centennial Olympic Park, among other places. Instead of reaping the benefits of lucrative libel suits, Rudolph has spent the last half decade running from an intensive manhunt in the rugged mountains of North Carolina. Instead of $2 million in his pocket, he has $1 million on his head as one of the FBI's Ten Most Wanted. Instead of being courted by movie producers, he's been hounded by armies of law enforcement agents, mercenaries, and bounty hunters.

What he hasn't been doing, however, is getting himself caught.

Rudolph is the flip side of protest era radicals like Angela Davis and Bernardine Dohrn, who populated the FBI's Most Wanted list in the late 1960s and early 1970s. Back then, the government was conservative and the militants hailed from various antigovernment ultraliberal organizations, many of which promoted the violent overthrow of the nation. In the 1990s, during the Clinton administration, the situation was reversed. The government became liberal, and the radicals were antigovernment, ultraconservatives, many of whom promoted the violent overthrow of the nation. Although the FBI is supposed to remain neutral politically, the truth is that they are far too often tools of the party and ideology in power. Thus, the preponderance of antiwar radicals, Black Panthers, and Students for a Democratic Society types on the Top Ten list back in the hippie days were replaced by the abortion clinic bombers, abortion doctor assassins, anti-gay-rights activists, isolationists, and white supremacists who populated the list during the Clinton era.

Eric Rudolph epitomizes this dichotomy. After the bombing of a single abortion clinic in Birmingham, Alabama, in January 1998 that killed an off-duty policeman and gravely injured a nurse, Rudolph was the subject of an unprecedented manhunt in the mountains of his native North Carolina. When that failed to prove fruitful, he was placed on the Top Ten list the following May, an eyebrow-raising jump for someone whose crime seemingly paled in comparison with scores of other criminals he leaped over. Was it politics as usual, or did the FBI know more about Rudolph's past bombing ways than they were letting on—i.e., that he was the much sought Olympic bomber? Whatever the answer, when the dust cleared and the damages were finally tallied up, the North Carolina mountain man became not only worthy of his listing, but of the vastly upgraded $1 million bounty the agency placed on his head.

An intensive study of the materials used in the bombings led the FBI to suspect the then thirty-four-

year-old in a total of four incidents, including the
deadly explosions at the Birmingham abortion clinic in
1998 and the Olympic Park blast two years earlier. In
between, the agency says Rudolph bombed a building
that housed a Sandy Springs, Georgia, abortion clinic
in January 1997, then hit a lesbian nightclub called The
Otherside Lounge in Atlanta a month later. What especially angered authorities was the nature of the bombings. At the Olympics, a caller from a pay phone
nearby warned the police that the bomb would go off
in thirty minutes. It exploded in twenty-two. At both
the Atlanta clinic and lesbian club, two bombs were
hidden, the second timed to go off forty-five minutes to
an hour after the first. The plan in all three cases, law
enforcement officials believe, was to lure in the police,
firefighters, and paramedics in order to kill and maim
as many as possible. The reason, apparently, was to
carry out the bomber's war against government agents.
Six officers were injured in the Sandy Springs blast—
all from the second bomb hidden in the parking lot
where they gathered. Five partyers were hit by shrapnel from the first bomb at The Otherside Lounge.
Learning from the prior incident, officers discovered
the second explosive device near the side of the club
and cleared the area before any additional police, paramedics, or firefighters could be killed or injured.

"There's nothing magic about Centennial Olympic
Park. The Centennial Park bombing was directed at
law enforcement," FBI Special Agent Jack Daulton
said, noting that it went off eight minutes earlier than
the caller had warned.

Rudolph's supporters in the militant antiabortion,
antigay, and other ultraconservative movements chal-

lenge that assertion, claiming that the FBI's suspicions are nothing more than an attempt to paint Rudolph in less heroic colors to discourage those the Feds feel may be giving him food and shelter. The government is afraid, they insist, that Rudolph will do what Bernardine Dohrn did decades before—remain a fugitive long enough to see the political tides change.

To determine which side is more on the mark, one must dig deeper into the bomber's background and possible psyche. Who is this handsome carpenter, Eric Robert Rudolph, what does he believe, and what is his mission? Hard to say precisely, especially when tossing in the Olympic bombing, an action that appears to lack the clear political motives of the other acts. Still, there are strong clues based upon his upbringing and geographical influences.

Rudolph's mother Patricia moved the family of four sons and a daughter from Homestead, Florida, a rural area about twenty-five miles south of Miami, to the sparsely populated Cherokee County region of western North Carolina after her husband died in 1980. Eric Rudolph was thirteen. The family settled on an isolated ridge near the tiny community of Topton. It's possible that Ms. Rudolph made the move to enjoy the peaceful isolation of an area that is popular with tourists seeking to become one with nature by backpacking through the Appalachian Trail. The majestic recreational area offers camping, rafting, and kayaking on the Nantahala River, or fly fishing in any of a host of cool mountain streams that cut through the dense forest. It's also possible, however, considering the family's religious beliefs, that Patricia Rudolph was specifically drawn to the area that borders Georgia and Tennessee because it's a haven for political and religious extremists, tax protesters, white supremacists, survivalists, Freemen, and others of their ilk.

Outside the small town of Andrews—population 2,800—across from Junaluska Gap and Rattlesnake Knob, an organization called the Northpoint Tactical Teams constructed a two hundred-acre armed compound in the early 1970s to prepare for the coming "New World Order Dictatorship," if one believes their leaflets. A guardhouse and iron gate limits access, while a thirteen-star U.S. flag flaps in the breeze overhead. Its founder, the late Nord W. Davis, Jr., was a well-known antigovernment type who wrote a newsletter that he diligently dispatched to like-minded subscribers. Davis's manifestos frequently made reference to the "Army of God." A favorite painting of his known as *The Faithful and True* showed Christ riding a horse with a diadem in his hand, leading the "Army of God."

The devil, in Davis's eyes, was the concept of "One World Government" that would drag the Earth into the biblical prophecy of Armageddon. Inside the retired IBM executive's compound, which includes a 1,000-foot underground bunker, was an impressive arsenal of shotguns, rifles, and assault weapons at the ready in case any snoopy Feds came around and tried to imprison him inside a United Nations concentration camp, as the belief went. The bunker was, and may still be, packed with enough supplies to ward off such United Nations storm troopers "indefinitely." Davis, who died of prostate cancer in 1997 at age sixty-five, was a pal of Colonel James "Bo" Gritz, the highly decorated Vietnam Special Forces commander who has since become an icon in the survivalist movement. Gritz, who ran for President in 1992 with neo-Nazi politician David Duke as his running mate, came to

Davis's compound a number of times to conduct highly publicized survivalist and paramilitary training camps.

Davis's death quieted the voice of the Northpoint Tactical Teams, but officials say his widow Ann remains at the mountainside compound located just a few miles from the Rudolph family home. She's accompanied by an unknown number of her husband's disciples. So far, it doesn't appear that anyone has emerged as the new leader—at least not publicly.

If Davis and crew weren't Rudolph's main inspiration, there were certainly others in the Cherokee County area who could have stepped in. One Andrews family has waged a decade's-long battle against the IRS. James Bruggerman, a white supremacist minister, has a congregation near the town of Murphy. Neighboring Macon County boasts a common-law court that's disconnected from any federal or state authority. The region's rugged isolation combines with its lack of ethnic diversity and "let people be" philosophy to enable such groups to thrive without interference.

How much the young Eric Rudolph was involved with such groups is not known. Several civil rights organizations, such as the Southern Poverty Law Center in Montgomery, Alabama, have gone on record as identifying Rudolph as a full-fledged member of Northpoint Teams. Others, including Davis's widow, claim that he wasn't. What's known is that he arrived in the close-knit community as an outsider, and may have gravitated to extremists like Davis as a way of fitting in. Whatever the influence, it wasn't long before the Florida beach boy was referring to the government as an oppressive force, questioning historic truths, writing school essays denying that the Holocaust happened, refusing to divulge his social security number because he viewed it as a form of government control, and avoiding anything to do with banks and checks.

Rudolph's family left the area for a brief time in 1985 when Eric was eighteen to seek refuge at the Church of Israel in Schell City, Missouri. Instead of purging Rudolph from the Cherokee County intolerance, that merely fortified it. The Church of Israel is part of the Christian Identity movement, an odd sect that harkens back to nineteenth century England. Members believe that Anglo-Saxons are the true descendants of the twelve tribes of Israel, and they brand Jews and blacks as "mud people" and creations of Satan. Christian Identity followers are also known to be antigay, militant antiabortion activists who view those political battles as a holy war. Rudolph's Northpoint Tactical Teams neighbor, Nord Davis, Jr., considered himself, among other things, a Christian Identity preacher. It would thus seem likely that the Rudolph family's association with the distant church may have come at Davis's recommendation, solidifying the link between Eric Rudolph and Davis.

The Christian Identity movement is also known to operate a thriving underground railroad that assists their "soldiers" in efforts to escape "persecution" from law enforcement officers.

Before it would come to that, Rudolph tried the Army. He spent eighteen months as an infantryman, learning additional survival and weapons skills. However, like Oklahoma City bomber Timothy McVeigh before him, Rudolph found that his ultraconservative, antigovernment, Christian Identity views were even too extreme for the military. He washed out "for conduct-related reasons" and was deemed to be "not compatible with military service," standard boilerplate jargon for someone who's given the boot for myriad psychological reasons. Afterward, he returned to his beloved mountains, possibly, like McVeigh, with a giant antigovernment chip on his shoulder.

More revealing are the notes sent to Atlanta newspapers after the 1997 bombings there. An organization called the "Army of God" claimed responsibility and wrote the familiar phrase "Death to the New World Order" in their letters. It also issued a dire warning to abortion clinic workers: "Let those who work in the murder mills around the nation be warned once more—you will be targeted without quarter."

That was apparently the goal when a man wearing a wig and driving a 1989 Nissan truck dropped off a package outside the New Women All Women clinic in Birmingham on January 29, 1998. An alert citizen took down his license plate number, providing police with the critical clue to the bomber's identity. (Unlike more savvy rebels and revolutionaries, Rudolph failed to simply steal another license plate prior to his act to mask his identity. It was a critical mistake.) Robert "Sandy" Sanderson, thirty-five, was the off-duty police officer killed in the explosion. The clinic's head nurse, Emily Lyons, forty-one, was blinded in one eye and disfigured, and now must suffer the indignity of having her discomforting photo displayed alongside the even more horrific pictures of mutilated babies on the Web pages of antiabortion activists. (See the open letter from Lyons to Rudolph at the end of this chapter, and a speech given by her, reproduced at the end of this book.)

Considering the bomber's beliefs and background, it's likely that a specific clinic was targeted because of the presence of Officer Sanderson. The veteran cop also moonlighted as security for a gay nightclub. A policeman—i.e., a tool of government oppression—who protected both an abortion clinic and a gay nightclub during his free time provided the bomber with a rare trifecta of his favorite targets.

Afterward, the Army of God once again took credit, using the opportunity to lash out at the French abortion tablet, RU-486, promising to fight anyone who "manufactures, markets, sells, and distributes the pill."

After the explosion, Rudolph was traced via the license plate back to Cherokee County, where he rented the sword and sorcery video *Kull the Conqueror* from a store in Murphy the following day, January 30. Raccoon hunters found his truck bogged down in mud under a thicket of woods outside the town. An "Army of Uncle Sam" comprising more than three hundred federal and state law enforcement agents of various stripes, from FBI to ATF, swarmed into the area searching for the elusive Rudolph. They used a combination of both modern and ancient technology—infrared tracking equipment, space-age motion detectors, and bloodhounds. At the time, it was the largest dragnet in American history, a show of force that easily crossed the border into extreme overkill when weighing it against the actual crime on record. However, as mentioned, the Feds very likely were already connecting Rudolph to the prior bombings—explosions that had targeted them. Whatever the truth, they spared no money or manpower, poring through Rudolph's previous residences and breaking into some outdoor storage lockers he had previously rented, looking for clues that would connect him to the bombings. The hunt initially centered around a thirty-square-mile area of northwestern Macon

County near Nantahala Lake, then expanded from there into the vast forests.

The costly government force, which was frequently accompanied by an equal number of media representatives, has remained in the area at various strengths ever since, setting up a large base camp while alternately amusing, enrichening, and irritating the locals. In the early years, the Feds buzzed around night and day in their government-issued pickup trucks, cars, and giant Suburbans, many towing state-of-the-art surveillance equipment. They packed the area inns and kept the waitresses and cooks in the local grills and diners hopping.

In contrast to the seriousness of the search, many residents took a lighter view. Local bingo halls displayed signs that proclaimed "Rudolph Plays Here." Restaurants, even those filled with hungry officers, announced on their billboards that "Rudolph Eats Here." The Lakes End Grill at the edge of Nantahala Lake sold bumper stickers that say "I Survived the Rudolph Manhunt." Different versions cover the years 1998-2002. The Cherokee Restaurant in Andrews added Rudolph Burgers, Wilderness Fries, and FBI Curly Fries to their menu. The natives' loyalties can be understood by digging deeper into the FBI potatoes: Curly, because home boy Rudolph was running the poor city slickers around in circles.

Rudolph, it is believed, is living in a cave, an old mine, an abandoned cabin, or in the comfort of a supporter's home. He may also be, as one weary tracker commented, catching rays on a beach in California. Still, the popular view is that he's out there in the 530,000 acre Nantahala National Forest, peering up at the Great Smoky Mountains, waiting for the government to forget about him and go home.

The FBI vows that won't happen. Although most of the original three hundred officers have been reassigned, enough have stayed to keep Rudolph from waltzing into town and returning *Kull the Conqueror*, the video he rented five years ago. (Comedians have cracked that if he rented it from Blockbuster, he would have been hunted down and apprehended years ago.) The agents insist that they will stay until they find him, leasing homes in the area, attending local churches and civic group meetings, and hanging out at popular restaurants and bars. When out searching, they sport bright orange hats to keep from being blasted by trigger-happy deer hunters. A permanent base of operations has been set up in an old sewing-machine plant next to a hospital and a public housing project in Andrews, a city that dubs itself "The Little Town With the Big Heart." No signs announce the building's purpose, but that hasn't stopped locals from referring to it as the "FBI building." Inside rests an impressive array of computers, telephones, and high-tech surveillance equipment that monitors every leaf movement in the area. When some local high school kids punched Rudolph's name into a registration computer during a blood drive as a lark, the agents appeared like magic within ten minutes. They weren't amused.

Nor were the agents amused in November 1998 when someone took a series of potshots at a command post across from a furniture mill. The bullets were fired from a dark street behind a soccer field three hundred yards away just after 8:00 P.M. One of the slugs brushed the hair of an agent working inside. It was never determined if the shooter was Rudolph sending a message that he was still around, one of his supporters, or simply a resident tired of the FBI's noisy presence, which was exacerbated by the coming and going of helicopters.

Some agents now expect to remain on the job until they retire, privately lamenting the task of finding a single, technology-avoiding man in a massive area that harbors hundreds of caves and a countless number of shacks and buildings. They're looking for an outdoorsman who even when he wasn't being hunted preferred sleeping in his truck, or in the woods, rather than wasting money on a motel room. A man at home in a geographical expanse so remote its county seat is closer to the capitals of seven neighboring states than it is to its own ruling clan in Raleigh, a factor that no doubt appeals to the antigovernment factions who reside there.

Why bother? Because despite the seeming isolation, this same man is said to be hiding a mere 125 miles away from Atlanta, the giant southern metropolis Rudolph chose to target for three of his four assaults.

Federal and state governments have already poured $50 million into the hunt for a fugitive they've found no sign of for more than five years now. The last confirmed sighting was in July 1998, when Rudolph took a truck and six months worth of supplies from the home of a seventy-one-year-old Andrews health-food-store owner who didn't report the encounter until two days later. Rudolph paid the man, George O. Nordmann, with five hundred-dollar bills for the haul, which included batteries, wheat, corn, raisins, and cayenne pepper, a hot spice used to foil search dogs and keep extremities warm in cold weather. Nordmann was described as a devout Catholic with a Franciscan monk son who kept mainly to himself. (Catholicism has remained fervently antiabortion.) The truck was found nearby not long afterward. There was no trace of Rudolph or the seventy-five pounds of supplies, and there hasn't been a sighting since—at least, not by someone who'd tell.

"In the hills, we live a littler different than anybody else," Steve Cochran, a former friend of Rudolph's, explained to the *Asheville Citizen Times*. "If Eric came down today and showed up at my granddaddy's place, [my granddaddy would] say 'Hi,' and offer him something to eat. The ATF and FBI call that 'aiding and abetting.' We just call it being friendly."

As the years have passed, many residents doubt that Rudolph is still around. Even the hardiest of locals question whether a skilled survivalist could exist that long without resurfacing for supplies. The winters are bitterly cold, and development and tourists have driven away much of the wild game. To survive, Rudolph would have to pop in and out of civilization, robbing stores and homes for food and supplies, or depend upon the kindness of strangers. The FBI initially found evidence that would seem to support this theory, discovering raisin and oatmeal boxes, vitamin bottles and tuna fish cans, in areas where they suspected Rudolph had been. Others scoff at such remarks and point out that if a lonely mountain woman took a liking to the handsome fugitive, he could live forever out there with her help. The area, they say, has no shortage of such independent women. Still others point out the various underground railroads and support groups among the extremists who view every day Rudolph is not caught as a victory against the hated federal government. Even some mainstream churches have trouble faulting

Rudolph for his antiabortion advocacy. "I doubt he will be found to be an unprincipled killer," Conrad Kimberough, a priest at St. William's Catholic Church in Murphy, told the Associated Press.

"I don't support him for killing people," an Andrews resident told Nicole Brodeur of the *Raleigh News and Observer*. "But abortion is kind of bad too."

"I don't believe he meant to hurt those people down there [in Birmingham]," agreed Margaret Bateman of Macon County. "I think he was just trying to save the babies."

Other supporters are even more overt, particularly those who erect Internet Web pages promoting various extremist and antiabortion views. One such page claims to have solved the mystery of the motive for the Olympic bombing, connecting all the acts to violations of the Ten Commandments. The abortion clinics, they say, obviously violated the Fifth Commandment against murder. The gay bar violated the Fourth Commandment regarding honoring one's parents (a stretch), and the Olympic Park action was for violating the First Commandment regarding false gods. The idea there is that the glorification of Olympic athletes is a form of idol worship, especially the worship of athletes from "pagan" countries. Another theory is that the Olympic Village, long noted for spirited couplings among the thousands of vibrant young athletes from around the world, mocked the Christian Identity's ban against interracial bonds.

If Rudolph has escaped the forests and returned to civilization with the help of such supporters, chances are he would have struck again. There was concern among many both in and out of law enforcement that he might have been planning an encore performance at the 2002 Winter Olympics in Salt Lake City, Utah. However, with so much added security following the 9/11 terrorist attacks, that seemed unlikely, possibly because Rudolph simply may have lost his appetite for such violent statements after the massive attacks in New York and Washington shocked the world, including his own ultraconservative world. Or he may have felt he wouldn't have received the support he did before from a nation that had suddenly grown extremely weary of such tactics.

Of course, the reverse is also true. The hunt for a homegrown rebel like Eric Rudolph doesn't seem so critical anymore now that the airwaves are filled with reports that armies of American-hating foreign terrorists are currently being trained in Cuba and the Middle East, eager to top Osama bin Laden's big score.

Whatever the reason, the 2002 Winter Olympics passed without incident.

Still, the FBI hasn't forgotten Rudolph, and remains committed to bringing him in. And the news, sidelights, and interest in Rudolph hasn't completely abated. To gain better insight, Jeff Stein, a reporter for the Internet magazine *Salon*, tracked down Rudolph's unabashedly gay little brother Jamie, a talented musician who lives in New York's Greenwich Village. Jamie Rudolph told Stein that Eric visited him in 1997 after secretly bombing the lesbian bar, and didn't display any antigay bias at all.

"He seemed comfortable. I could talk to him openly," Jamie told Stein. "I knew he was conservative and antigovernment and anti-Clinton, but I didn't know he was antiabortion."

Jamie confirmed that the Rudolph brothers were seen as outsiders in Andrews and that Eric may have

embraced the extremist views as a way of making
friends. He also confirmed that the stint in Missouri
with the Christian Identity movement deeply affected
Eric. Interestingly, none of that influenced Jamie
Rudolph. He literally ran from the Cherokee County
bullies and symbolically ran from their closed-minded
social and political views.

The reaction of another Rudolph brother, Daniel, has
been tragically bizarre. In March 1998, Daniel
Rudolph purposely cut off his hand with an electric
saw, videotaping the gruesome event at his home near
Charleston, South Carolina, to "send a message to the
FBI and media." It's not clear just what the message
was. Daniel Rudolph is the oldest brother who assumed
responsibility for the family after their father died.

As the search progressed, the normally tight-lipped
FBI gradually released detailed information that helps
explain how they worked backward to connect Rudolph
to the four separate bombings. They charged him with
his first and most famous act, at Centennial Olympic
Park, in late 1998 after spotting a pattern that linked
him to the three others. The formal accusations followed the release of their laboratory findings during a
press conference—and on the Internet—in late 1997 as
an attempt to spark the memories of people who may
have sold the then unknown bomber his supplies. To
do so, the agency gave a description of how each bomb
was made, the components used, and the similarities of
design and supply source. The exercise provided the
public with a fascinating insight into forensic criminology Y2K style.

For example, the Olympic bomb was concealed in
an olive green military-style backpack known as an
ALICE pack. Black tape was wrapped around the

buckles on the front, and the pack contained an impro-
vised handle made by inserting a round wooden rod at
the top, a common alteration made by Army soldiers.
An eleven-gauge (one-eighth inch) steel plate fifteen
inches long and twelve inches wide, cut from a larger
piece using an oxyacetylene torch, was used to direct
the shrapnel. The plate was padded with olive green
foam used in military sleeping mats. The foam, the
FBI said, had been laminated together. The bomber
also used three metal pipes, two by twelve inches,
threaded on each end, with two-inch metal end caps on
each pipe. The explosive was three to four pounds of
Accurate Arms brand number 7 or 9 smokeless gunpowder. For shrapnel, the bomber used size 8d concrete or masonry nails 2½ inches long. The detonator
was comprised of a blue, Eveready twelve-volt lantern
battery, a Westclox "Big Ben" wind-up alarm clock,
gray duct tape and black plastic electrical tape.

Moving on to the twin Sandy Springs bombs, the
FBI noted many similarities as well as differences.
These devices were set in olive green military ammunition cans and contained eleven-gauge steel plates cut
with an oxyacetylene torch. This time the shrapnel
was 3½ pounds of size 4d 1½-inch flooring nails. The
detonator was a Westclox "Baby Ben" alarm clock
and Duracell D-cell batteries wrapped in gray duct
tape and black plastic electrical tape. A major difference was that the bomber used a hundred feet of
twisted galvanized wire, and relied upon dynamite as
the explosive.

For The Otherside Lounge, the bomber went back to
olive green polyester backpacks with back straps, and
placed them in 1.3 gallon storage containers. The familiar steel plate was there, only these were a quarter

inch instead of an eighth, and were cut with a plasma arc cutter. The shrapnel here was a total of 6½ pounds of size 6d, two-inch-long galvanized wire nails. While the nails differed, the detonator was nearly identical— six-volt Eveready Energizer lantern batteries, a West-clox "Baby Ben" alarm clock, gray duct tape and black electrical tape. The explosive was dynamite, about fifteen to twenty half-pound sticks.

In Birmingham, the bomber built a similar, dynamite-based device packed with 1½-inch flooring nails, and placed it just outside the door. Only this one was detonated by remote control, indicating that Rudolph was growing more sophisticated in his design skills. The nails, however, were said to have come from the same manufacturing batch as those discovered at the Atlanta clinic—and in Rudolph's storage shed. The same Cherokee County shed produced a book entitled *How to Build Bombs of Mass Destruction*. All of Rudolph's bombs were described as "antipersonnel devices," meaning they were intended to kill and maim people rather than destroy property.

The FBI asked that if anyone remembered somebody purchasing these unusual supplies, to contact them at 1-888-ATF-BOMB. They've also asked those who were at the Atlanta Olympics and took pictures to scour their film for anyone who might look like Rudolph. He was said to be wearing khaki-colored shorts, a dark T-shirt, dark ankle-length boots, and light socks.

Releasing the detailed information proved fruitful. A Nashville couple in the ammunition business contacted the FBI and said they believed they sold Eric Rudolph fifty pounds of that specific type and brand of gunpowder in 1994. The metal sheets have been traced to matching steel found at a plant in Franklin, North

Carolina, where a friend of Rudolph's worked.

Combining all of this with the license plate in Birmingham, the FBI finally had their man in all four bombings.

Yet, as noted, the work continues, both in the field and inside the FBI's state-of-the-art labs. In March 1999 a small bomb exploded outside the Femcare Clinic in Asheville, North Carolina, causing little damage and no injuries. Asheville is about seventy-five miles from the region where Rudolph was last seen. The previous October, two other female-oriented medical facilities had been hit in nearby Fayetteville—the Carolina Women's Medical Clinic and the Hallmark Abortion Clinic. Both had been set on fire a month before, sustaining minor damage. As of yet, the FBI's white coat types have not tacked these on Rudolph, thinking more in terms of a copycat. Since the Rudolph hunt began, many area abortion clinics have received threatening calls that promise additional violence until the FBI gives up the search. (Nationwide, there have been more than fifty arsons and nearly twenty bombings at abortion clinics.)

A number of abortionists have been slain as well, including Buffalo, New York, Dr. Barnett Slepian in October 1998, and Dr. David Gunn, who was shot at his Pensacola, Florida, clinic in 1993. Dr. Slepian's assassin, antiabortion activist James Charles Kopp, was placed on the FBI's Ten Most Wanted list eight months later—thirteen months after Rudolph was so honored on May 5, 1998. Rudolph is fugitive Number 454. Kopp, who was captured in France in March 2001, was Number 455. Interestingly, Kopp was placed on the list the same day as Number 456, terrorist Osama bin Laden, then sought for the American embassy bombings overseas.

The abortion controversy, with or without Kopp and Rudolph, continues to rage on. In the end, the pair did nothing but throw more fuel into an already blazing inferno, one that shows no sign of abating. The intensity of each side's views can be vividly seen in following divergent responses to Rudolph's actions. Ann Rose, a women's health consultant from Atlanta, saw the connection between the first bombing at Centennial Olympic Park and the abortion rights battle right from the onset. Rose, who left the park earlier that evening before the bomb went off, proved to be prophetic in her immediate reaction:

Now, the entire world knows how it feels to work in an abortion clinic. For years, the abortion clinics in this country have been living under the mandated daily routines of: be wary of strange packages, interrogate suspicious people, investigate your mail, install metal detectors, wear bulletproof vests, evacuate due to bomb threats, carry guns, and worry about death threats. We saw short-haired guys in camouflage near the clinics years ago and nobody cared to investigate. Medical professionals had to become "security experts" along with performing their routine medical duties. My last death threat was over the Internet last week . . . I've personally seen antiabortion terrorism escalate. Picketing in the seventies was largely peaceful groups of nuns and quiet religious types . . . In the eighties we saw "Operation Rescue" type events, the same events that crippled Atlanta for six weeks during and after the 1986 Democratic Convention. It also brought us bombings, burnings, acid attacks, invasions, and other domestic terrorism. Then, the nineties brought us murder . . . Another right-wing militaristic Christian wing nut at work here [in Atlanta]? You bet I think so.

Rose proved to be correct. Her sentiments are contrasted by an equally impassioned Army of God letter left at both a Cherokee County boot store and newspaper in March 2002:

Eric Robert Rudolph
May God Be With You!

The Army of God by definition is composed of Christians who utilize and/or endorse physical action including lethal force against those in the abortion industry . . . Beginning officially with the passage of the Freedom of Choice act, we the remnant of the God-fearing men and women of the United States of Amerika do officially declare war on the entire child killing industry. After praying, fasting and making continual supplication to God for your pagan, heathen, infidel souls, we then peacefully, passively presented our bodies in front of your death camps, begging you to stop the mass murder of infants. Yet you hardened your already blackened, jaded hearts. We quietly accepted the resulting imprisonment and suffering of our passive resistance. Yet you mock God and continued the Holocaust.

No longer! All the options have expired. Our most dread sovereign Lord God requires that whosoever sheds man's blood, by man shall his blood be shed. Not out of hatred for you, but out of love for the person you exterminate, we are forced to take arms against you. Our life for yours—a simple equation.

Dreadful. Sad. Reality, nonetheless. You shall not be tortured at our hands. Vengeance belongs to God only. However, execution is rarely gentle.

In the middle of this relentless war of words, ideologies, religions, and actions, are the innocent victims. John Hawthorne, husband of the woman who died at Centennial Olympic Park, doesn't want that to be forgotten.

"I want accountability for what happened to Alice. That's what I want," he told Gannett News Service columnist Mike Lopresti on the eve of the 2002 Winter Olympics. "There is no closure. There's this one scene where everyone is standing there drinking beer or whatever, and you see the blast and their reaction. Every time I watch that, I was watching the exact moment my wife died . . . There was only one life lost. But it was important to me."

Eric Robert Rudolph was born September 19, 1966. He's five-eleven, 180 pounds, with blue eyes, brown hair, and medium build. He has a noticeable scar on his chin, but may be wearing a beard to mask it. He works as a carpenter, roofer, or handyman.

The Reward

Chances of the average Joe spotting Rudolph and collecting the $1 million reward? Excellent. Rudolph is said to be hiding in the mountains of western North Carolina near Andrews. However, he may have grown weary of the lonely survivalist lifestyle and returned to civilization, most likely a small southern town in North

Carolina, Alabama, Georgia, or Tennessee. He may be living with a woman.

An open letter to Eric Rudolph from Emily Lyons, his victim in the Birmingham clinic bombing:

Eric,

You may think that you have gotten away with murder. You have not. When someone commits a crime, they are removed from society. As long as you are in hiding, you cannot be near other people. You cannot go to the grocery store. You will never have another date. Your mother has lost a son, as she will never see you again. Should you become sick, no doctor or hospital is available to you. You dare not show your face in public.

The day that you planted your first bomb, you committed suicide. The life that you could have had is gone. You may still have a pulse, but you are as good as dead. I believe a person should be thought of as innocent until proven guilty, but your self-imposed exile has sentenced you without a trial. You have been removed from society without ever being able to tell your side of the story.

Two people died as a direct result of your bombs and another died from a heart attack. Well over a hundred were seriously injured. For what? Perhaps you felt that you had a point to make. If so, you failed to make it. If your actions had something to do with Waco, there is no evidence of a connection. Your brother is a homosexual, and has said that you have no problems with his lifestyle. If so, why bomb a gay nightclub? Is it ok for your brother but not strangers 400 miles away?

It is true that many disapprove of my working in a clinic that provided pregnancy terminations. However, I have no idea what abortion has to do with bombing a gay nightclub. What does abortion or homosexuality have to do with bombing the Olympics?

I was substituting for a coworker who delivered her baby the weekend before you set off the bomb at the clinic where I worked. If you had been a week early, you would have killed both mother and fetus. How is that preserving the unborn?

The attack changed nothing regarding the clinic. It was open for business one week later. No staff members quit. All of the patients either rescheduled or went to another clinic. Another officer replaced the policeman you murdered. Another nurse replaced me.

I understand that your father died when you were young. Now, Officer Sanderson's children share your fate of having to grow up without a father. A daughter in Atlanta has grown up without her mother. Your mother has lost her son. Your brother was so upset that he made the insane decision to cut off his own hand. Is this what you consider your life's greatest accomplishment?

I have endured 18 operations, and will never be physically near what I was before. I was blind for almost a year, and only have limited vision in the one eye that remains. However, you failed to destroy me. My husband and I enjoy a wonderful life together while you constantly look over your shoulder in fear of being captured. You are a one million dollar walking Lottery ticket.

I do not ask you to turn yourself in. You are already serving your sentence. You would be much better off in prison with three hot meals, a warm bed, and available medical care. You could see your family again.

You will either be caught one day or you will die in hiding. I only ask that you send word in as to what you hoped to accomplish. You have caused so much pain to so many innocent people, and nobody has any idea as to why. All that I am asking is that you send a note with your reasons along with proof that it came from you. Letters have been sent in claiming responsibility, but nobody knows if they came from you or not. Those of us who have suffered so much by your hand deserve to know why.

Emily Lyons, R.N.
267 W. Valley Avenue #365
Homewood, AL 35209
emily@emilylyons.com

Update!

After five years of eluding an intense manhunt, Eric Rudolph was arrested by a lone police officer on May 31, 2003. He was caught foraging for food behind a store in Murphy, North Carolina—the same rugged, western North Carolina region where law enforcement officials believe he'd been hiding all along. See *Captures and Replacements*, p. 292, for more on Rudolph's apprehension.

Chapter 5

Glen Stewart Godwin—
Murderer/Escape Artist

• •

Reward: $60,000

One factor that becomes apparent when studying the history of the FBI's Ten Most Wanted list is the extraordinary attention given to prison escapees. This was especially true in the first decade, when it seemed eight out of ten listees at any given time were wanted more for what they did after committing their original crimes than they were in their criminal heyday. The list in those bygone days was populated with comparatively small-time crooks who, like Woody Allen's protagonist Virgil Starkwell in the movie *Take the Money and Run,* wouldn't have been able to even sniff the list had they not done something to rise above the sea of common criminals. The easiest way to do this was to orchestrate, or at least be part of, a prison escape.

There are numerous reasons the Feds pay special attention to escapees. First, it's seen as a direct, personal insult to law enforcement and law and order. An escapee is a con who beat the system, beat the law, beat his punishment, and beat society. Feeding an already bad person that kind of ego boost can do wonders to prompt him or her to make the jump from the criminal minors to the major leagues. A nonviolent home burglar who escapes might quickly graduate to armed robbery and murder.

Second, the frantic nature of the escape doesn't end once the con is outside the prison walls. The process of escaping all too frequently involves carjacking, hostage-taking, home invasions, and other violent acts against the general populace. That's why prison escapes are big news, and tend to place entire communities on fearful edge, not knowing where the outlaw will pop up next. Think of the classic Humphrey Bogart movie *The Desperate Hours.*

Along similar lines, a prison escapee is a special breed of desperado who needs to commit some quick, immediate stickups to get the necessary stake that will ensure their continued freedom. The reckless nature of these crimes often results in violence and death, even from crooks who have never been violent before.

Adding to the unstable mental state of an escapee is the hands-on knowledge of the despised prison life they left behind, contrasted with the glorious rush of newfound freedom. Toss into this combustible mix the fact that the escapee knows that if caught, his or her prison life will be even more suffocating and restrictive than before, and you have the classic makings of a desperado who vows not to be taken alive.

Intensify this tenfold if the escape itself involved violence against a corrections officer or administrator— as they often do. To carry out the escape, corrections officers are frequently immobilized, disarmed, tied up, beaten, and even killed. Thus, the escaped felon has already become a different kind of animal from the moment he or she steps foot outside the facility. Take everything from the miserable prison life scenario in the paragraph above, then toss in the personal hatred and sworn vengeance of the guards who were duped, humiliated, or beaten, not to mention the fury of the friends and sometimes even relatives of any officers who were killed. A violent escapee of this breed who is captured and returned can expect to give new meaning to the concept of "hard time."

In essence, a bad man on the run is a very bad man.

Of course, the FBI will straighten their starched ties and simply say it's a matter of jurisdiction. Escapees generally like to make tracks, crossing county and state lines as quickly as possible to put the hated prison and herds of angry local police and corrections officers as far in the rearview mirror as possible. This may explain why the FBI takes jurisdiction over escapees, but it doesn't explain why they so often place these particular fugitives on the vaunted Top Ten list. See "all of the above" for that.

In summation, as a prosecutor might say, even though it seems a bit quaint to put a common escapee on the list today alongside evil incarnates like James Bulger, Eric Rudolph, and Osama bin Laden, there's a method to the FBI's angriness.

Glen Stewart Godwin is a prime example. Until he became only the third man in history to escape historic Folsom Prison in 1987, he was just a common hopped-up California murderer, destined to serve his time in obscurity. After gaining a measure of fame for fleeing Folsom, he added to his résumé south of the border. Captured in Mexico, he killed a man in jail to avoid extradition, then escaped again. The second Houdini act lifted him into the big-time, hitting the FBI list in 1996 at slot Number 447.

Life started out on an entirely different path for Godwin. Darkly handsome, personable and preppy, the Alabama-born, Miami- and California-raised Godwin was the son of a forty-year-old chef and his eighteen-year-old Canadian wife. The well-dressed, tennis-playing, Palm Springs High School graduate completed two years at the University of California at Irvine in the late 1970s before trying his hand at being an entrepreneur. He operated a tool-distribution business in Palm Springs, and was living at the pricey Mission Hills Country Club in Rancho Mirage, the place where they hold the Dinah Shore golf tournament, one of the majors on the LPGA tour.

Godwin was on his way to a successful, upscale life when drugs and impatience took hold. It's possible he may have been living too high too fast and needed some quick cash to keep his playboy lifestyle going. His good friend Kim Robert LeValley, twenty-six, was seen as the solution. A pilot who smuggled marijuana, LeValley was known to flash large wads of bills. Godwin and his roommate, Frank Soto, hatched a scheme to lure LeValley to their pad on the premise of investing in a condominium. Once inside, they'd jump the bewildered dealer and snatch his money. It was a quicker and more direct attempt to profit than a previous plan to sell out LeValley to the Drug Enforcement Administration for a percentage of the haul.

The simple robbery turned into something entirely different when Godwin was said to have gone berserk. Soto was so shocked he testified that he froze in panic, observing a chilling side of his roommate he'd never seen before. "Glen Godwin stood up and started stomping on his head and kicking him in the chest and abdomen," Soto recalled. After unsuccessfully trying to strangle LeValley with a towel, Godwin then dashed to the kitchen and retrieved a knife, frantically stabbing LeValley twenty-eight times in the chest, stomach, and neck while the man pleaded for his life, according to Soto. The carnage was such that the walls were splattered with blood and the condo's tile floor became a pool of red. Friends speculate that Godwin was probably under the influence of drugs when he snapped. If that was the case, it was a bad trip that would forever change the course of the once promising young man's life.

Stuck with a badly mutilated body, Godwin and Soto recruited a third man, Roy Dickey, to help them wrap the body in sheets and a plastic tarp and stuff it inside LeValley's pickup truck. Dickey was an employee of Godwin's company, and claimed that he was forced at gunpoint to participate after being summoned to the condo on an unrelated matter. Dickey said Godwin, shirtless and covered in blood, pulled a pistol on him and threatened to kill his girlfriend and her five children unless he assisted in dumping the body. "He [Godwin] said, 'You've got thirty seconds to make up your mind to help me, or Jamie and the kids will be dead within the hour,'" Dickey later testified.

Dickey and a fourth man carted the corpse to the Chocolate Mountain Aerial Gunnery Range located just east of the Salton Sea, about fifteen miles southwest of Desert Center. At the military range, the pair tried to blow both the truck and body into intermingled atoms using a crude but powerful device made from fuel, oil, nitrogen fertilizer, and dynamite. (A similar mixture would later be used by Timothy McVeigh to destroy the Oklahoma City Federal Building.) The idea was to blame the death on the U.S. Army and Marines who used the range for artillery training. A few practice sessions might involve enough government explosives to obliterate the site and erase all evidence of what really happened.

It didn't work out that way. LeValley's body, although charred and in pieces, was intact enough to produce a dental match. When the badly bungled plot unraveled and the men were rounded up, an angry Frank Soto took an unusual step. He agreed to testify against Godwin for no other purpose than to make sure his bloodthirsty roommate was put away. Soto didn't buy the excuse that Godwin was acting uncharacteristically because of drugs. The way he saw it, Glen Godwin had unleashed a murderous demon that had been inside him all along. Soto foretold things to come when he testified at the 1981 trial in Indio: "I believe the most dangerous man I have ever met is sitting in the courtroom." Fifteen years later, the FBI would agree with that assessment.

Soto accepted a twenty-five-year sentence, earning no consideration for his damning testimony. Dickey, thirty-six, pleaded guilty to an accessory count and received a two-year term. Charges against the fourth man were later dropped.

Godwin's attorneys, Dudley Gray and Jerry Shuford, vehemently disagreed that their client was the out-of-control brains behind the scheme. "I thought then and I still believe he was framed," Shuford told reporter Mike Kataoka in 1998. Shuford and Gray argued that one or more of the three other men killed LeValley in a Palm Springs parking lot and pinned it on the younger, twenty-three-year-old Godwin. Gray referred to Soto and Dickey as "liars, scum, and filthy people" and urged the jury to view them as such.

For his part, Godwin tried to convince the court that he wasn't even there at the time. He testified that he was having drinks with a local woman at a Palm Springs bar when his roommate and employees murdered LeValley without his knowledge. The woman was never called as a witness by either the defense or prosecution. "I didn't kill anybody," Godwin nonetheless insisted.

Godwin's mother Denise testified that she had been at the condo earlier in the evening, and her son was dressed for a night on the town. Soto and Dickey countered that he was wearing nothing but bloody tennis shorts. Superior Court judge Richard Marsh viewed the evidence against Godwin as "overwhelming" and didn't find the bar drinking alibi the least bit credible. Neither did the six-man, six-woman jury. After three days of deliberations, Godwin was convicted of first-degree murder and sentenced to twenty-six years to life.

"Mr. Godwin is smooth, smart, articulate, and on the ball," prosecutor Joe Gibbs acknowledged. "But he was too smooth and ended up convicting himself. He has the image of a nice guy, but he's anything but a nice guy . . . The motive for this murder is dollars, it's bucks, it's greed, envy, jealousy."

It took the "smooth, smart" Godwin just six years to figure out a way to dramatically shorten his sentence. Somehow, the crafty con got his hands on the blueprints of the prison. The old drawings revealed that a 1,000-foot drainage pipe extended from the original area of the much expanded, 5,000-inmate prison to the

American River nearby. The problem was, the pipe had
iron grates and bars placed at various intervals to prevent a Folsom resident from doing exactly what Godwin was thinking. To overcome the obstacle, Godwin
recruited a former cell mate named Lorenz Karlic to be
his man on the outside. The loosely wired Karlic had
spent time at Charles Manson's old nuthouse, the California Medical Facility at Vacaville, before serving out
a ten-year sentence for second degree murder, robbery,
and escape.

As is the flaw with many prison and security designs, the pipe had been rigged to keep prisoners from
using it to get out. There were no checks in place to
keep someone on the outside from cutting their way in.
That assignment was given to the unstable Karlic. With
the path to freedom open, Godwin swung into action.
He had previously bribed a trustee clerk to switch his
classification from the maximum security psycho
killer he was to a low-risk model prisoner worthy of
special privileges. That pen dance enabled him to snare
a coveted job as a gardener in the older section of the
facility that was not as tightly watched or guarded.
More important, that was the place where the newly altered drain began.

Godwin ducked into the formerly padlocked pipe
sometime after 9:30 A.M. on June 5, 1987, bent down in
a crouch, and dashed unimpeded to the river. A rubber
raft was waiting there, along with civilian clothes. Using the raft to cross the calm water, Godwin was met on
the other side by a rented, reddish-orange Ford Bronco
with a chestnut-colored top. Lorenz Karlic was behind
the wheel. The pair drove to a designated location
where Godwin's young wife, Shelly Rose Godwin,
was waiting. Mrs. Godwin had rented both a truck and

a Lincoln Town Car on instructions from her husband for reasons she later claimed were never specified. She professed to be shocked when her husband suddenly appeared inside the Bronco, and later described him as acting crazed and violent, ordering her to be quiet and slapping her around when she protested. (Officials disputed Shelly Godwin's version.)

Simple as the plan seemed, it was only one of three successful escapes ever made from the century old prison Johnny Cash immortalized in the 1968 tune, "Folsom Prison Blues." Corrections officers didn't realize Godwin was missing until he failed to show for a work assignment at 11:10 A.M. It took them another hour to discover the broken drain gate. By then Godwin had gotten a solid head start. Not even helicopters from the California Highway Patrol and Sacramento County Sheriff's Office could make up for the lost time. In addition, having a raft and cars immediately available quickly negated the abilities of the prison's trained bloodhounds.

The dim-witted Karlic was nabbed three days later still lingering around his apartment. He had left tools with his fingerprints on them near the pipe, and deputies merely had to stake out his residence to make the pinch. Inside, Karlic had aerial photos of Folsom scattered about. The far more clever Glen Godwin, along with his "surprised" wife Shelly, got away clean. Godwin had pulled a fast reversal on his old bunky, basically trading the ex-con's freedom for his own. While Godwin roamed around unfettered, Karlic spent the next two years back inside taking the brunt of the corrections officers' wrath.

The escape made the *America's Most Wanted* television show, but the splash of publicity failed to turn up any solid leads. That's because Godwin was cleverly hanging out in a place the program didn't air—the old outlaw cowboy destination of Mexico. Such cleverness soon gave way to routine escapee desperation. The tool salesman immediately went back to the same drug business that caused all his problems to begin with. Six months after making history by exiting Folsom, he was busted for being caught with thirty to forty grams of cocaine and found himself locked up inside the Puerte Vallarte Prison in Guadalajara. After being convicted and sentenced to seven years, he was transferred to the Jalisco State Penitentiary.

Americans imprisoned in Mexico have long told horror stories regarding the conditions there. Not Glen Godwin. He much preferred Mexico to California. When the FBI finally tracked him down through fingerprints a year later—he was booked under a different name, Stewart Michael Carrera—and began the extradition process, Godwin responded by murdering a fellow inmate for no other reason, the Feds believe, than to delay or void the extradition. Godwin used the time to set up his next escape. First, he ingratiated himself with members of a powerful Mexican drug cartel. Then he apparently helped orchestrate the contract killing of a second prisoner in return for assistance with his escape, repeating the inside/outside formula that had been so successful at Folsom.

Unlike Folsom, however, the precise details of how he bolted the Mexican prison aren't known. "There were no official records, or that's what we were told," laments Tom Anzelmo, one of the FBI's case agents in Sacramento. "It's not like America down there." Anzelmo added that through interviews with other prisoners and friendly officials speaking off the record, the "impression" they received was that Godwin "was secreted in a vehicle of some type" and was driven out to freedom.

"Mexico is quite a different story," adds Sacramento case agent Bill Nicholson. "There's a lot of corruption there. They will tell you the official party line, the BS, because they know if they're trying to throw us a curve ball, we'll see through it if they reveal the specifics of the escape."

Similarly, the agents were never able to determine the method of or weapons used in the prison murders attributed to Godwin.

Whatever the particulars this time around, when the Mexican authorities took roll call one day in September 1991, the "gringo" was gone.

The saga of Godwin's wife-turned-accomplice, the former Shelly DeLeeuw, is an odd tale on its own. She had met Godwin nearly three years before while working at a hamburger joint in Irving, Texas. She was a sixteen-year-old high school sophomore, and he was the proverbial dashing older mystery man from Palm Springs. He told her he was working as a restaurant equipment salesman. The naive teen described her suitor as "the perfect gentleman" who was handsome enough to be a model. DeLeeuw made the fateful decision to give him her phone number, a knee-jerk reaction that would change her life. Godwin courted the pretty teen, and they began a relationship just two months before he returned home and became mired in the mess with LeValley.

Godwin hid his problems from his young sweetheart for as long as possible, dutifully maintaining the long distance relationship. He wrote and called, then everything stopped. DeLeeuw wasn't told the truth until early 1982, after Godwin's murder conviction. She recalled that LeValley had been one of her boyfriend's best friends.

Figuring that was the end of that, DeLeeuw went on with her life, graduating from high school, getting a job as an appeals clerk, and dating a marshal. Godwin, however, had other plans. Like all cons, he needed help on the outside, and continued wooing his former girlfriend through the mail and phone. DeLeeuw told journalist Jack Fischer of the *San Jose Mercury News* that she saw no future in the relationship, but "I still cared for him and what happened to him." Those sentiments prompted her to visit Godwin at California's Soledad Prison, another well-known jail. Godwin had a big surprise to greet her arrival.

"He already had everything set up for me to marry him," she recalled. "He had the minister and the family visit set up. The more I sat and talked to him, the more it seemed real. Now I can't believe it." His years in prison apparently did little to tarnish Godwin's charm, because the next thing Shelly DeLeeuw knew, she had herself an imprisoned husband. She also had a frustrating new life as the wife of a convicted murderer serving a long sentence. (Godwin told her the whole thing was a mistake and he would soon be set free on appeal.) She spent the next two years moving from prison town to prison town as Godwin was shifted around the system, mostly because of escape attempts. After a failed effort to bolt from the Deuel Vocational Institution in Tracy, he was promoted to Folsom, a joint with a rock-solid reputation for keeping flighty cons inside.

On the day of his escape, DeLeeuw maintains that she was totally in the dark. The 1987 Town Car was rented at the Budget Rent-A-Car stand inside the San

Jose airport for her to use during the visit. The orange-red 1987 Bronco was checked out from a Sacramento auto dealer so Karlic could go camping. DeLeeuw used her credit card for both transactions, insisting everything was on the up and up. Corrections investigators weren't swallowing it. They noted that a number of items found near the escape route drain had been purchased by her. If that wasn't bad enough, DeLeeuw had been arrested for shoplifting wire-cutters and pliers from a department store in Cupertino. At her office, police found travel brochures pitching the wonders of Mexico and notes taken during conversations with travel agents. Godwin's mother, who was living with her daughter-in-law at the time, maintained the company line and told skeptical authorities she didn't believe her son's wife had anything to do with it.

Whether she was duped or a full-fledged co-conspirator, the authorities knew one thing for certain—the pair were on the run together.

In Mexico, DeLeeuw said that she and her husband stayed on the move for six months before he was nabbed on the drug charges. Having enough of the con's wife life, she told reporters and authorities that she took advantage of Mexico's liberal divorce laws and returned to Texas, washing her hands forever of her troublesome husband. That apparently remained true even after his second escape. There's no indication he's tried to look up and win back his former bride.

Which is not to say he's been lonely. FBI agents say Godwin has since been living high on the lam hog, using drug proceeds to play big spender and seduce many new girlfriends. He travels first class, beds down in four-star hotels and dines in expensive restaurants.

Reports have him hopping between Mexico, Central America, America, and other countries, and even popping in for brief periods back home in Palm Springs. More recent information offers the intriguing possibility that he's turned bohemian artist, traveling the art festival circuit from Hawaii to Key West, operating a woodcarving booth hawking loons, Christmas tree ornaments, Santas, elves, reindeer, and such. (The wares probably change to reflect other holidays.) The Christmas booth sighting was part of the 1999 Stone Arch Festival of the Arts in Minnesota.

"He's probably in some mountain village somewhere where people have no reason to expect him to be anything but what he appears to be," speculates Sacramento FBI agent Carole D. Micozzi. "I think he is catchable if we somehow can tap into the community he's living in."

Agents Nicholson and Anzelmo are more skeptical of that sighting, despite the fact that it came from numerous sources. (Details are sketchy as to whether the man in question was ever located and questioned by local authorities.) The Sacramento case agents say it simply doesn't fit Godwin's profile as a wealthy, high-living playboy drug dealer. "We've received literally thousands of tips on Godwin, especially after the airings of *America's Most Wanted*," Anzelmo cautions. "Can we rule this out? No. We have to consider that any tip could be accurate."

"When we weigh the information that we receive, we look at the whole picture," adds Nicholson. "How much weight did we give this tip? Not a lot. But until we get this guy, we're leaving all doors open."

Nicholson and Anzelmo feel that Godwin spends

most if not all of his time in Mexico or Central America, where he's grown comfortable. They believe, however, that it's possible he visits America on occasion.

"He's proven to be a very elusive and savvy prey," Nicholson admits. "Based on what we've learned, they [former associates] say that this is what he's all about. He can drop out of sight the moment he feels us closing in. He's savvy enough to remain out of sight as well."

While Godwin has proved to be slippery, the same can't be said for his former accomplices. A subsequent airing of *America's Most Wanted* in early 1990 resulted in Shelly Rose DeLeeuw being recognized in East Dallas. To the FBI's surprise, she had remarried and was five months pregnant. She wasn't exactly in hiding either. The bewildered former teen was working as a waitress in an area steakhouse under her own name. The Feds extradited her to Sacramento County, where she was charged with conspiracy, conspiracy in a prison escape, and aiding and abetting a prison escape—all for her part in the original Folsom plot. "He's destroyed enough of my life," an emotionally overwrought DeLeeuw told reporter Fischer as she awaited trial. "I just want to be with my husband and have our baby."

DeLeeuw eventually pleaded no contest to the aiding and abetting charge and was given time served (five months) along with five years probation.

Lorenz Vilim Karlic, the ex-con who also helped Godwin escape from Folsom, made the news again in 2002 when he was convicted of various weapons and resisting arrest charges while being sought for murder. Karlic is suspected of killing his ex-wife's husband, Philip Benjamn Ackely, fifty-two, of Idyllwild, Cali-

fornia. Ackely's body was found in a shallow grave in
the Marion Mountain area near Idyllwild above Palm
Springs. During Karlic's trial, the graduate of prison
mental wards had to be chained to a weighted chair
and guarded by a trio of bailiffs. Depressed over the final dead-end prison sentence, Karlic subsequently
killed himself in the L.A. County Jail.

For the curious, the first successful escape from Folsom Prison occurred way back in 1880. It was nothing
more than a "walk away" from a work detail on a
foggy morning. Back then, the prison boundaries were
just lime marks on the ground. The man, identified
only as "Northrup," was caught in a bar in Sacramento
a few days later trying to pick a fight. Since that time,
many others have tried to break out of Folsom in ingenious and not so ingenious ways, including through
the same storm drain used by Godwin.

In 1920 three cons jumped the engineer of the train
that served the prison (and so tormented Johnny Cash),
crashed the engine through the front gates, and leaped
into a nearby quarry—where they were immediately
captured.

In 1932 a bored con built a diving helmet from a
football. It had a single goggle eyepiece and a breathing tube. The man filled his pockets with scrap iron to
weigh him down, cut through a fence, and jumped into
an adjacent canal. The air hose wasn't long enough and
he promptly drowned.

In 1937 seven felons stormed warden Clarence
Larkin's office and took him hostage. The prison had a
"no hostage" policy then, so the guards were instructed
to shoot at the inmates without regard to Larkin's life.
Larkin tried to escape during the confusion, but a bitter
inmate fatally slashed him before being shot himself.

A second inmate and a corrections officer were also killed, and the five remaining inmates were wounded.

A small group of hopeful Folsom prisoners once tried to build a helicopter in the prison's machine shop. Not surprisingly, the crude, quizzical contraption was discovered before the escape attempts could be made.

The most successful escape prior to Godwin followed a familiar pattern seen at prisons everywhere. In 1968 murderer Stephen Leslie Wilson jumped on a truck while corrections officers had their attention diverted by the crash of three inmate-operated forklifts inside the prison's warehouse. Wilson then used metal clippers to hack his way out of the enclosed truck after it left the yard. He was never seen again.

Glen Stewart Godwin is forty-five years old, six feet tall, 170 pounds with black or salt and pepper hair and green eyes. He's probably well-dressed and comes across as a man of wealth, education, and influence. He has no known scars or tattoos. He often portrays a Latin and speaks Spanish well. He goes by the names of Michael Carmen, Michael Carrera, Nigel Lopez, and Dennis Harold McWilliams, among others.

The Reward

Chances of the average Joe spotting Godwin and collecting the $60,000 reward? Excellent. He's around somewhere out there, skipping between Mexico and the United States, often returning home to Palm Springs. It's possible that he could be manning a booth and showing off his holiday-themed woodcarvings at an area art festival—any area. The FBI says the best tips have come from those traveling to Mexico and/or Central America and encountering a friendly American who strikes up a conversation. These people didn't realize who they were dealing with until they came home and saw *America's Most Wanted*, or went on the Internet. "They are usually quite astonished to discover that was the person they ran across," agent Anzelmo says. "The public is still one of our best assets."

Chapter 6

Donald Eugene Webb—
Cop Killer

· ·

Reward: $50,000

Cop killers have always produced the most determined posses. No surprise there. Whether it's a Mayberryish two-man sheriff's department or a federal police army like the FBI, law enforcement officers of any stripe can't help but take it personally when one of their own is callously gunned down. Even more than prison escapees, cop killers are hunted with a relentless intensity that knows no limits.

Some have questioned this, wondering why the search for a cop killer should be any more intense than the dragnet for any other type of murderer. After all, a life's a life, and everyone should be treated equally. Why shouldn't the police search as intensely for a robber who shoots a convenience store clerk as they do for someone who takes the life of a peace officer?

In theory, maybe things should be equal. In reality, the differences in effort and manpower are understandable. If society hopes to maintain order, there must be unqualified respect given to law enforcement agents (as well as firefighters and paramedics). They are the first-line protectors of the public. When one of them is assaulted, injured, or killed, it should be viewed as a personal attack against all of us.

The FBI takes a special interest in cop killers because even among the criminal fraternity itself, the above-mentioned respect generally holds true. The words "Freeze! Police!" more times than not will make the most desperate killers toss down their weapons and throw up their hands. If instead the person turns and fires, the police know they are dealing with someone who has gone beyond the point of no return. A felon willing to kill a police officer is a person who will kill anybody, anywhere, anytime, for the most trivial of reasons. It's also a person who is keenly aware of the intensity of the manhunt that will follow—but doesn't care and pulls the trigger anyway.

Not the kind of human you'd want running around in your neighborhood.

In Chapter 4, this rationale explained the mystery of why the initial manhunt for Eric Rudolph was so uncharacteristically overwhelming when he was publicly being sought for nothing more than "questioning" in the bombing of a single abortion clinic. The FBI and Atlanta police knew that Rudolph might be the same politically motivated zealot who not only bombed a number of other places, but set secondary devices to literally go off in the responding officers' faces. That made it personal—and thus the massive show of force in the forests of western North Carolina.

This also explains why with each passing day, a small-time jewel thief named Donald Eugene Webb sets a new record for the lengthiest stay on the FBI's Most Wanted list. Webb, placed on the chart in May

1981 at the archaic sounding Number 375, has long shattered all previous records. His nondescript face has adorned post office walls for so many years his Top Ten number is closer to 1960s protest era radicals like Angela Davis, 309; Bernardine Dohrn, 314; Katherine Power, 315; Native-American activist Leonard Peltier, 335; political assassin James Earl Ray, 351; and by-gone era serial killers Ted Bundy, 360, and Christopher Wilder, 385, than it is to fellow current listees Osama bin Laden, 456; James Bulger, 458; James Spencer Springette, 471; and Robert Fisher, 475.

It would have been easy for the FBI to quietly remove Webb from the list long before he toppled the record in 1999. He hadn't been heard from in decades, and some agents believe he's passed away. Instead, the FBI endures this constant insult to their abilities for one simple reason—Donald Webb is a cop killer. To its credit, the FBI continues to keep Webb listed as an enduring assurance to all law enforcement officers everywhere that the hunt for someone who takes the life of one of their own will never end.

The Oklahoma-born Webb was a known jewel thief and burglar already on the run when he rolled his white Mercury Cougar into the small community of Saxonburg, Pennsylvania, on December 4, 1980. The well-traveled forty-nine-year-old was half Native American from a father who abandoned the family when he was young. Webb had his name officially changed from Donald Eugene Perkins to Donald Eugene Webb in 1956 in Bristol County, Massachusetts, where he settled after a stint in the service. When moved to do an honest day's labor, he worked as a butcher, restaurant manager, vending machine repairman, jeweler, car salesman, and real estate agent. He was known to leave large tips, dress flashy, associate with prostitutes despite being allergic to Penicillin, hang out at racetracks, and enjoy the company of dogs.

It's not know why he changed his last name in 1956, but the process in doing so would later help him take on as many as ten different aliases and become a master of assumed identities. He needed those new names in 1980 because he was dodging a federal warrant for interstate flight to avoid prosecution and was being sought in Colonie, New York, for skipping bail after a burglary. Webb had come to the small town of Saxonburg, to case the local jewelry stores. He was apparently looking for an easy score to help finance his getaway, and was also acting as an advanced scout for a band of burglars he ran with. Saxonburg, a rural, Butler County borough twenty miles north of Pittsburgh, had a population barely over 1,000 back then. It was protected by a three-man police force.

Webb, possibly distracted by craning his neck searching for stores, ran through a stop sign. Saxonburg police chief Gregory Adams was patrolling the area and observed the Cougar commit the routine traffic violation. He hit the lights and pulled the car over.

"Routine" traffic stops are every policeman's nightmare. Walking up to a parked, idling vehicle can be one of the most dangerous aspects of their job. Even with computer-equipped patrol cars that can do almost instantaneous license plate checks, the officers still can't be sure who they will find waiting in the driver's seat. It could be an absentminded senior citizen, a harried businessman, a terrified teenager operating with a learner's permit, a fellow officer, a pretty girl trying to flirt her way out of a ticket, or the mayor's wife. Usually that, or something equally harmless, is the case.

Unfortunately, in far too many instances, the stopped car contains a nervous drug dealer with a trunkload of illegal narcotics, a serial killer wanted in multiple states, a carjacker, a heavily armed felon on the FBI's Most Wanted list, or any number of armed and dangerous bad guys. Captain Gregory Adams had the misfortune of stumbling upon one of the latter that afternoon.

Adams had spent the morning helping care for his three-year-old son Ben and eight-month-old baby Greg, Jr. because his wife, MaryAnn, twenty-eight, was ill with a breast infection. He went outside for a while to hit pinecones baseball style with a broomstick, one of his favorite backyard activities. He did that so often his latest bat had become worn and tattered from months of the stress-relieving activity. He came back inside for lunch, then left for his afternoon shift shortly before 1:00 P.M. He swung by the house a couple of hours later to bring in the mail and check on his young family. "Hi, Fat Boy," he cooed to Greg, Jr., calling the cherubic child by a pet nickname before hoping back in his patrol car and continuing his rounds.

Minutes later he spotted Webb running the stop sign. What followed started out normally enough. Instead of flooring it, Webb pulled into the parking lot of an Agway feed store and waited for the officer to approach. It was around 2:55 P.M., broad daylight. After a short conversation, all hell broke loose. The two men began a life and death brawl, both with their fists and guns, firing at close range. Bullets flew everywhere, into nearby trees and various parts of the two cars, indicating that the hand-to-hand battle continued throughout the shooting.

Adams was hit in the side and the chest, the small,

.25-caliber slugs collapsing a lung and chewing through the bottom of his heart. He was also brutally pounded on the head and face with an unidentified blunt object. After taking the second bullet, he fell to the pavement incapacitated. Webb, bleeding profusely himself, jumped back into the car and drove away. A lady who lived nearby called for help at 3:00 P.M. Paramedics arrived, but there was nothing they could do. Captain Gregory Adams, thirty, never made it to Butler Memorial Hospital, dying in the ambulance on the way.

MaryAnn was alerted by a neighbor monitoring a police scanner. "Greg's been shot," the woman announced. A borough secretary came by to give her a lift to the hospital. The neighbor volunteered to watch the kids. MaryAnn quickly threw on some clothes and was taken to the medical facility.

"I remember thinking how slow the secretary was driving," she recalls. "When we finally arrived, I was told that Greg had died. My stomach dropped out of my body. I thought I was going to pass out."

Greg and MaryAnn had met on a bus in Maryland in 1972 when she was in town to visit her sister. Instantly smitten, Greg made a nuisance of himself, begging for a date while MaryAnn was "trying to blow him off." Undeterred, the young Metropolitan D.C. police officer convinced her brother-in-law to give him their phone number. Greg called, and MaryAnn agreed to go out. The persistence paid off because MaryAnn discovered she liked him after all. They married four years later. Since they were both natives of Pennsylvania, Greg jumped at an opportunity to transfer to the small, rural town to seek a less dangerous environment to continue his law enforcement career. He had intended to become an attorney, enrolling in law school, but dropped out after being quickly promoted to Saxonburg police chief.

"He wanted a quieter life," MaryAnn explained. "It was just a routine traffic stop . . ."

State troopers swarmed to the scene to look for clues. They found two separate trails of blood. At the lab, one was found to be type A, like Adams. The other was type O, which matched Webb's. The radio mouthpiece had been ripped from Adams's car, and his clip-on tie was found on the trunk. Investigators also found the biggest clue a law enforcement officer could ever hope for. In the scuffle, Webb had dropped his ID card. The New Jersey driver's license listed him as Stanley J. Portas. It was an alias, but one that was not only known to be used by Webb—it came complete with a bizarre twist that would make it even easier to identify him.

Police initially began looking for Portas, tracing the name to St. John's Cemetery in Dartmouth, Massachusetts. The real Stanley Portas had died February 28, 1958, from a heart attack. Generally, when a alias ends at a gravestone, that means a con did an arbitrary search of the cemetery or area death notices and assumed a random identity. Not so with Webb. Stanley J. Portas was the name of his wife Lillian's deceased former husband. Add a "Jr." and it was also the name of his adopted son, a police officer in New Bedford, Massachusetts.

It wasn't the best choice of aliases for a man on the run from the law, especially a man who drops his identification card at the scene of the crime. Whether Donald Webb or Stanley Portas, the trail led to the same place.

Prior to his ill-fated trip to Saxonburg, Webb had

stayed in a Greensburg, Pennsylvania, motel. He returned to his room sometime afterward, quickly packing his things and leaving cash on a dresser with a note to the maid to pay his bill. Odd that a man wanted for murdering a police captain would turn around and be so diligent about paying a small lodging bill. Odder still that he'd leave extra as a tip for the housekeeper. Both actions, however, were said to be in character.

At this point the odds seem strong that Webb wouldn't make it to sundown without being caught. Alias aside, he was identified, was shot and bleeding, and was driving a known car of a make and color that stood out on the road. The police had arrived within minutes of the murder, and had the "flash" information on the wires within a half hour. Still, Webb managed to elude capture. The leased Cougar was eventually found parked outside a Howard Johnson's motel in Warwick, Rhode Island. Pools of drying blood on and under the carpet beneath the steering wheel indicated that Webb had most likely been shot in the leg. Although injured, short of blood, in obvious pain, and possibly even carrying a .38 slug inside his leg, Webb was nowhere in sight. A quick check of area doctors and hospitals determined that he had not sought treatment anywhere in the vicinity.

Further investigation determined that the stepfather of a policeman was a member of the Fall River Gang, a group of skilled burglars that operated out of New Bedford/Fall River and extended their reach to New York, Canada, and Pennsylvania. A few weeks before the shootout with Adams, Webb and two others had been nabbed red-handed in Colonie, New York. They each posted the $35,000 bond and skipped town. Webb shot Captain Adams and fled the scene in Saxonburg, police theorized, because he faced a mandatory ten-year sentence based upon his previous record and was afraid of being recognized.

"Greg asked tough questions," Pennsylvania State Police corporal James Poydence, a friend of Adams, told reporter J. Kenneth Evans of the *Pittsburgh Post-Gazette* in 1993. "If he started asking too many questions, Webb may have figured he was going to be arrested and had to kill Greg to stay out of jail in New York."

After that the trail went ice cold. The last bit of evidence was discovered three months later when Adams's .38-caliber handgun was found in a wooded area three miles from the Agway store. A group of children playing among the trees discovered the weapon.

Although Webb has been featured repeatedly on *America's Most Wanted* and *Unsolved Mysteries,* as well as newspapers and magazines, there hasn't been a sign of him in decades. Tips have poured in, especially after the television programs, but nothing ever checked out.

Meanwhile, a young policeman's family was left to carry on alone. "It was tough on me, but you have to say, 'Well, I have to deal with it,'" MaryAnn says. "My kids kept me going. They kept me busy. But my oldest, Ben, he was so angry for a long time. He couldn't understand why his father wasn't coming home. He directed that anger at me. It took him a very long time to deal with it. I can't even say when he came to terms with it, or if he has even to this day. There's still anger in him."

Ben Adams, now twenty-five, admits that he was an emotional child, but says he was probably destined to become an "angry young man" regardless. Losing his father certainly didn't help. Exacerbating things were the whispers around town that Webb was just a fall guy, and his father's murder involved the kind of deeper, small-town motivations that reminds one of the popular movie *Walking Tall*, or an episode of the memorable 1980s television series *The A-Team*. From what Ben was told, his father was snooping around the local crime syndicate and had to be eliminated.

"There's a lot of people around Saxonburg who believe it wasn't this Webb guy at all, that it was a Mafia type thing," Ben says. "My father found out about them, and did or heard something that he shouldn't have. I was told all my life to get out of Saxonburg the first chance I got. To move away and stay away. They didn't want to tell me why specifically. They tried to protect me. I guess they were afraid I was going to grow up and seek revenge."

Law enforcement officials admit that Webb may have been part of a bigger gang with organized crime ties, but remain convinced that he's their man and that the shooting was a random act set off by the unplanned traffic stop. Either way, Ben Adams was forced to grow up angry and fatherless.

"I still have fleeting pictures in my head of things we used to do together, but they're fading and getting harder and harder to remember as the years pass," he says. "I recall playing in the snow in the backyard, riding in his police car, and the night he took me to the hospital when my brother was born. I remember him holding me and playing with me. One evening, I rolled out of bed and hit my head on the floor. My dad came running over and held me and stayed with me until I stopped crying and went back to sleep."

Although Ben claims to have no burning desire for

personal vengeance other than to see Webb captured and tried—if Webb was indeed the shooter—he paints a bleak picture of life without his father. Like many children, he was upset when his mother eventually began trying to rebuild her life by going out and dating again. In turn, he was disappointed when the new faces in their world, including the man she finally married nine years later, didn't immediately step in and become as caring as his father.

"I was angry, reckless, and emotional in my youth," he says. "I lashed out at people a lot, not just my mom. I needed a strong father figure that wasn't there. My uncle told me that I had ADHD"—attention deficit hyperactivity disorder—"and the progression was triggered by my father's death. If he was around, he could have controlled it and controlled me. Then again, I might have rebelled and had problems with my real dad. It's hard to say."

One thing the Adams family does agree on is that Webb deserves his place in criminal history.

"I was glad when they put Webb on the Top Ten list," MaryAnn says. "I'm slightly disappointed that I don't receive periodic updates directly from the FBI. I believe they're still looking for him because my husband was one of their own."

The last possible hint of Webb's existence was a letter sent to then FBI director William Sessions in 1990. The author, claiming to be Webb, apologized to his victim's family and said he was contemplating surrendering. If it was Webb—handwriting analysis was inconclusive—the sentiments quickly faded. There was never any such surrender.

"I think he realized that was the end for him," speculates Poydence, who headed the investigation after it happened. "He has to sit back, get a new identity and a little job, and hope to live out his life."

Retired Pittsburgh FBI Special Agent Larry Likar believes Webb has already lived out his life. The former head of the Greater Pittsburgh Fugitive Task Force feels a career criminal like Webb, who would now be in his seventies, would have been busted long ago if he were still alive.

"His job was to do a burglary, not to kill a police chief," Likar points out. "He screwed up. If it was just him working alone, that would have been different. But he was part of the Fall River Gang, which had organized crime ties. The first thing a guy like that usually does when he's caught is to look for a way to lessen his time. He had a lot of information he could have given us regarding the inner workings of that gang and how they cased jewelry stores in small towns. He could have laid out a number of things. His associates may have figured he was too hot. Why would they help him or keep him around? I recall that not far from where his car was found, there was an incinerator and automobile demolishing plant. When the car was recovered, that was it. That was the last link to Donald Eugene Webb."

On the other hand, Likar acknowledges that Webb could have received help in hiding and in creating a new identity from his more loyal friends in the criminal underworld. Still, the agent finds it hard to overlook the fact that organized crime groups don't like to deal with someone who brings a lot of "heat" and may lead a posse to their doorstep. Webb very well could have been turned away by his old gang and received no help at all. This is especially true of cop killers.

"There's been a huge investigation on this case over

a long period of time," Likar added. "The Boston office is still investigating. We've had numerous leads, but nothing ever panned out."

Agents have shadowed Webb's family members with no luck. They even tailed some all the way to Canada to see if that's where he was hiding, but nothing came of it. The relatives insist they haven't heard from Webb in decades.

"The amount of manpower expended on the Webb case has been rather substantial," Likar told Michael Fuoco of the *Pittsburgh Post-Gazette* in 1999. "It's been sporadic, but every time the case is publicized, there's a rash of activity across the country. But that's the way it should be for the murder of a police chief. We should never give up."

MaryAnn hopes the FBI will always feel that way. "He's gotten away with murder. Until they have proof positive that he is no longer among the living, I think they should keep him on the list."

Most of those in Saxonburg who remember Adams agree. Officer Mark Antoszyk joined the force the very day his new boss was killed. He spent his harrowing first afternoon and evening combing through area neighborhoods with the State Police and FBI searching for Webb and/or the white Cougar. "It was nerveracking," he recalled at a ceremony honoring Adams on the fifteenth year anniversary of his death in December 1995. The ceremony was held near a monument that was erected in Adams's honor outside town hall.

"When I see everybody honoring my father, I know he did his duty and was very good at it," Greg, Jr. said. "He did a good job and was a good man. It makes me proud. I wish I could have known him."

Longtime Saxonburg mayor Reldon Cooper remembered the chief as being "a great guy who was always fair," and couldn't believe the quick passage of time. Others in the community shared MaryAnn's dismay over not hearing more about the investigation from the FBI.

Unfortunately, there hasn't been much to tell. "If a person is able to gain solid false identification, that is not going to show up," Likar explains. "You have to have a name. The only way to make a case is that somebody has to tell you if he is alive and be able to say where."

Webb set the Top Ten record on September 14, 1999, when he overtook the previous Top Ten champ, another cop killer named Charles Lee Herron. The former black militant made the list on February 8, 1968, after he and three accomplices ambushed two police officers during a traffic stop in Nashville. One of the officers was killed. Herron's associates were captured within months, but he remained free until June 18, 1986. Herron was caught after one of his former cohorts, William Allen, escaped from prison in 1974 and looked up his old pal. Allen and Herron, placed on the Top Ten list together, became roommates in Jacksonville, Florida. When Allen applied for a driver's license in April 1986 using a badly designed fake identification, police arrested him on the spot. Investigating Allen's residence for additional evidence, they were greeted by the long-lost Herron, who they initially didn't recognize. Herron remained cool. When detectives returned to the station, one spotted Herron's poster on a wall. The FBI was notified, and a federal SWAT team swarmed the house and took Herron without incident—eighteen years, four months, and nine days after being listed.

Webb has since topped that record by another four years and counting.

"In reality, the leads are dead," admits Likar, currently a criminology professor at a Pennsylvania university. "Was he murdered by his own gang, and his body gotten rid of, or did he have help, escaped, and remains on the run? We may never know the answer. The only reason he's still on that list is the fact that he murdered a police officer."

His widow wants everyone to remember that, and more. Although she eventually remarried, and the boys turned out well and are both currently attending Pennsylvania universities, the scars remain. "He took away our lives," MaryAnn says. "He took a father away from two young boys who never got to know him. He took my life as I knew it, because from that day on I had to rebuild a new one. The life I thought I was going to live vanished. I was planning to stay home and raise my two sons. After that, I needed to get a job"—to supplement his pension and survivors benefits—"and for my own sanity. I was having to deal with day care, babysitters, and working. He took everything from us. I hope they catch him."

Greg, Jr. feels the same way—to a degree. "He took away the other half of my life. I grew up without a father, without a male role model. I didn't have a dad like the other kids, so that hurt. At this point, however, I don't think it matters that much if they finally catch him. When he dies, if he hasn't repented, he'll get what he paid for. If he's sorry for what he did, he'll be forgiven. It's up to God now. I'm not bitter about it. As far as the Top Ten list goes, if there's a chance he's still alive, I'd say keep him there. If he's dead, they should use the position to spotlight another criminal."

As the decades-long search continues, Ben Adams stays busy working toward getting a law degree and becoming a prosecutor. He insists it's not for the obvious Freudian reasons. "If I wanted to fight back and get revenge, I'd become a bounty hunter or a police officer. I can't use that as motivation, just as I can't look back with resentment and say my life would have changed in this or that direction. My life is good now. I like the way things turned out. There's only one event in my life that I would change, because if I could change that [the shooting], a lot of the other bad stuff wouldn't have happened. I view being a prosecutor as a positive goal, a way of helping people."

Should Webb eventually be captured anywhere in the world, he would be brought back to Pennsylvania for trial. Those jumping ahead and looking for a *Madam X* Hollywood ending should note that the legal system generally frowns upon proceedings with personal prejudices attached. It's doubtful that a district attorney, or a judge, would allow a young prosecutor to handle the case against the man who killed his father. There is, however, no law forbidding it.

Donald Eugene Webb was born on July 14, 1931. He is half Native American, five-nine, with brown eyes and either brown or gray hair. He weighs about 165 pounds. These descriptions, however, go back two decades and could be very different today. He has small scars on his right cheek and right forearm, a larger scar on his leg where he was shot, and a pair of tattoos. "Don" is inked on his right hand, and "Ann" is on his chest. He'd be in his mid-seventies today, possibly working as a jeweler or a butcher. He might be accompanied by a dog.

The Reward

Chances of the average Joe spotting Webb and collecting the $50,000 reward? Remote. Webb has not been seen for nearly a quarter century. If he's alive, he has a well-established new identity and probably looks little like his old mug shots. However, the tattoos on his hand and chest could be revealing if someone were to notice—and if he hasn't had them burned off.

If Webb is dead, you can still collect the reward by locating his remains. One theory is he was killed by his own gang after dumping his Cougar at a Howard Johnson's motel outside Warwick, Rhode Island. If true, his bones may be in a wooded area nearby.

Chapter 7

Hopeton Eric Brown—
Jamaican Drug Baron/Murderer

Reward: $55,000

Drug smugglers and narcotics dealers have had a major presence on the FBI's Ten Most Wanted list for the past quarter century. In conjunction with the politically charged "War on Drugs" that has frustrated so many previous presidential administrations, the FBI has done their part to track down and help prosecute the worst of the dealers and smugglers. It can be exasperating work. Drug cartels, like La Cosa Nostra mobs, are nearly impossible to stamp out. Cut off their head by capturing their leader, and a new head immediately pops up, carrying on business as usual. Wipe out a whole gang, and a rival organization jumps into the vacuum and picks up the slack.

As long as the demand for illegal drugs remains so insatiable, and the money involved so astronomical, there's little the FBI, the local police, the Drug Enforcement Administration, or a hundred presidential campaign speeches can do.

With hordes of dealers and pushers scattered on

every inter-city corner supplying up to twenty million recreational or addicted customers per week, it can be difficult for the FBI to signal out the worst of the bad. That's why those who do make the grade have almost always committed additional crimes, usually murder. In an odd sense, that makes them no different than any other businessman—except that the police aren't after the neighborhood car repairman for plying his trade.

As with mobsters, high level dealers would prefer to remain geographically stable so they can conduct their highly lucrative business in their designated territory for as long as possible. The smart ones stay in the shadows and avoid doing anything out of the ordinary to attract attention. Although better equipped than their goomba counterparts to live on the lam if it comes to that, a dealer or smuggler can't get much business done that way, nor can they police their tumultuous, dealer-eat-dealer landscapes.

Invariably, before the FBI brings in the power of their famous list, a smuggler has to do something extraordinarily bad that forces them to leave the comfort of home and take flight. In more cases than not, this involves a highly publicized shootout or murder. The gunplay generally occurs when a rival gang tries to take over, or the corporate structure of a boss's own ambitious crew needs a bit of deadly housecleaning.

Once on the run, a drug baron can be extremely difficult to catch. Unlike their fish-out-of-water mobster counterparts, the nature of their business has made them skilled at both standard and clandestine travel. Years of using false identification, overseeing border-crossing smuggling operations, and moving in and out of foreign countries undetected has prepared them well for a life in exile. An American drug kingpin who sud-

denly finds himself the subject of a grand jury indictment need only catch that afternoon's regularly scheduled uncharted cargo flight to South America, Mexico,
the Caribbean Islands, or anywhere else, and whoosh,
they're gone. Often, the more powerful smugglers prepare homes and hideouts in foreign countries, a place
where they are not only familiar and comfortable, but
protected as well. Penetrating a smuggler's vast private
security force, while at the same time overcoming the
"assistance" of corrupted local police, can prove to be
difficult and dangerous.

In addition, drug smugglers rarely have to deal with
the financial desperation that plagues other fugitives
and forces them into the open. Instead, these cash-
laden criminals usually have millions in overseas bank
accounts that are easily accessible and can't be frozen
or seized by the Feds. And money, as the saying goes,
can buy anything and anybody.

If it sounds like hunting drug smugglers is more
trouble than it's worth, you'd get no argument in some
circles. The entire overtaxed law enforcement and court
system would breathe a huge sigh of relief if somehow
the stifling illegal drug business would simply go away.
Overcrowded prisons would suddenly be taking down
their "no vacancy" signs and welcoming new residents,
the kind of "real crooks" that many legalization activists believe are far more worthy of incarceration.

Now, back to reality. The scourge of drugs that has
ravaged America and other nations can't be ignored.
Along with the innumerous health and social ills it has
brought, it's caused a multitude of feeder crimes to
soar in its wake. Desperate addicts will do anything to
fund their next fix, making drugs, burglary, robbery,
and murder a routine quartet. The "War on Drugs,"

however hopeless it might seem at times, can never be surrendered. The FBI, as a reminder of this, has been doing their part by making sure a drug kingpin or two is almost always represented on their Most Wanted list.

Hopeton Eric Brown, an otherwise undistinguishable young Jamaican smuggler who operated out of tropical Montego Bay and arctic Minnesota, was pushed into slot Number 462 in March 2001. The most immediate response to the fame given this little known poison pusher was the vexation it brought to philosophy professor Eric Brown of Washington University in St. Louis. Brown, like many people in the Internet age, operates a Web page that traces the successful careers of those who share his common name. There's a biochemist, an artist, a science fiction writer, an actor, a photographer of nude women, a comic artist, a test pilot, a rock band drummer, a trumpeter, the lead singer of the Peabodys, a labor lawyer, a gospel preacher, a pastor, an alternative cancer treatment doctor in the Bahamas, a college basketball player, an NFL safety, two college baseball players, a producer at Foxsports.com, and a magician, among other notable Eric Browns.

And now, much to professor Eric Brown's chagrin, there's a murdering drug smuggler on the FBI's Ten Most Wanted list.

This dark side of the Eric Brown force started out as a sweaty, unhappy goat farmer desperate to expand his horizons beyond a hardscrabble existence on his beautiful but poverty-stricken island home. Brown left the farm in the mid 1990s and set out to make a fortune in the drug business. He hooked up with the Jamaican Posse, a menacing, homegrown gang of vicious thugs that handled the marijuana and cocaine supply route to

many American cities, including Minneapolis/St. Paul.
An opening developed in the embryonic Twin Cities
branch, and Brown grabbed it, eventually moving to
the bitterly cold climate to run the operation on-site.
There, the burly, ambitious twenty-one year old organized a subfaction known as the Rude Boys. Success
came fast. Soon, the Rude Boys were shipping $45,000
a month back to the island, and seemingly spending
similar amounts partying in America.

The Rude Boys, just like their Jamaican Posse over-
lords, were a particularly violent, ruthless, and brain-
less crew that attracted way too much attention. Brown
and top associates Mosiah Omar Wright and Christopher St. Aubyn Headley ruled their icy kingdom with
tire irons, lead, and fear. They supplied, then tightly
squeezed, the local dealers, bullied those who complained, brutalized anyone who looked at them cross-
eyed, and threatened everyone else to keep quiet.

Instead of following their own advice, the unsophisticated Jamaican farmers and street kids used their sudden riches to live lavish, highly public lifestyles.
Smarter drug barons have long learned that endurance
in the business comes from shielding themselves behind their subservient street dealers, letting the underlings take the risks and attract the attention while they
lay low and suck up the money. Not so with the Rude
Boys. The high-flying Jamaicans tooled around in the
prerequisite "pimpmobiles," roared through the streets
on candy-colored "crotch rocket" motorcycles, courted
equally fast and expensive women, and held court in
area nightclubs and restaurants. The glitzy Red Sea
Club in Minneapolis was a favorite hangout.

Suffice it to say, the local authorities were alarmed.
Transporting steamy, Montego Bay–style violence and

domination to the easygoing, Scandinavian-rooted twin metropolises was a match made in crack house hell.

The beginning of the end came for Brown on March 21, 1997, when he and four of his goons burst into the St. Paul apartment of one of their prized dealers, James Rodgers, ranting and raving about some missing marijuana. Rodgers's pad was a crucial drop-off point for postal shipments and couriers. Up to that moment, he had been a loyal junior Rude Boy. Didn't matter. A paltry five to eight pounds of marijuana was missing from the latest shipment, an amount worth about $12,000 on the street, and Brown and crew were going to teach Rodgers, and the whole neighborhood, a lesson. They secured his hands behind his back with duct tape, slapped a smaller piece over his mouth to mute his screams, then shot his kneecaps in an attempt to get him to fess up. Trouble was, Rodgers had nothing to fess. A "friend" had stolen the marijuana from the apartment shortly after it arrived, and Rodgers had no clue where to find it. In fact, he wasn't even aware that it was missing! Unable to convince his attackers that he was innocent, he watched in horror as the barrels were raised and the bullets hit higher, killing him.

"Brown was making a statement," FBI case agent Jim Tucker confirmed. "Nobody was going to rip him off. I'm sure poor Mr. Rodgers wished he had taken the drugs."

The hapless dealer's girlfriend, Mary Tabor, had the bad luck of being at the Birmingham Street apartment that day. She tried to hide under a mattress, but was discovered and shot five times from behind, including twice in the head, as she tried to run away. It was sloppy work. Tabor regained consciousness, found her way to her car, drove to her own apartment on Forest Avenue, and called the police. "She's one of the most fortunate victims I've ever seen," Tucker acknowledges. "She was acting on sheer adrenaline. When the Jamaicans left, they thought she was dead." The police sent an ambulance for Tabor, then went to check out her wild story. Arriving at Rodgers's apartment, they drew their weapons and announced their presence. No one responded. They could hear a television playing loudly inside, and the door was unlocked. Easing their way in, guns still drawn, they saw blood on the hallway carpet. The source was soon apparent. Rodgers's battered and bullet-riddled body was propped up against a couch.

The apartment had not only been ransacked, but bullets were sprayed everywhere, splintering walls, shattering glass, and spider-webbing mirrors. Dozens of shell casings dotted the floor. A few rocks of crack cocaine sat on an end table. The crack pipe lay on the floor below. At first glance it looked to be just another small-time drug deal gone bad. Only this one had an added element to tie it all together—Rodgers's forty-two-year-old girlfriend. She survived, recovered, and sang very loudly to the police.

With a motivated witness under wraps, the police had the smoking gun they needed to go after the Rude Boys. A full-fledged investigation was launched. Realizing the scope of Hopeton's organization, the St. Paul detectives called in the Metro Gang Task Force, then summoned the Minnesota Gang Strike Force, which included city, county, state, and federal law enforcement officers like Agent Tucker. Targeting the Jamaican Posse, they connected with the U.S. Marshals in Hartford, Connecticut, and Leon County sheriffs in

Tallahassee, Florida, both areas where the Posse also operated. One of the suspects in the St. Paul murder was discovered in a Florida prison. Two others, Wright and Headley, were eventually tracked down and arrested as well.

By the end of the decade, the focused, interagency campaign had eradicated the entire troublesome gang. Those who weren't imprisoned or killed left town to avoid the heat.

"If you follow Jamaican gangs, they are some of the most vicious we have in the United States," Minnesota Gang Strike Force commander Ron Ryan said when Brown made the FBI's list. "These are major people who have committed major crimes. We eliminated the group here."

In "eliminating the group," Ryan, Tucker, and company were able to catch virtually all of the major players in the gang—all except Hopeton Brown. The boss, tipped about the foul-up with the girlfriend, abandoned his cold-weather kingdom before the SWAT teams swooped in.

The St. Paul murder was indicative of what can only be described as some kind of violent mental meltdown that afflicted the young man, possibility because he was sniffing too much of his own product. On a tepid Sunday night, January 14, 2001, Brown and a friend named "Pambo" exited a dance hall in the Mount Salem section of Montego Bay, Jamaica, around 2:30 A.M. and found Arabian "Ugly Man" Taylor, twenty-two, casually leaning up against Pambo's car. Brown took offense, and Taylor took offense to Brown's offense. Brown, already in a foul mood, let fire with his 9mm, not only murdering the offending leaner, but snuffing out the life of Clement "Washie" McLean, twenty-seven, who was sleeping peacefully inside his nearby home on Piggott Street. A stray bullet cut through Washie's wall and slammed into his chest. Nobody even knew Washie had been hit until his stunned girlfriend found him dead in his bed. Both Pambo—who was later identified as Francis Young, aka Duval Smith—and Brown successfully eluded Jamaican police.

Special Agent Tucker traveled to the tropical island to investigate. "My goal was to seek new information on Hopeton Brown based upon the shooting there, and to determine how close the Jamaican authorities were to catching him," he explains. "Drug dealers can be very influential down there with various police departments." Tucker said his Jamaican counterparts were cooperative, but have been unable to locate either Brown or Pambo.

Despite his volcanic temper and penchant for violence, Brown has managed to evade long-term capture on any island or continent, mainly by changing identities and staying on the move. He's traveled throughout the United States, Europe, and the West Indies. Specifically, he's been spotted in Victor Gerena's old hometown of Hartford, Connecticut—where he has a wife and two children—as well as Orlando, Tallahassee, Pensacola, Miami, back to Minneapolis, San Diego, Jamaica, and Antigua.

Even when caught, Brown has exhibited an uncanny ability to slide through the cracks. He was arrested in London, England, in June 2000, under one of his numerous aliases, but was released before he could be extradited due to an "administrative error" in the paperwork trail between the police and prosecutor. That blunder came despite Brown being nabbed with drugs and a fake passport, and with the London authorities knowing he was a major Caribbean bad guy.

Prior to that, Brown was picked up in Orlando in 1998 after pistol-whipping his girlfriend and future wife, Tamara, because he suspected that she was cheating on him. Following a brief armed stand-off with the police, he was freed when Tamara refused to press charges. Officials believe the subsequent marriage was a payoff that had the added benefit of giving Brown resident status in America.

Agent Tucker suspects that Brown may be hanging out somewhere in England, with occasional trips to Jamaica and Miami. "I have reason to believe that he still has acquaintances in England and feels comfortable there," he says. Tucker also feels that Brown has remained active in the drug business, working through operatives in Miami, Tallahassee, New York, Hartford, Houston, and San Diego. He was last seen in January 2001 in Miami and London.

"He seems to have unlimited access to false documents that appear legitimate," Tucker explains. "That's common with drug dealers. He changes his identities on a regular basis. In the UK, his passport listed him as Simon Plested. With his authentic looking IDs and documentation, he's able to travel freely. When he takes off the gold jewelry and flashy clothes, he doesn't stand out. The only thing that distinguishes him is the mole or dark spot under his left eye. It's about half the size of a pencil eraser."

Although Brown has been successfully run out of Minnesota, the devastation he left in the lives of his customers lives on. Cocaine deaths in the Hennepin County, Minneapolis/St. Paul, area peaked during Brown's brief reign in the mid-1990s. From 1995 to

A Blast from the Top Ten Most Wanted Past

The Radicals: Weather Underground pin-up girl Bernadine Rae Dohrn and American Indian enforcer Leonard Peltier.

Photos courtesy of the FBI.

The Serial Killers: Gay stalker Andrew Phillip Cunanan and suave sociopath Theodore Robert Bundy.

Photos courtesy of the FBI.

The Trailblazers: Bankrobber Willie Francis Sutton, the first celebrity listee, and spouse murderer Thomas James Holden, the first ever most wanted criminal.

Photos courtesy of the FBI.

A Tale of Two Families

One family left to go it alone. Police Captain Greg Adams with his wife and sons shortly before he was gunned down during a traffic stop near Pittsburgh.

Photo courtesy of the Adams family.

Another family destroyed by a father's unexplained rage. Robert Fisher and the family he murdered.

Photo courtesy of the FBI.

The Destroyers

Robert William Fisher
DOB: April 13, 1961

Robert William Fisher slit his wife and children's throats as they slept, blew up his home, then vanished in the northern Arizona forests.

Photos courtesy of the FBI.

Donald Eugene Webb shot and killed a police chief in 1981 to escape scrutiny, forever changing the course of a young family's life. The second photo is an age enhancement showing how he might look today. Webb's been on the FBI's list longer that any fugitive in history.

Photos courtesy of the FBI.

Rebel With a Mysterious Cause

Eric Rudolph set the bomb at Centennial Olympic Park in 1996, then followed up by exploding similar deadly devices at abortion clinics and gay nightclubs. He vanished into the forests of western North Carolina. Rudolph was arrested on May 31, 2003.

Photos courtesy of the FBI.

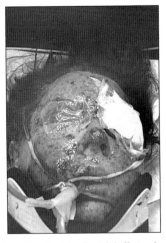

Nurse Emily Lyons, shown with her devoted husband Jeff, took the full force of one of Rudolph's anti-personnel bombs. It's been a long, hard recovery (See Victim's Corner).

Photos courtesy of the Lyons family.

The Drug Barons

Hopeton Eric Brown
DOB: September 26, 1974

High-living Jamaican "Rude Boy" Hopeton Eric Brown brought steamy Montego Bay-style violence to Minneapolis/St. Paul.

Photos courtesy of the FBI.

James Spencer Springette
DOB: August 18, 1960

Virgin Islands superfly James Spencer Springette, aka Jimmy the Juice, shipped one hundred thousand pounds of cocaine into Augusta and Atlanta, Georgia during the 1990's. Springette was arrested on November 5, 2002.

Photos courtesy of the FBI.

Murderers Row: Gangsters and Prison Escapees

Boston Mob Boss and FBI informant James "Whitey" Bulger is on the run with his second choice girlfriend, Catherine Greig. Whitey is one of the most vicious mobsters in New England's storied organized crime history.

Photos courtesy of the FBI.

Glen Stewart Godwin
DOB: June 26, 1958

The many faces of murderer/escapee Glen Stewart Godwin, one of only three men to ever successfully break out of legendary Folsom Prison.

Photos courtesy of the FBI.

1996 the rate shot up from forty-six to sixty-four. In 1997, when the Minnesota Gang Strike Force started turning the tide, the deaths dropped to fifty-one. The following year, after Brown's flow was curtailed, it sank to pre-1995 levels, just thirty-nine. Then, as new gangs and suppliers began filling the void, it slowly started to creep back up. Forty-three people lost their lives to cocaine, mostly the crack variety, in Hennepin County in 1999.

Similarly, Minneapolis/St. Paul's six methadone maintenance programs filled to capacity in the mid-1990s and have operated with a waiting list ever since.

Another telling result of Brown's sojourn in Minnesota is seen in the skewed figures pertaining to marijuana. The intoxicating plant is harder to ship and smuggle due to its larger bale size, it's less profitable per pound, and is a milder drug that usually has far less health-related side effects than cocaine, heroin, or methamphetamine. Yet in Hennepin County, during the years when Brown was carting in the weed by the truckload, the treatment rate for the "mellow" drug soared, outnumbering cocaine, methamphetamine, and heroin combined. More disturbing still, half of those seeking treatment for marijuana-related illnesses were under eighteen. Talk about poisoning the minds of our children.

As an aside for legalization proponents, the high marijuana treatment rate that held over to 1999—3,847 cases—nonetheless paled in comparison with alcohol, 10,202. Injuries and sickness caused by a legal liquid that can be readily purchased in supermarkets and corner convenience stores far outweighed all illegal drug-related medical problems combined. That's a sobering thought.

Unwilling to legalize an additional series of health-destroying drugs to go along with alcohol, nicotine, and caffeine, the government battles on against their unregulated street cousins. The latest tactic in the public relations sector of the "War on Drugs" is the effort to make people aware of the link between narcotics and terrorism. This has been one of President George W. Bush's major pushes, especially in the aftermath of 9/11.

"It's so important for Americans to know that the traffic in drugs finances the work of terror, sustaining terrorists, that terrorists use drug profits to fund their cells to commit acts of murder," Bush stresses. "If you quit drugs, you join the fight against terror in America."

To prove this point, the State Department has released reams of information to support its claim that drugs "form an important part of the financial infrastructure of terror networks." Twelve of the twenty-eight terror organizations identified by the State Department are said to traffic in drugs and use the income as their primary source of revenue. Some surprising organizations made the cut:

Abu Sayyaf Group (*Philippines, Muslim homeland*)	Growing
Basque Fatherland and Liberty (*Spain, communist separatist*)	Trafficking
Hezbollah (*Lebanon, Islamic homeland*)	Trafficking
Islamic Movement of Uzbekistan (*Afghanistan/Middle East/Central Asia, Islamic militants*)	Trafficking

Kurdistan Workers Party (*Turkey, Kurdish homeland*)	Trafficking
Liberation Tigers of Tamil Eelam (*Sri Lanka, separatists*)	Couriers
National Liberation Army (*Colombia and Venezuela, leftists*)	All aspects except international movement
Palestinian Islamic Jihad (*Gaza Strip, Islamic homeland*)	Trafficking
Al Qaeda (*Anti-American, anti-Jewish Islamic militants*)	Trafficking
Revolutionary Armed Forces of Colombia (*Marxists*)	All aspects except international movement
Shining Path (*Peru, communists*)	All aspects except international movement
United Self-Defense Forces of Colombia (*right-wing paramilitary*)	All aspects except international movement

Where is the bulk of the terrorist support money coming from? The United States Office of Drug Control Policy estimates that between 1988 and 2000, Americans alone spent between $57 and $91 billion on illegal drugs—each year! That's enough to fund the full-scale militaries of a score of mid-size nations, much less scattered terrorist groups.

The revolutionary Armed Forces of Colombia (FARC), for one, is said to pull in about $300 million from drugs per annum. And what about those "strict" fundamentalist Muslim Taliban in Afghanistan, the religious-based government party assisting despised terrorist Osama bin Laden in his relentless "holy wars"? They relied upon money from opium and heroin to stay in power before American soldiers ran them out in 2002. The Taliban and their al Qaeda operatives are still using drug money to fund their hidden base camps. Muslim Afghanistan is credited with producing seventy percent of the opium sales in the entire world.

When it comes to violence, there is little difference between drug cartels and terrorist organizations. Bombings, kidnappings, torture, and the killing of innocent civilians are the standard modes of operation for each. So are money laundering, arms-for-drugs trades, and the use of aliases and doctored travel documents.

The Hopeton Eric Browns of the world often profess to be "merely providing a service" as they cruise around each and every town like Super Fly in their gleaming cars, fancy threads, and with their high-upkeep, soul-selling ladies on their arms. The FBI doesn't share that view. The agency can see through the Drug Emperor's flashy new clothes. Underneath is just another Most Wanted Public Enemy.

Hopeton Eric Brown was born September 26, 1974 (or August 26), in the Canterbury area of Montego Bay, St. James, Jamaica. He's black, five-eight, 175 pounds, with black hair and brown eyes. He has a mole or dark spot below his left eye, and a scar on his chest. He has a large forehead and low-set ears. He often sports heavy gold jewelry and carries himself like what he is—a newly rich drug dealer. He uses the aliases Anthony Brisco, Simon Plested, Omar Kennedy, "Sandokam," "Sando," "Angel," and "Shawn."

The Reward

Chances of the average Joe spotting Brown and collecting the $55,000? Excellent. Brown is traveling around the States, West Indies, and Europe, and no doubt continues to play the big-spending, lady-killing drug kingpin the moment he feels the heat is off. With his lilting Jamaican accent, facial mole, thick rolls of cash, and flashy gold jewelry, he shouldn't be hard to spot.

Chapter 8

James Spencer Springette—
Caribbean Drug Kingpin
. . . .

Reward: $50,000

Imagine, for a moment, how one of the world's largest and most profitable agriculture businesses is run. Every aspect of the day-to-day operation involves doing something highly illegal. The planting, farming, and harvesting of the raw materials, all illegal. The refining, manufacturing, and packaging, all illegal. The trucking, shipping, marketing, distribution, promotion, and sales, all so individually and collectively illegal that in some countries, particularly the Middle Eastern Islamic nations, getting caught carries an automatic death penalty.

Now imagine that, on top of this, you've got to move a product worth hundreds of millions of dollars without the least bit of police protection. Waiting outside your gates are swarms of thieves, armed robbers, and business rivals eager to relieve you of your inventory, cut into your profits, force you to pay tributes, steal all your cash on hand, or swarm in and take over the entire operation.

Should any of that occur, you have absolutely no legal recourse to do anything about it. Not even O.J. Simpson's Dream Team of attorneys could help you get your company returned.

At least you can fall back on the past earnings, right?

Not so fast. If the local government's army of computer hackers, regulators, tax collectors, investigators, law enforcement agents, and bean counters find out which bank, savings and loan, or mattress is holding all the company's past profits, they can jump in and "tax" it at 100 percent, draining away a lifetime of back-breaking labor with a few clicks of a keyboard.

Bizarre as this sounds, that's the way it is in the business of illegal narcotics.

The previous chapter addressed the societal ravages of drugs along with the difficulty of tracking down those who manufacture, distribute, and sell them. It also noted that the FBI likes to keep a dealer or two on their Top Ten list as a reminder that the War on Drugs will never be surrendered. Which is why, when a spot opened in April 2002 after the capture of child molester Michael Scott Bliss, the agency didn't hesitate to place another smuggler on the list, one with a similar background to Hopeton Eric Brown.

Actually, James Spencer Springette was picked from the crowd and plugged into slot Number 471 because his criminal résumé expands well beyond smuggling into areas that could have put him on the list either way. Born in St. Thomas, Virgin Islands, Springette, also known as "Jimmy the Juice," is not only a drug dealer, he's an attempted cop killer and a prison escapee. The trifecta makes direct hits on three of the FBI's prime individual qualifications for getting listed.

Springette, forty-two, is said to be the boss of a violent drug cartel known as the "Island Boys," which loads tons of cocaine into planes in Colombia, airdrops it by the bale into the Caribbean, fishes it out into boats and ships, then divides it into smaller packages and transports it to the United States. Springette's main territory in the U.S. throughout the 1990s was the gardenlike golfing Mecca of Augusta, Georgia, home of the annual Masters tournament. Like a prized high school golfer being sought by colleges, Springette was recruited to Augusta in 1991 by three area distributors who gave him a tour of the steamy, magnolia-and-azalea-lined old southern city, particularly the less delicate Barton Village area, and sold him on the benefits of shipping his product to soul singer James Brown's adopted hometown. Springette agreed, producing a whopping 400 pounds of cocaine worth $4.6 million in the very first "good faith" deal. Thus, another Colombia to the Caribbean to the United States drug connection was made.

With big money came bigger trouble. Within months two of Springette's three newly rich partners were gunned down by jealous rivals in Decatur, Georgia. One was paralyzed, and the other, Askia Rojas, was killed. The pair were roommates in Augusta—Georgia's third largest city, behind Atlanta and Columbus—and had yet to find the time to buy individual mansions with their spoils. It was a sign of things to come.

Jimmy the Juice, known to be an expert at mapping out trafficking routes from South America to the United States, soon began experiencing the same problem Hopeton Eric Brown encountered in St. Paul. A lilting-accented "Island Boy" living high on the hog among the blooming dogwoods in pollen-saturated Augusta stood out like a neon-colored one iron in Tiger

Woods's golf bag. The authorities got wind of the un-
welcome stranger and set about trying to get rid of him
and his violent cronies. As in Minnesota, they banded
together to form an impressive gang of their own, bor-
rowing agents from the U.S. Customs Service, FBI,
Drug Enforcement Administration, Georgia Bureau of
Investigation, the Richmond County Sheriff's Department, and police officers from throughout the Caribbean. Assistant U.S. Attorneys J. Michael Faulkner and
John T. Garcia were the overseeing prosecutors.

In 1998, after busting and squeezing some of
Springette's associates, the task force was able to in-
dict the Island Boys on charges of importing cocaine
hydrochloride and cocaine base, conspiracy to distribute cocaine, and money laundering. It was the biggest
cocaine case in the history of the U.S. District Court in
Augusta. "Monstrous in size," as Faulkner put it,
stressing that the operation had given the Colombian
drug cartels a direct line into their once tranquil city.

"The conspiracy took on the form of a loose-knit
business organization with different members assuming different roles and performing different duties," the
indictment explained. "Manager, organizer, supplier,
recruiter, cocaine processor, cocaine courier, currency
courier." And in every position, as explained above, a
criminal.

At a bond hearing for Kevin Shawn Blyden, thirty-
eight, the first of the seven indicted "Island Boys" to be
arrested, federal agents told disturbing tales of how the
gang tried to fight the government. One potential witness was choked and left for dead. A $5 million bounty
was placed on the head of another. In a testament to the
viciousness of drug mobs, the bounty was said to double to $10 million if the witness's entire family was

murdered in the process. After hearing such testimony, U.S. Magistrate Judge W. Leon Barfield denied Blyden bond—despite the fact that Blyden had voluntarily turned himself in.

"This court will not take a chance . . . He will be detained pending trial in this case," Judge Barfield explained. Barfield added that in twenty years on the bench, he'd never had a case that involved so much cocaine, money, travel, and violence.

Blyden later cut a deal and testified about the gang's operations and financial reach. He pocketed $3,000 his first day for doing nothing more than acting as a lookout during one of the Caribbean drops. He was promoted to unloader, and made $10,000 lifting sacks of cocaine from a boat. As he gained the gang's trust, he was allowed to become a courier, transporting as much as $1 million in cash from Augusta to the islands. In all, officials suspect that more than 100,000 pounds of cocaine worth $12.5 billion was dumped into the Atlanta/Augusta area by the Island Boys during the 1990s.

Prior to the indictment, and the subsequent compromising of his underlings, Springette felt the heat intensifying and began spending less time in Augusta, possibly setting up his escape and exile. He used his Virgin Islands driver's license to acquire a passport from the Federation of St. Kitts and Nevis in the name of Elmo Brandy. Despite the fancy new paperwork, he began encountering even more trouble outside his estranged Georgia territory. On June 19, 1996, police in the British Virgin Islands became suspicious of a van and pickup traveling together at 3:30 A.M. on one of the island's highways near Tortola and set up a roadblock. Cornered, the occupants, including Springette, fired automatic weapons at the officers, severely injuring one. "As we alighted from the vehicles . . . all hell broke loose," recalled Chief Inspector Alvin James of the Royal British Virgin Islands Police. The gang got away, leaving James's superior officer on the ground in a pool of blood. To make their escape, the Island Boys were forced to abandon 2,772 pounds of cocaine, assault rifles, ammunition, magazine clips, navigation equipment, radios, scanners, and infrared night vision goggles.

A week later the gang gathered in Springette's hometown of St. Thomas, U.S. Virgin Islands, to access the damages. They concluded that one of the group had to be a rat. Rodney Isaacs drew the symbolic short straw and was soon executed. He was found in a rural area covered with lime, two bullets inside his skull.

A pair of Colombians suspected of taking part in the shootout were later located and arrested. They promptly escaped from a St. Thomas prison bus with the assistance of armed associates, one of which, officials believe, was Springette. A corrections officer was severely assaulted during the breakout. FBI agents also found evidence of two bribe attempts in St. Thomas. The Island Boys offered $75,000 for police investigative files, and promised $40,000 to anyone who would destroy the evidence gathered against them.

Things were heating up in Georgia as well. Four months later, investigators intercepted an Island Boy courier in Lowndes County and confiscated a cool $447,466 of Jimmy the Juice's cash. The new year brought more bad news. Panama officials seized nine tons of Springette's cocaine in 1997.

Seeking refuge at his supply point—Medellín, Colombia, the drug capital of the world—Jimmy the Juice was arrested, surprisingly, on January 30, 1999, by the Colombian Administrative Department of Security. He was targeted as part of a joint United States/Colombia crackdown of smugglers. However, before he could be extradited, he escaped from the well-oiled La Picota maximum security prison in Bogota on March 1, 2000. Springette had complained bitterly about his lumpy old mattress, then slipped his 5'11", 250-pound body inside as it was hauled out to be replaced. The extra heavy mattress was tossed in the back of a truck and driven off, going through seven checkpoints before exiting the grounds. Prison director Fabio Campos told the Colombian media that he suspected Springette had help. Fifteen corrections officers were subsequently suspended after a follow-up investigation.

"He requested a new mattress. The mattress was delivered, and when the old one was taken out, he was apparently wrapped up inside," confirmed La Picota spokeswoman Rocio Devia.

Jimmy the Juice's feathery escape came on the same day U.S. President Bill Clinton certified Colombia as a "cooperative ally" in the War on Drugs. It was the second straight year Clinton had so honored the cocaine-laden South American nation. In turn, Colombian president Andres Pastrana renewed extradition agreements between the countries. For decades, extraditions had been forbidden by various local laws that were lobbied for and promoted by the major smuggling families.

In a testament to his wealth and influence, Springette was able to escape, with help, from the same prison that has held Miguel and Gilberto Rodriguez Orejuela, the former leaders of the infamous Cali Cocaine Cartel. The Cali Cartel once included the biggest, richest, and most powerful drug producers and distributors in the world.

Back in James Brown's Augusta, things weren't going as well for Springette's former home boys. On July 13, 2001, Caribbean Kings Marrissa Torres, twenty-eight, Patrick Farrington, thirty-one, and Ivan Williams, twenty-eight, were sentenced for their roles in the drug ring. Torres received eight years, Farrington twenty-four, and Williams seventeen.

"This conspiracy was a major-league importation," U.S. District Chief Judge Dudley H. Bowen, Jr. announced. "It seems almost the product of fiction rather than reality, the sort of thing that would make a good book."

Farrington testified that his main function inside the gang was to navigate the boats used to fish the cocaine from the warm Caribbean waters after it was dropped from passing planes. He directed more than thirty fishing expeditions of that nature.

Additional court testimony revealed that Springette's gang operated in Georgia's Richmond (Augusta) and neighboring Columbia counties, as well as Atlanta, Virginia, Florida, the U.S. Virgin Islands, the British Virgin Islands, the British East Indies, Panama, Colombia, and Venezuela. The Island Boys even ventured all the way to Ireland, where they haggled over the purchase of a $305,000 cargo ship.

The convictions, the result of ten years of work on the part of the local, state, and federal government, were tempered by the fact that the gang's ringleader, Jimmy the Juice, remained free. U.S. Customs agent Larry Sapp has vowed that the investigation will continue until Springette is brought to justice. Sapp testified that Springette remains active in the smuggling business and continues to operate out of Colombia and the Caribbean. "What we understand now is that Mr. Springette does his own supplying."

"We think he's a threat to the public," adds FBI Special Agent Theodore Jackson of Atlanta. "He needs to be off the street."

Drug Enforcement Administration agent Pat Clayton spent much of the 1990s on the front lines trying to do just that, mostly by hamstringing Springette's minions in Augusta.

"Springette wasn't around here himself that much," Clayton said. "He never lived in Augusta. He'd visit from time to time and check out the operation, but he mostly let his associates handle things. That's what the smarter, upper echelon smugglers do, they insulate themselves. Even so, it wasn't hard to find his boys. These Virgin Islanders stick out like sore thumbs around here with their accents and flashy dress. They'd hang out at a place called the Caribbean Club."

Clayton added that Springette preferred to stay in Miami, where he owned a house, boat, and had a girlfriend stashed, or in the Virgin Islands, where he had the same trifecta in place along with some children. "He also had smuggling pipelines going to Miami; Norfolk, Virginia; and New York. He'd fly the drugs into Miami or Atlanta, then have couriers drive them to Augusta, Norfolk, or New York. Often they'd use females to drive, some underaged."

The veteran DEA agent said that aside from the drugs, the Island Boys "brought a new kind of violence to Augusta." Not content with the lucrative smuggling business, the gang would sometimes don masks and invade the homes of rival dealers and buyers to take their drugs and money. Other times, when Springette was slow in supplying them, they'd move fake cocaine to keep the cash flow going. Although such tactics aren't generally good for business, the demand for cocaine is such that the Island Boys knew they could always find an eager new buyer no matter how many locals they alienated. One such heist resulted in a three-way chase through Augusta after a duped buyer, duct-taped to a chair during a rip-off, broke free and started out after the masked gang. The police got wind of the chase and queued up as well. The dangerous road race ended with one of the Island Boys being run over by the angry American dealer. He survived, but was scooped up by the police and put out of business.

Clayton said the Augusta DEA worked closely with their counterparts in St. Thomas, St. Croix, and Puerto Rico and were eventually able to disrupt Springette's operation and strangle the supply line. "We pretty much put a big damper on the operation in Augusta," Clayton says. "There's a small Jamaican population that's picked up some of the slack, but it's nothing like it was before."

Unfortunately, Clayton agrees that mastermind Jimmy the Juice has simply moved his operation elsewhere. "We have some ideas where he might be, but we'd rather keep it to ourselves right now so as not to spook him."

The Island Boys may be gone from Georgia, but the damage they left behind remains. The influx of 100,000 pounds of cocaine into a state from a single source was bound to cause trickle-down problems, and it has. Statistics from the Office of National Drug Control Policy covering Georgia for the year 1999 tells the story of what happens when a particular area taps into a vibrant supply line from Colombia. From the police blotter: 76.7 percent of adult males arrested in Atlanta for any crime tested positive for drugs. The rate was even higher among females: 77.2 percent. If it was a drug offense, 85 percent of the men and 95.5 percent of the women were using what they were holding at the time of their arrest. Among prostitutes, 92.3 percent of the females were high when arrested, as were 70.7 percent of the males.

In 1998 and 1999 there were 11,276 cocaine-related emergency room visits in Atlanta alone. Of the 5,980 in 1998, 166 were carried out on a slab.

Prior to 1998 there were only three courts in Georgia that dealt exclusively with drugs. By the year 2000 there were six. Two years later there were eight.

In 1999, Georgia had the largest number of prison admissions in nearly a decade, 20,628. The number doubled the total prisoner count to 41,630. Thirty-eight percent of the 41,630 arrived with a drug problem and had to be sent to a taxpayer-funded detox unit.

Expanding to the entire state population, 57.5 percent of all those who entered a drug treatment facility in the second half of 1997 were using Jimmy the Juice's product—cocaine.

Those numbers could go on and on, state by state, city by city. Which explains, once again, why the Hopeton Eric Browns and James Spencer Springettes of the world keep showing up on the FBI's Ten Most Wanted list.

James Spencer Springette was born in St. Thomas, U.S. Virgin Islands, August 18, 1960. He's African American, five-eleven, 250 pounds, with thinning black hair (possibly graying by now), a receding hairline, a pencil-thin mustache, and brown eyes. He often wears a gold loop earring in his left ear. He travels frequently throughout the U.S. and British Virgin Islands, Venezuela, Panama, Colombia, France, and the United Kingdom.

He speaks English and Spanish. In America, he frequents the Southeast, particularly Atlanta and Augusta, Georgia; Norfolk Virginia; and Miami. He also goes by the names of Elmo Brady, Elmo Brandy, Kyle Pierce, Elmo Spencer, Kent Worwell, Kent Worrel, Shawn Pickering, Brian Miller, Jimmy Springette, Jimi Springette, James Spencer, Spencer Springer, Efram Zoran Johnson, Everson Weberson, Spencer Springette, Jimmy, Juice, Segal, Jimmy the Juice, and Uncle.

The Reward

Chances of the average Joe spotting Jimmy the Juice and collecting the $50,000 reward? Excellent. The Juice is out there, traveling from the islands to South America and America. He's probably established, or trying to establish, a new territory somewhere in the southeastern United States, most likely in a mid-sized, secondary city like Augusta near a bigger metropolis. He's estimated to be worth hundreds of millions of dollars, so he will probably be tossing cash around like gumdrops. If he's spotted overseas, contact the nearest U.S. Embassy or Consulate. (Note: See Captures and Replacements for an update on Jimmy the Juice.)

Update!

James Springette was spotted, surrounded, and eventually apprehended near Caracus, Venezuela on November 5, 2002. He was taken into custody by the Venezuelan military, working in conjunction with U.S. officials, and was immediately extradited to America. See *Captures and Replacements*, p. 292, for more on Springette's arrest.

Chapter 9

Richard Steve Goldberg—
Child Molester
· ·
Reward: $50,000

Sex crimes can be a sticky situation for law enforcement. Today's illegal act can be tomorrow's acceptable practice. Yesterday's illegal act can be a source of laughter or angry derision. As comedians and humor writers love to point out, many states have some very odd sex-related laws still listed on their books. Others only recently have done away with them after being held up to ridicule. Examples abound.

Sixteen states have, or recently had, laws outlawing heterosexual fellatio, cunnilingus, anal sex, and the use of dildos—even between married couples in the privacy of their homes.

Detroit's forefathers, noting that they were the car capital of the world, quickly banned sex in autos—much to the chagrin of drive-in movie owners. A more free-thinking Idaho city, Coeur d'Alene, did the reverse, protecting "paradise by the dashboard light" types by forbidding police officers from rudely walking up and knocking on a Lover's Lane couple's window. Liberty Corner, New Jersey, also ruled that it's okay to do it in a car—as long as you don't bump into the horn. Blow the horn and you could be jailed. Carlsbad, New Mexico, forbids "nooners" in cars during employee's lunch breaks unless their vehicles are equipped with tight curtains. Cottonwood, Arizona, legally frowns upon people making love in cars with flat tires, preferring they kill the time before the Triple A truck arrives doing more chaste activities.

It was a crime in Illinois for a male to have an erection in public. Erect female nipples, a more obvious sign of arousal, are okay. Maryland prohibits the sale of condoms from vending machines except in places where alcohol is sold. Kentucky, Idaho, and Maine require a license to sell condoms. In Kentucky and Idaho, the license can't be displayed. In Maine, it must be.

A federal law makes it illegal to send used, unwashed underwear and other unmentionables through the U.S. mail. Sweet talkers in Alabama are banned by law from seducing "a chaste woman by means to temptation, deception, arts, flattery or a promise of marriage." That would pretty much make felons of every Alabama male who ever set foot in a roadhouse. Those into S&M are warned to stay out of Mississippi, where the leather and whips stuff remains a no no.

Cleveland, Ohio, bans patent-leather shoes on women so as not to tempt men with salacious reflections. Politicians, FBI agents, and everybody else in Washington, D.C., can only have sex in the missionary position. In Oxford, Ohio, a woman is forbidden by law from undressing in front of a picture of a man. In Romboch, Virginia, it's illegal to make love with the lights on. A man pleasuring a women in Connorsville, Wisconsin, better not get overly excited about it. It's against the law there to shoot off a gun to celebrate a woman's orgasm. Married couples in Cattle Creek, Colorado, can't fondle each other while bathing in a "lake, river, or stream." Apparently, getting down and dirty in a cattle creek is okay.

In Tremonton, Utah, a woman can't have sex in an ambulance. Husbands in Willowdale, Oregon, can't talk dirty while making love to their wives. Other cities go further and regulate the freshness of a man's breath during the act, targeting garlic, onions, and sardines as specific culprits. The law doesn't state whether the "victim" can be held responsible if she's the one who cooked dinner. In Sioux Falls, South Dakota, you can be arrested for trying to keep warm by making love on the floor space between the twin beds in a hotel room. Similarly, one must watch out for the cops in Newcastle, Wyoming, if you have designs on bonding inside a store's walk-in meat freezer. That's not allowed. Battering the ribs Rocky Balboa style is okay.

It's a felony in Indiana and Ohio for a male skating instructor to have relations with a female student. The reverse is allowed. A female toll collector on the Pennsylvania Turnpike is expressly forbidden from having sex with a truck driver in her tollbooth. Again, the reverse is okay. North Carolina bans male Peeping Toms from peering in at women. Women are free to look all they want at men. So are homosexuals, as long as they're looking at the same sex. Oral sex remains a no no in the liberal Hollywood state of California. A coast away, the same act was once punishable by a whopping twenty-year sentence in Florida. "Highway hummers"—getting oral sex while driving—are outlawed in Skullbone, Tennessee. Single folks engaging in any kind of sex can be fined $5,000 in Michigan and slapped with a five-year prison sentence. It's cheaper in Texas, only $500. Cheaper still in Virginia, twenty to a hundred dollars. Cheapest yet in Rhode Island, a mere ten dollars. But don't add oral sex to the equation in Rhode Island. That's termed an "abominable, detestable crime against nature" and can get you seven years behind bars.

Buckfield, Maine, allows cab drivers to trade a ride for sex if the fare is picked up at a nightclub or other drinking establishment, but makes it against the law for the cabbie to double dip by keeping the meter running and charging the person for the lift.

A badly written old law in Washington prevents men from having sex with a virgin under any circumstance, even on his wedding night. The same woeful writing plagues Connecticut's statues. A law there prevents any "private sexual behavior between consenting adults" whatsoever, even among married couples. Louisiana passed a law against "streaking" during the 1970s "running bare" craze, and lists different punishments depending upon who saw the streaker.

Other states have gone beyond merely regulating human bonding. Cats and dogs in Ventura County, California, must have a permit to engage in coitus. (That doesn't mean with each other.) Filling out the proper forms there must be a major hassle for them. Moose in Fairbanks, Alaska, can't mate on a city street. Kingsville, Texas, prohibits pigs from having sex at the airport.

Many state laws were aimed at curtailing homosexuality, outlawing various forms of sex between men, but allowing the same acts between women. Other states ban all variations of partners having anal sex, quizzically known as the dreaded "buggery" in legislative lingo.

To complicate matters, playful Internet surfers and hackers have spiced such historically accurate lists with exaggerated versions of their own, making it nearly impossible in some cases to determine what is fact and what is fanciful fiction. (Those attempting to weed out the scattered plants have discovered that some of the most outlandish-sounding laws have turned out to be the real ones.)

Obviously, the FBI doesn't waste its time and resources chasing after those who knowingly, or most likely unknowingly, break these silly, archaic laws. While many a car thief has made the Top Ten Most Wanted list, nary a single serial Lover's Lane visitor has been so honored—flat tire or fully inflated. Still, despite the ever loosening social mores, there remain sexual practices that are universally scorned. Because of this, the FBI continues to maintain what has essentially become the sex-crime spot on their hallowed list. Today, the qualifications have been narrowed to basically two things: serial rape and child molestation.

It's hard to imagine either of these psychically and psychologically scarring acts ever being erased from the law books, or being overlooked as nonsense from a different era. Rape is a violent assault against an unwilling partner, mostly women, and pedophilia is one of the last remaining sexual taboos. Criminals of this ilk can pose a particular risk because in the strange moral world of prisons, rapists and child molesters are viewed as the lowest of the low. Child molesters, known as "chomos" in prison language, are usually ostracized and preyed upon by their fellow inmates, and frequently must be segregated from the general prison population. This can make a child molester on the run a particularly dangerous character to deal with. Similarly, the public shame that comes with being outed as such can move a man to violent desperation.

A string of felons inhabiting the unofficial Top Ten sex crime slot in 2002 illustrates both the breed and the FBI's determination to keep public awareness high by continuing to place this type of criminal on the list. (As mentioned in the Introduction, the FBI officially maintains that there are no specific positions designated for any particular crime, despite "coincidences" that might point to the contrary.)

The second year of the new millennium opened with a Vermont con named Michael Scott Bliss making the sex deviant big-time by being placed on the list January 31, position Number 470. He was Vermont's first ever top-tenner, and the third accused child molester to make the cut. Bliss, who had served a nine-year term for viciously beating a Brattleboro, Vermont, woman's three children with an aluminum baseball bat after she scorned his advances, was accused of repeatedly sexually molesting a nine-year-old female relative over the course of the previous year. The thirty-six-year-old delivery truck driver traveled with his victim through three different states—Vermont, New Hampshire, and Massachusetts—and went so far as to commit some of his indecent acts at his mother's home in Vernon, Vermont. Subsequent assaults occurred at another relative's house in Chesterfield, New Hampshire, hotels in Brattleboro and Holyoke, Massachusetts, and a rest area along Interstate 91.

"We notified every field office of the FBI, FBI legal attachés in Mexico and Canada, and Interpol," Vermont FBI supervisor John Kavanagh announced at the time of the Bliss listing. "We're trying to make his world a lot smaller. There's always a fear when you have a pedophile on the loose that there will be more victims."

"He's a predator and a menace to society," added FBI Special Agent Louie Allen of Albany, New York, the region that oversees Vermont.

As is the pattern with modern pedophiles, Bliss couldn't keep his grossly antisocial behavior to himself. Thanks to computer technology, these once isolated outcasts have found acceptance and refuge on the Internet, where literally hundreds of Web pages are tailored to their particular perversions, many owned and operated by pedophiles themselves. Along with offering visual satisfaction, the pages also link pedophiles with each other, enabling them to share stories, pictures, videotapes, and even live cam shots of their latest conquests. Bliss was no exception. Investigators found videotapes of his molestations, video camera rental receipts, along with computer file conversions being prepared for apparent Internet release. While such dissemination might titillate a fellow pedophile, the poetic justice is that the Web sharing can backfire to a staggering degree. The tapes, photos, and disk files provide prosecutors with slam-dunk cases in an area where convictions were once difficult due to the age of the victims and the unwillingness of parents to have them testify in court.

On the other hand, the tapes and computer files, once captured, can turn an already desperate pedophile into an even more dangerous felon who knows that not even Perry Mason could overcome the shocking photographic evidence. Combine this with how much they're hated in prison, and you have the classic makings of yet another genre of criminal who might choose to shoot it out with the police rather than be taken alive.

The balding, left-handed Bliss, known to roll his own cigarettes and race automobiles, was tracked by the FBI through rental car records. A vehicle he acquired at Bradley International Airport in Windsor Locks, Connecticut (near Hartford), on April 7 turned up at Los Angeles International Airport two months later on June 6. The FBI suspected that Bliss either left the country or wanted to make it appear as if he'd skipped. Los Angeles agents, going with the second theory, stepped up their search. The L.A. Feds were part of a larger, multiagency child exploitation task force known as the Southern California Regional Sexual Assault Felony Enforcement Team (SAFE), which included detectives and investigators from the Los Angeles Police Department's Sexually Exploited Child Unit, the Los Angeles Sheriff's Department Family Crimes Bureau, the California Bureau of Investigation, and the Department of Corrections, Parole and Community Services. If Bliss was hiding in the L.A. area under this diligent agency's watch, it was a mistake that rivaled that of his videotaping.

On February 9, *America's Most Wanted* aired a segment on Bliss, as they do on all new top-tenners. A viewer called the Albany, New York, FBI offices and said a man resembling Bliss had been working construction at the Olympic Hotel in Los Angeles a few months before. SAFE investigators jumped on the tip and determined that it was indeed Michael Bliss, and the airport car drop had been a ruse. Bliss was no longer around the Olympic, but by chance had recently contacted the hotel on South Westlake Avenue about doing some work in exchange for a room. The task force followed that trail and located him not far away at the Nutel Hotel on West Third Street on April 23. He was cornered and arrested without incident.

Ronald Iden, assistant director of the FBI's expansive L.A. Field Office, credited the tipster for the capture: "The arrest of Bliss by the SAFE Team in Los Angeles is another example of the importance of citizen involvement and cooperation between law enforcement at the local, state, and federal level."

Wasting little time, the FBI placed another sex criminal in Bliss's empty slot a week later. The dishonor went to Ruben Hernandez Martinez, thirty-five, a Mexican laborer being sought for a series of at least four armed home invasions, burglaries, and rapes committed in the Nashville, Tennessee, area from 1997 to 1998. Martinez's mug shot was pasted into Top Ten slot Number 472. (Prior to Bliss's arrest, James Springette from the previous chapter took position Number 471. The FBI put a Nevada murder/rape suspect named Timmy John Webber on the list shortly after Martinez, but Webber was captured in late April 2002, before the listing was announced. Webber still will be officially listed as Top Ten suspect number 473.)

A bilingual Hispanic with wavy, shoulder-length hair and a goatee, Martinez was working in America as a resident alien (green card). He used his job as a painter, drywall installer, or landscaper to case neighborhoods for single or divorced women living alone. Usually working with an accomplice, he broke into their homes or apartments in the Hickory Hollow, McMurray Drive, and Edmondson Pike area of Nashville and mentally abused, tortured, and raped the women for hours at gun- or knifepoint. One accomplice, Luis Castanon, was arrested, tried, convicted, and sentenced to sixty years.

"We're hoping that increased publicity and notoriety of these heinous acts he committed will lead to the one call that gives us the right tip to lead to his arrest," explained FBI Special Agent Phillip Thomas, head of the Memphis division. "He is the worst of the worst. He is involved in a number of aggravated assaults that we know of here in Nashville, and our behavioral analyst advised me that we can assume he is engaged in the same behavior elsewhere."

Thomas got his wish—in near record time. In yet another testament to the power of the FBI's list and communication channels, Martinez, who had been on the lam four years, was arrested in Mexico the day after he was listed. He was captured on a firearms charge by the Agencia Federal de Investigaciones and the Tamaulipias State Judicial Police at a home in Rio Bravo, a city just across the border from McAllen, Texas. Martinez was known to frequent the town, best known for the John Wayne movie of the same name. The arrest was credited to cooperation between the FBI, Nashville police, and Mexican authorities.

"People out there who have been raped need to realize that it is not anything to be embarrassed about or to be shy about," one of Martinez's victims told Craig Boerner of the Nashville *City Paper*. "There are so many sexual assault victims out there who have not come forward."

A month and half later the FBI kept the "unofficial" sex slot active by giving the diligent L.A. SAFE team a selection of their own. The L.A. gang successfully suggested a particular thorn in their side named Richard

Steve Goldberg, a former Boeing aerospace engineer. Goldberg is accused of luring six small girls between the ages of five and eight into his gaily decorated Long Beach, California, home on varying pretenses, and then sexually molesting them, some repeatedly. Just like Bliss, Number 474 Goldberg couldn't keep his good fortune to himself, videotaping or photographing some of the activities and keeping the pornographic pictures in his computer—once again for potential dissemination to fellow pedophiles. That was his undoing. Two young girls—possibly future victims—playing on Goldberg's computer saw images of naked children flash on the screen, some of whom were recognizable. The girls told their parents, who called the police.

Goldberg was arrested in May 2001, but the police and prosecutors immediately encountered typical roadblocks in nailing down the case. They were initially unable to acquire the proper warrants needed to seize the computer because the victims were so young, and the girls continued to view Goldberg as their friend. Apparently, as intelligent and skilled pedophiles in the child-care business so often do, Goldberg couched the nudity, picture-taking, and molestations in the form of a game, not only deceiving the children, but convincing them that it was all in good fun. In between, he took them on exciting field trips to Disneyland and local parks and lakes, further blurring the abnormal with the normal. The waters were so muddied that the police were forced to release him without charge.

"It was the same situation we find when it's a father or close relative," explained Long Beach Police detective Mike Holguin. "The children knew him for a long time. A trust relationship had been built."

Unwilling to give up, Detective Holguin and the Long Beach sex crime squad stuck to it, eventually gathering enough evidence through additional interviews to convince a judge to sign a search warrant. "It's just a matter of putting in the time and effort and talking to these and other children, and friends of friends of friends, to get all the bits and pieces and tie them together," Holguin says.

Despite the month-long delay, the police were still able to find the damning photographs in Goldberg's computer, some of which portrayed him in sexual situations with the children. "That was a surprise," Holguin admits. "Maybe he thought we'd never get the search warrant, or the children would never turn on him." The seemingly baffling and self-destructive oversight is nonetheless typical of pedophiles. They cherish their pornography and are loath to erase, throw away, or even move it out of easy reach. "You hear about them never destroying their collections," Holguin acknowledges. "They need to relive the events. Plus, this kind of material is hard to get hold of."

Goldberg was present with his attorney during the search, but was not arrested. A short time later he made a regularly scheduled summer visit to his parent's home in Rumson, New Jersey. Not surprisingly, he failed to return to California and has been at large ever since. Wherever he's hiding, chances are he's carrying copies of his prized pornography collection with him.

Police eventually charged the missing aviation engineer with six counts of lewd acts upon a child and two counts of possessing child pornography. Ironically, he did a Bliss in reverse, escaping from the Los Angeles area to the Northeast coast. The Brooklyn native was last seen in late June 2001 at his elderly parents' house.

"He's a predator who poses a risk," warns Holguin.

Goldberg presents an unnerving case that serves as a warning to parents everywhere. A tall, thin, gangly, clownish-looking man with long, dyed-black hair accented by a deeply receding hairline and a bushy dyed-black mustache, he managed to ingratiate himself with area adults, particularly single parents in his middle-class, northern Long Beach neighborhood who were desperate for babysitters. In a classic "too good to be true" scenario, he offered to watch their kids for free, all due to his abounding love for children. To further set the trap, the laid-off engineer transformed himself into something of a local "Willie Wonka," an eccentric but seemingly harmless soul who turned his home into a children's playland. He programmed his computer to make it easily accessible to Web pages and video games that appealed to young girls. He built a swing set in his backyard, and kept cuddly ducks and rabbits in cages for the girls to play with. He had CDs of playful children's music, a television tuned to Nickelodeon, Disney, Fox Kids, or other children's channels, and a large assortment of arts and crafts supplies. The bathrooms were furnished with colorful soaps and shampoos.

Although he proclaimed to "love all children," there were few things in the home that would interest a boy. "We didn't find baseball mitts, bats, or basketballs," Holguin confirms. "He was definitely interested in little girls."

Any red flags Goldberg's behavior raised were apparently dashed by his impressive degrees, his prestigious background at Boeing, and the acceptable social status of being the president of a popular local gun and fishing club. Everything appeared to be on the up and up.

It most certainly wasn't.

"People still assume that the child molestation problem is mostly about strangers, the guy on the park bench," Holguin said. "That's usually not the case. It's someone you know and trust. Parents need to be more diligent about checking where their kids are going, and who else is around. If they are spending the night with a friend, are there uncles or older brothers in the house? And be aware that if something bad does happen, chances are the child won't discuss it."

FBI case agent Tim Stanislawski of Long Beach said the multiple airings of Goldberg's story on *America's Most Wanted* produced a wealth of tips, but nothing panned out. "He's a very distinctive-looking person, tall, thin, receding hairline, large nose, it's surprising how many other people look like that."

Stanislawski suspects that Goldberg may have dramatically changed his appearance to distance himself from the "distinctive" photos the FBI has spread around. "If I was him, I'd alter my looks. Dye his hair, shave his head, something. He's a smart guy. I don't expect him to tell anybody he's wanted like some others do. He'll arrive in an area, keep to himself, and handle his money carefully because he doesn't have a lot and needs to make it last. I wouldn't expect him to be driving a new car. My speculation is that he's grown accustomed to a warm climate as well. I don't think he'll go to a winter city. He's not a winter guy. He's listed as 'armed and dangerous,' and with his gun club background, we have to assume that's the case. This guy needs to be caught."

When that time comes, Goldberg and others like him may have a defense that wasn't available when he first chose to flee. On April 16, 2002, the U.S. Supreme Court overturned a 1996 law banning virtual child porn on the Internet on the grounds that it prohibited speech with "serious literary, artistic, political, or scientific value," and that it violated the First Amendment, which "bars the government from dictating what we see or read or speak or hear." The decision caused an uproar among child protection advocates, including Attorney General John Ashcroft, who saw it as a blow to prosecutors. Ashcroft said it would make prosecuting child pornographers "immeasurably more difficult."

During the same session, the High Court overturned an Arizona law that enabled "sexual predators" to be committed for treatment indefinitely after completing their prison sentences if doctors ruled they were still a threat to society. Arizona state representative Jeff Hatch-Miller told the *Arizona Republic* that the twin rulings were "a blow to the fabric of the country's soul."

A disappointed Hatch-Miller added: "I understand freedom is important, but we don't need to lower our values in this country to provide for freedom. This [virtual porn] ruling is particularly distressing coming on the news that our sexual predators may be released. It's almost like the Supreme Court is saying we'll give them a little child pornography to take with them when they're freed. In this new era that the Supreme Court has pushed us into, people can go shoot live video of children involved in sex, say in Yugoslavia or Asia, and come back here and say it's virtual. It will be totally up to the police to prove the identity, and, quite frankly, there's no way for the police to enforce that."

The virtual child porn ruling enables Web-page operators to use advanced computer technology to alter the images of adults having sex to make it appear as if they are children. The technology also makes it possible to create fabricated images of children that are almost indistinguishable from the real thing. In specific, Goldberg could argue that the nude photos weren't really of his young neighbors, but were computer creations using their faces from regular photographs. Similarly, he could argue that he spliced in nude photos of himself frolicking with the computer creations.

"I see this as a real setback in trying to rid our society of sexual perverts," Lieutenant Larry Jacobs, head of the Phoenix Police Organized Crime Bureau, told the *Republic*. "We see some real potential problems that this is going to open to us both in the investigations and the prosecution. People get all hung up on whether it is actually victimizing a real child," Jacobs cautioned. "Whether it's produced in a computer-generated world or the real world, its purpose is to do one thing and that is to satisfy the needs of sexual perverts. It's preparing that individual to the point where he will go out into the real world and victimize a real child."

As the FBI can attest, there's already too much of that as it is.

Richard Steven Goldberg was born November 9, 1945. He's six feet tall, 160 pounds, with brown eyes and a deeply receding hairline. He may have long, curly, dyed-black hair, or shorter gray hair. He usually sports a mustache to match his hair, either black or gray, and wears glasses. He's intelligent, with engineering and aviation skills, and is good with children. Goldberg enjoys the outdoors, camping, hunting and fishing. He's known to frequent Rumson, New Jersey; Las Vegas, Nevada; Bullhead City, Arizona; Colorado and Georgia. He has an ex-wife and two adult children who all live in Atlanta. As the former president of a Long Beach gun club, Goldberg is no doubt proficient with firearms. Police confiscated a shotgun from his California home, but found nothing else.

The Reward

Chances of the average Joe spotting Goldberg and collecting the $50,000 reward? Excellent. Pedophiles tend to be repetitive in their actions due to their relentless need to satiate their abnormal sexual desires. Look for a thin, scraggly-haired, well-spoken, overly friendly, odd-looking man pushing sixty whose residence quizzically looks like a little girl's bedroom. He's probably working in a no-questions-asked, blue-collar job that is way beneath his intelligence and skills level.

Chapter 10

Robert William Fisher—
Familicide

Reward: $50,000

Switch on a police scanner in a randomly selected city on any given night and the old expression, "There's a thin line between love and hate," will spring dramatically to life. More times than not, the majority of radio calls that send squad cars crisscrossing across town signal the code for a "domestic." That's law enforcement lingo for a loud, often violent squabble between husbands and wives, or among lovers of all possible mixes, matches, and genders.

Toss in confrontations between parents and children, cousins, aunts, uncles, or any other pairing of relatives, and it's hard to imagine how the overburdened police find the time to do anything else.

If the sheer numbers aren't bad enough, "domestics" can be the most unpleasant house calls for responding officers to make. Often, another cliché comes into play: "Blood is thicker than water." The victim getting the worst of the skirmish frequently turns on the police officers who come to the rescue, suddenly becoming violently protective of their abusive husband, wife, or lover.

Prosecuting domestics can be a colossal headache as well. Couples tend to make up long before the snail-paced judicial system can deal with the original complaint. That frequently results in the otherwise legal rarity of having the victim appear in court as a hostile witness for the prosecution, and as a supportive witness for the accused. Family, financial concerns, and/or overpowering *amore* prove to be more powerful motivations than justice over some long forgotten confrontation.

These misplaced sentiments can be a deadly trap, especially for women at the physical, emotional, and financial mercy of an unrepentant husband or boyfriend. That's why many states now have domestic abuse laws that give the prosecutor, not the victim, the right to drop or proceed with a case. Prosecutors are encouraged by women's rights and antiabuse organizations to go forward even if the victim is uncooperative and the conviction of a breadwinner brings long-term hardship to the family. That, activists say, is still preferable to a lifetime of beatings and possibly death.

In turn, as women become financially independent and emotionally strong in our progressive society, the roles have reversed. Police are seeing more women stepping into the role of the batterer. Since men tend not to report such incidents and are physically better equipped to endure the punishment in silence, the statistics that exist are thought to be only the tip of the iceberg.

Taken as a whole, domestics are a muddled mess that law enforcement agents, almost to the man and woman, would prefer not to have to deal with. Police officers are trained to battle criminals, not function as marriage counselors who make house calls. Unfortunately, there's no away around it. Considering the overwhelming number of domestic incidents, and the fact that most violent crimes, including murder, occur between people known to each other, domestic violence is a crime category that isn't going to go away.

Despite all the problems with arrests and prosecution, the FBI has not hesitated to put the worst domestic abusers—murderers—on their Top Ten list. In fact, it may be the one constant on the list over the last half century. While technology and sociology have changed the face of other crimes—yesterday's radical revolutionaries are today's college professors and politicians—the very first list in 1950, as noted in Chapter 1, included two men who killed their wives and one who stabbed his girlfriend. A half century later, the FBI still holds a slot open for those who do likewise.

Some might question this, arguing that such killers only pose a danger to their spouse or lover. Once the "heat of passion" has cooled, they have no reason to injure or harm anyone else, and thus pose no further danger to society. While that may be true with some, others have repeated their violent ways with subsequent partners. A scattered few, after snapping and "tasting blood," have gone on to become serial killers. Regardless, as noted above, domestic violence, even on an individual, one-time-per-person basis, is so rampant in society it would be hard to convince the FBI that it no longer warrants a regular Top Ten spot.

The historic 2002–2003 list reiterates this. After months of talk about reorganizing the FBI to better emphasize the fight against terrorists and cyber criminals, when a slot opened in June 2002, the FBI went back to the traditional well and slapped a spouse killer's picture right next to that of world-renowned public enemy Osama bin Laden. The message sent was clear—domestic violence will not be tolerated any more than terrorist attacks.

The current holder of the domestic violence position, Robert William Fisher, is one of the more fascinating cases. A churchgoing Navy veteran, former firefighter, and cardiovascular technician at the world famous Mayo Clinic—based in Rochester, Minnesota, but with a facility in Scottsdale, Arizona—Fisher represents that strange breed of human who goes home one day and, seemingly out of the blue, kills his entire family. Usually, the assailant then turns the weapon on himself. Fisher didn't, instead choosing to use his outdoor skills à la Eric Rudolph and escape into the wilds of northern Arizona, where he may or may not remain today.

Fisher's case gained national notoriety for the brutality that was piled on top of the typical shock and bafflement. Sometime on the night of April 9 or in the early morning hours of April 10, 2001—the Monday and Tuesday after Palm Sunday—the forty-year-old hospital technician shot his wife Mary, thirty-eight, in the back of the head, slit her throat, then crept into the rooms of his son Bobby, ten, and daughter Brittney, twelve, and slit their throats to the bone with a hunting knife. Medical examiners suspect they were all sleeping when they were murdered. Whether Fisher intended to kill himself as well and got cold feet has been the topic of much debate. What is known is that at some point, Fisher decided he needed to cover his tracks and make the inexplicable murders look like an accident. Tampering with the natural gas lines of his modest home he rigged it to explode. At 8:42 A.M. on April 10, it did, rocking the densely packed south Scottsdale neighborhood and destroying most of the structure. When police unraveled the mess, they discovered that Fisher, the family's Queensland heeler dog Blue, and Mary's Toyota 4-Runner were gone.

Convinced he was responsible, the Maricopa County attorney's office charged Fisher with three counts of homicide and one count of arson on an occupied structure on July 19, 2001. Nearly a year later, on June 29, 2002, the FBI made Robert William Fisher the 475th addition to their Top Ten List.

"It's a mixed blessing," said Scottsdale Police Sergeant Douglas Bartosh. "We are happy for the attention given to a fugitive from our area who committed such a horrendous crime, but it's unfortunate that we had to experience this horrendous crime in Scottsdale."

Rumors swirled that jumping Fisher over 8,000 other candidates was a "makeup call" to the Phoenix FBI office after headquarters in Washington failed to respond to the famous "Phoenix Memo" sent by Arizona Special Agent Kenneth Williams. Prior to 9/11, the alert Williams had warned higher-ups in Washington that fervently anti-American Arab nationals were training at Arizona flight schools, possibly for ill intent, and he suggested investigating similar schools nationally to see if a pattern was emerging. Headquarters didn't run with the ball, citing the manpower involved and rules forbidding the ethnic profiling of particular groups. (See Epilogue for more on this.)

FBI spokesman Ernie Porter denied that jumping Fisher to the head of the class was a payback to Phoenix or a reward for their insightful work. The Top

Ten list, Porter insists, isn't used that way. Whatever the true machinations, the intricacies and nuances of the Fisher case make him a worthy representation of his small but alarming breed of criminal—those committing "familicide."

Robert William Fisher was raised in Tucson, Arizona, the brown, tumbleweed-dotted, Old West city that's currently undergoing a population explosion. Back in the 1960s and '70s, however, it remained a relatively rural, sleepy college town. It was in this "living desert" of Tucson that Fisher first learned to love the great outdoors, roaming the deserts searching for jackrabbits, coyotes, roadrunners, wild pigs, mountain lions and bobcats. Camping trips to the cool mountain forests in northern Arizona further instilled him with a deep respect for nature.

When he wasn't outside exploring, the rangy youth also enjoyed music and choirs. Fisher pulled a few hitches with the Tucson Boys Chorus Town Singers.

The few dark clouds in his idyllic young life were caused by human nature and twentieth century society. His parents divorced when he was fifteen, a domestic upheaval that hit him hard. Surprisingly, psychiatrists say it's the older children who are scarred the most by divorce, and Fisher serves as a textbook example. Decades later he often recounted his despair over his parents' problems and freely admitted the scars lingered. His mother, Jan Howell, told police investigators that she left because her husband was too controlling and she needed space to escape her "yes sir" existence and live her own life. Fisher and his two sisters stayed with the father, a local banker. Although the shattering of the family unit only affected the last three years of his teenage childhood, he often speculated that his life would have turned out differently if his mother had been around until he was at least eighteen.

After high school he joined the Navy and served as a petty officer second class on the USS *Belleau Wood* for most of 1979 through 1982. It is believed he learned to be a firefighter in the Navy, and used the training after his discharge to secure a fireman/paramedic position at the Borrego Springs, California Fire Protection District located two hours northeast of San Diego. He met his wife-to-be, Mary Cooper, not long afterward at a Baptist church social. A peppy blonde from an unbroken, close-knit family, she filled a void in his life that was missing since his mother's departure. With the full blessing of her parents, Bill and Ginny, the couple married in the mid-1980s.

Fisher's career hit a bump when he hurt his back on the job and had to file for disability. Longing to return home to the desert, he moved his young wife to Scottsdale, a growing city adjacent to Phoenix. After searching the area, they purchased a ranch-style home in the 2200 block of North 74th Place for $80,000. As with most young couples, they had different ideas on how to decorate. In the spirit of compromise, clean and orderly Mary allowed him to christen the dining room with the massively antlered head of a bull elk he'd proudly downed on one of his hunting trips.

When not out trampling the woods searching for new wall decorations, Fisher attended Gateway Community College in order to focus his medical technology training into a more specialized area. This enabled him to work under less "heavy lifting" conditions in hospitals, as opposed to the constant physical strain of being a streetwise paramedic. Known to be calm and collected under fire, he excelled in the often stressful world of a cardiovascular technician, an occupation that involves placing shunts and catheters inside the hearts of patients prior to surgery. Friends and coworkers say they never observed any signs of him cracking under the pressure of the intricate task, nor did they observe any other mental defects. He enjoyed the work and atmosphere so much that one year he doubled his salary through voluntary overtime.

Unlike many in the medical field who become hardened to human suffering out of a psychological necessity, Fisher was said to have clung to his humanity, remaining caring and patient-friendly. He always strove to be cognizant of the fact that he was dealing with an entire person and not just a mechanical pump beating inside a biological unit. "He was walking the walk of a Christian," a workout buddy told Nena Baker of the *Arizona Republic*. "It wasn't a convenience item."

Despite his strong "your body is a temple of God" religious beliefs, coupled with an extensive knowledge of health, medicine, and fitness, Fisher was quizzically fond of chewing tobacco, a nasty, addictive, good ol' boy vice that can be repulsive to others while at the same time playing deadly havoc with a user's health. Friends said that in between spits, he displayed a dry sense of humor, was easygoing, and didn't have any strong political leanings.

His first child, Brittney, was born in 1988, followed by Robert, Jr. in 1990. The children were happy, outgoing, and playful. Brittney was a brainy, compassionate type, and Robert, Jr. was more of a prankster and cutup. The family was closely tied to Scottsdale Baptist Church and its myriad tributary activities. Mary

sometimes taught Sunday school and organized re-
treats and outreach events like camping trips.

Mary Fisher's penchant for a sparkling clean home
survived the addition of two lively kids, along with her
husband's preference for a rustic but orderly hunting
lodge setting. The Fishers continued to keep things
pristine, going so far as to spread out blankets under
the elk's long, protruding nose to protect the carpet
whenever Bobby or Brittney invited their friends over
for frequent pizza or Chinese food feasts.

Secure with his rebuilt family, Fisher was said to be
nonetheless paranoid about history repeating itself.
"He was adamant about not going through a divorce,
of putting his family through a divorce," Fisher's pastor, Gregg Cantelmo, told Baker in June 2001. "He had
strong feelings about it and a bad experience." His
feelings were so deep that he steadfastly avoided taking his children to Disneyland because decades before
his parents had an ugly public shouting match at the
popular theme park prior to their final separation.

Fisher's mother-in-law, Ginny Cooper, told the same
Republic reporter that Fisher didn't socialize with his
family very much because he had a fear of "getting too
close to people and losing them."

Six months before the murders, friends and church
members say Fisher began to withdraw from many of
his former activities and distance himself further from
his family. His attendance at church was spotty, and he
stopped working out at the World Gym, where he had
been a regular. However, he continued to make regular
stops at various area hunting, fishing, and outdoor
stores. Comfortable in those environments, he often
lingered to chat with owners and employees about

everything from his family to the ins and outs of various animal-calling devices. His interest in his outdoor life seemed to be increasing in direct proportion with the deemphasizing of his church and family activities. In response, Mary began hinting to friends that she was "at the end of her rope" and was seriously considering getting a divorce.

The night before the murders, Fisher went to his daughter's school to show support for her induction into the National Junior Honor Society. Teachers and administrators told police that he sat by himself, away from the rest of the audience, and was cold and blasé when approached. Brittney's young friends tell a different story, saying he was very much the proud father beaming over his daughter's academic accomplishment and freely interacting with them.

Afterward, Fisher took Brittney with him on a small shopping excursion to a Popular Outdoor Outfitters store and the Checker Auto Parts shop next door. At the Popular, he spent ninety dollars to purchase a water purification kit that consisted of a microfilter and pump, a sixty-four-ounce container, and two bottles of iodine tablets. This has given rise to speculation that he planned his escape in advance. If so, bringing along a cheerful, just awarded daughter he would soon kill like a wild animal was an especially ghoulish twist.

Checker, citing customer privacy, has refused to divulge what he bought there. However, he had changed the oil in his prized 2001 Dodge Ram 2500 Cummins diesel pickup truck a few days before, and may have been replenishing the stock. Either way, the father-daughter excursion, oil change, and possible resupply doesn't speak of a man planning to murder his family a few hours later.

While Robert, Sr. and Brittney shopped, Mary Fisher and Robert, Jr. were at the church attending a hunting class focusing on rifle and bow safety. It was an apparent effort to bond the family closer by sharing in the sometimes emotionally distant husband and father's interests. Fisher had taken similar classes previously, and could always be counted on to register for the annual, state-sponsored lotteries set up to grant a limited number of big-game-hunting permits to go along with the easily obtained small-game licenses.

Later that day, at home, Fisher's mellow mood changed dramatically around 10:00 P.M. when neighbors reported hearing him arguing loudly and angrily with his wife. The topic was not known, but may have been about Fisher's past and present infidelities, which he blamed on his wife's admitted sexual cold shoulder. The guilt-ridden medical tech had confessed about a lascivious encounter at a massage parlor two years before, when he briefly moved out at his stunned wife's request. That time, he similarly headed for the mountains, intent on camping for a month to sort out his life and serve penance for his sin. He returned after four days spiritually renewed and promised to rededicate himself to his wife, children, and church, telling friends the experience proved that he couldn't exist without his family. He readily confessed his indiscretions and lustful desires to pastors and peer counselors at his church, seeking their help in overcoming the relentless temptations of the flesh.

Things went smoothly until he stumbled a year and half later. As was his habit, and possibly his downfall, he again sought absolution through confession. He began telling friends and fellow employees at the Mayo Clinic about a bizarre, back therapy session with yet another supposed "professional masseuse" that got out of hand and left him with a urinary tract infection or some kind of sexually transmitted disease. Although the medical problem was quickly and quietly alleviated, thanks to the perks of his profession, he was terrified that his wife would somehow get wind of his latest betrayal and kick him out for good, throwing the family into the divorce he so dreaded. Months passed without the unlikely discovery, but Fisher remained nervous and on edge. Concerned friends cautioned that the only way he could be exposed was if he felt compelled to make another ill-advised confession to Mary. That, or if he continued to hang himself by seeking forgiveness and sympathy among a widening circle of acquaintances and associates.

Slapped back into the straight and narrow by that brief moment of backsliding, colleagues told investigators he began showing up at work with his Bible in hand, reading it during breaks along with his usual array of hunting magazines. Unfortunately, the paranoia over his sexual tryst being discovered began to spread to the more unhealthy area of believing "people" were poring through his "records" for unknown reasons. The creeping dementia was exacerbated by the fact that Fisher regularly carried a .38 caliber pistol in a specially designed fanny pack, taking advantage of an archaic Arizona law harkening back to the Old West, which allows citizens to purchase permits to pack such heat.

Neighbors said Mary Fisher and her gun-toting husband argued often, usually about sex and money—the standard domestic potholes. He wanted more of the first, she wanted more of the second. One tiff was so heated that the cops had to intervene. Scottsdale police, however, have no record of responding to such a

call, speculating that an officer may have cooled things
down and chose not to write it up to protect the family.
Another spat ended with Fisher dousing his fuming
wife with a garden hose.

Friends and junior high classmates of Brittney say
that Fisher was nice for the most part, but had spells
where he became controlling, abusive, and mean.
Some recalled an incident when he showed up at her
school ranting about something and appeared to be either intoxicated, on pain medication, or both.

Whatever the topic of the April 9 argument, Fisher
apparently didn't simmer down after his family gave it
up and went to sleep that night. The six-foot-one, 190-
pound, buzz-cut medical tech stormed off at 10:40 P.M.
in his wife's silver SUV and visited a nearby bank
teller machine, withdrawing the $280 daily maximum.
Security cameras show him wearing a silver and black
Oakland Raiders baseball-style hat, along with an RC
Cola T-shirt. He returned home sometime later, his
emotions percolating like a boiling coffeepot until he
was kicked over the edge of paranoia into a cauldron of
violent insanity.

He systematically went about murdering his wife of
sixteen years, daughter, and son, giving Mary the double treatment of being shot and having her throat cut to
the vertebra like a slaughterhouse cow. Fisher then set
a candle burning at the end of a hallway, disconnected
the furnace line, shut all the windows, and filled the
house with gas to the point where it became a ticking
time bomb. The three-bedroom, two-bath, ranch-style
home exploded in a fireball that collapsed a brick
fence, shot streaks of flame twenty feet into the air, and
shook the foundations of houses for a half mile. Firefighters from a nearby station responded within three

minutes, but there was nothing they could do but valiantly fight to keep the fire from jumping to the residences on either side and hop-scotching through the tightly packed subdivision. Despite a searing heat that melted their plastic face shields and frequent explosions from ammunition and aerosol cans, they were able to keep the blaze contained.

Ironically, a fireman injured his leg when he fell while battling the inferno, an unsettling reminder of how Fisher hurt his back and had to give up his own firefighting career seventeen years before.

It was initially believed that the explosion was a tragic accident and the deaths were unintentional. Fisher, thought to be away on a hunting trip, was the recipient of a huge outpouring of sympathy from those who expected him to drive up at any moment and discover his home and life in ruins. His father-in-law, Bill Cooper, his pastor, Reverend Cantelmo, and friends and coworkers were all concerned for his mental state when he found out. "He was the best husband you could ever ask for and the best son-in-law we ever wanted," Cooper assured when suspicions concerning Fisher's absence first arose.

Returning in such a manner may very well have been Fisher's plan. If the bodies of his wife and children were incinerated to the bone, it may have obliterated the blood and knife wounds, and prevented the medical examiner from finding an absence of smoke in their lungs—the telltale sign that they were dead before the fire. However, in yet another baffling aspect of the case, even if everything had gone perfectly, the extra, unneeded bullet to his wife's head would have still exposed the murders.

As it happened, the bodies weren't consumed

enough to mask any of the prefire activities. "It's difficult to do that in a house fire," notes former Phoenix
medical examiner Dr. Jeffrey Nine. "Unless a person
is completely burned cremation style, we can find the
evidence." That oversight resulted in the shocking
news from the medial examiner's office released the
following day that Mary, Brittney, and Bobby had been
murdered before the house exploded. Fisher, no doubt
monitoring the media, was thereby alerted that his
poorly designed scheme had literally gone up in smoke.
Any chance of rolling up and giving an Academy-
Award-winning performance as a devastated husband
was dashed. Instead, he headed for the hills.

Stunned friends, neighbors, fellow congregation
members, and classmates, many still refusing to believe
that Robert Fisher could be responsible, began making
a pilgrimage to the site, leaving candles, posters, cards,
Mylar balloons, Easter baskets, lilies, crosses, flowers,
and stuffed animals on the sidewalk and fence to the
right of the charred remains of the home. The notes
from the children were particularly moving, with mes-
sages like "Friends forever Bobby" and "Good-bye
Brittney, we'll miss you" scrawled by small hands on
large poster board. Some of the young misses who
came were still wearing the colorful polish and flowers
that Brittney had painted on their toenails during a
sleepover a few days before. One of the many topics the
chattering girls covered that night was the preferred
method of their future deaths. Brittney—and most of
the others—mentioned that if given a choice, she would
prefer to die in her sleep.

Behind the colorful and oddly cheerful display was
the darkened image of the gutted house where Brittney's wish tragically came true far too early. Fed by

the knowledge of the horror that happened inside, the once spic-and-span home seemed to radiate an eerily evil presence. Perched at the one o'clock position in a tightly packed urban cul-de-sac, the ravaged home emanated bad vibes for months, until it was eventually leveled to its still charred cement base.

At Supai Middle School, similar memorials were erected. An oak tree was planted outside in Brittney's memory. One young boy was found crying in a classroom, tortured over the guilt of having been mean to her on her last day. Tears streaming down his face, he told a teacher that despite his immature behavior, Brittney stayed after school once to help him with a homework assignment he was having trouble with. The boy, like many others at the diversely populated school, knew something was wrong from the moment Brittney failed to show up for class that morning, noting how proud she was of a near perfect attendance record that dated back to grammar school.

Similar stories emerged from Scottsdale Baptist Church, where services were held in the family's memory. One was attended by more than 1,300 people, and included boxes of tissue at the end of each row to dab the river of tears that fell, particularly from the children. Plainclothes Scottsdale police officers were sprinkled through the crowd just in case Fisher himself quietly appeared.

"Reasons and answers are not always available and may never be," Reverend Cantelmo told the congregation in an attempt to comfort the mourners. "While God doesn't tell us why, he does tell what. What are we to do? And that is to continue to love and cling to him and one another."

A music stand where Brittney played bells was left

empty up front, except for her twin instruments and decorative roses. Photos of the family adorned the lobby, minus the missing father. Sunday school teachers recalled how Brittney disabled a small race car she had built so a younger competitor could win a competition.

"From our finite, human point of view, Brittney's life was cut short," said her youth pastor, Jim Roden. "According to God's word—and I don't understand it on an emotional level—her life was just as long as God intended it to be. Her life was the perfect number of days. It was time to finish the race. It was time to go home."

Bobby was remembered as an outgoing boy who always picked the car token when he played Monopoly, enjoyed having friends sleep over, and had a knack for creating rhyming catch phrases, things like "funky monkey."

Some children, both at Brittney's and Bobby's schools and at the church, were having a hard time dealing with the brutal deaths, particularly with the reports that the father was the culprit. They had nightmares, and started questioning the nature of their own families, asking if something similar could befall them. Grief counselors were provided to quell their fears.

Little by little the truth about the seemingly "perfect," devoutly religious family that lived inside the gutted house began to trickle out publicly. The news slowly surfaced of Fisher's affairs, including a less tawdry hookup with a Scottsdale–HealthCare North nurse three years before. Also exposed was his brief separation, the marriage counseling sessions, his abnormal fears of divorce, his controlling nature, and his final, paranoia-inducing encounter with the second masseuse. Transcripts of police interviews revealed the precise, Clintonesque sexual act Fisher sought from the rubdown girls, something his disinterested wife apparently refused to do.

Along the same lines, there was Mary's verbal shrug to a girlfriend regarding how she endured her marital responsibilities in a grimace-and-bear-it style. "I think basically he wanted sex, um . . . I think every day!" the friend told police detectives. "I can't remember if it was every day or every other day they agreed on, but I mean now we're talking for fifteen years of their marriage . . . like at least every other day, and I said 'God!' I go, 'Why do you think?' You know, I mean yeah, I could see at eighteen, but at forty? Who wants to have sex every day? . . . She said, 'I think he just wants to because he can.' Because he wants to prove he still can or something like that. And I said, 'Well, how do you do it?' And she goes, 'No big deal, just KY Jell . . . and five minutes and it's no big deal.' She kinda talked about it like it was, you know, it was like dishes, laundry, sex . . . It wasn't like she was upset about it or anything. She was just kinda irritated with it, like, you know, she didn't enjoy it.

"One thing, though, she had said," the friend recalled. "I mean there was another couple in the church that a few years before had gotten a divorce . . . I wasn't there at the time but she had told me that one of the reasons why was because this woman didn't wanna have sex and the guy did and so he went elsewhere and she [Mary] had said, 'You know, I feel it's a small price to pay . . . it doesn't matter if I don't like it . . . If that's something Robert wants to do . . . ' You know, kind of a compromise for her marriage type thing."

Fisher's stash of pistols and rifles was also a popular topic among friends and the media. A long forgotten incident in which Fisher used a 9mm pistol to shoot a vicious pit bull brawling with his Labrador in the backyard under the children's swing set was brought out to give supposed insight into his darker side. Worse still, other reports stated that Fisher apparently lured the pit bull into the yard so he could stage the fight and justify executing the dangerous animal that he felt was a threat to his and other neighborhood children.

Another ominous tale had him heaving his terrified kids out of a boat into nearby Bartlett Lake to teach them to swim "tough aquatics" style. He quickly had to drag them back on board when they floundered and cried.

Strung together, the revelations piercing the hidden underbelly of a typical American family have been used in an attempt to give a logical motivation to an illogical and heinous crime. In reality, titillating as they sound, they're all common threads in the tapestry of life that millions of people experience and overcome on a daily basis. In no way do they even remotely explain what this man did. Saving one's beloved children from the pain of a broken family in our heavily divorced society may be a noble cause, but shooting their mother, slitting their throats, and blowing up their home to accomplish it is pure madness.

With a city in shock, a church in tears, and questions in the air, the hunt was on to find Robert Fisher, seemingly not so much to apprehend a fleeing felon as to provide a grieving community with some answers that would be easier to comprehend than the ones they were receiving.

To gain insight into Fisher's mind-set, police

combed through the remains of the home, carting out an extensive gun and knife collection that included four long-barreled hunting rifles, a pistol, a shotgun, and three knives. The arsenal survived intact because the weapons were locked inside a protective safe. Investigators found videotapes and home movies of Brittney's and Bobby's birthday parties in the safe as well. The rifles posed yet another dilemma. The only weapon that appeared to be missing was the .38 caliber pistol he carried in the fanny pack. The question arose as to why a hunter intending to live off the land in the wilderness would leave behind his extensive collection of hunting rifles? Complicating matters were flyers that seemed to contradict the weapon inventory and warned that the fugitive could be armed with a .223-caliber rifle, a shotgun, and a pistol.

Similar paradoxes were raised regarding his freshly oiled truck. Why would he choose to blow up his beloved, Ram-tough Dodge and instead take his wife's "soccer van" type 4-Runner? It's possible that he felt the light-colored SUV stood out less on the highway than the massive, more unusual truck, and required gas instead of diesel, giving him better refueling options.

Investigators also found a strange device in Brittney's room that consisted of a battery attached to some wire and tinfoil. This may have been created to ignite the blast. Parts of a candle holder were also discovered, presenting the possibility that the items were set to work in tandem.

The best way of getting the answers and solving the mysteries, of course, would be to find Robert Fisher himself. A break in that direction came ten days later. A hiker spotted Mary Fisher's Toyota 4-Runner at 11:00 A.M. perched deep in the Tonto National Forest north of Cherry Creek on the edge of the White Mountain Apache Reservation in the Naeglin Rim. It was parked near a cratered dirt fire trail, one of many that cut through the thick timber. The Fisher's dog, Blue, hungry and discombobulated, was running around between the SUV and nearby Acorn Cave under a roof of ponderosa pine, painful porcupine quills jutting out from his snoot. The once friendly, fetch-playing canine that inspired a loving short story from Brittney (see end of chapter) and licked the faces of neighborhood children was now fearful and spooked, and wouldn't come to anyone or allow them to approach. Animal control agents had to be summoned to capture it.

"I walked down the road and I see the nose of this car poking out of the bushes," the hiker told the police, according to a five-hundred-page report investigators later released. "This guy was parked hiding . . . You wouldn't camp like that. He didn't have a campfire going. It looked to me like the passenger side door might have been open, but I couldn't really tell. I turned around and walked in the other direction. Right off the bat, I figured that's the car. That's Fisher."

Despite widespread reports to the contrary, the man never actually saw Fisher himself, just the SUV. All that remained inside was the Raider cap he was wearing the night of the murders.

A platoon of 150 law enforcement officers swarmed to the rugged, 6,200-foot plateau located northeast of Young and thirty miles east of Payson as the crow flies or fugitive runs. They were convinced that Fisher was holed up in one of the nearby caves. "A dog won't leave his master. That's what we're banking on," explained Bill Fogle, a chief deputy with the Gila County Sheriff's Office. A fresh mound of human waste found

near the SUV passenger door was taken as another
sign by police that they were closing in on their prey.

One of the task force's first acts was to flatten the
SUV's tires, apparently fearing that Fisher might explode from a pile of leaves Rambo style, leap into the
Toyota, and try to floor his way out of there. When that
failed to occur, investigators narrowed the search to a
long, winding, splintered underground cavern known
as "Cave 41," which had footprints near its main en-
trance. News reports indicated that it would only be a
matter of time before Fisher was forced out. Officers
used bloodhounds, cadaver dogs, dropped tear gas can-
isters, and even cautiously slid around the damp,
murky, muddy passageways on their bellies, all to no
avail. The direct confrontation avenue had to be used
judiciously, if at all, as the caves in the area go on for
miles and are full of narrow passages and crannies
where a desperate criminal could get a Samsonlike
drop on an army of pursuers.

Instead of sacrificing officers, a specially designed
sewer camera attached to a plumber's snake was poked
through the labyrinthine networks. It revealed nothing
either. Additional footprints, some tracked for miles in
and around the oaks and pines, led nowhere. Freezing
weather, including a late season snowfall, complicated
efforts further. Police were eventually forced to abandon their activities after searching for less than a week,
conceding that Fisher may have simply left the SUV
and dog as a decoy and hitched a ride out—or had help
from a mysterious friend.

It was later revealed that the spot where Fisher
dumped the car and dog was the same place he had
camped before. Members of a nearby Buddhist colony

reported seeing a man resembling Fisher rummaging around as little as a week before the murders.

Regardless of Fisher's familiarity, the Hell's Gate/Red Lake Cave area was still a good forty-five road miles from the nearest town, with much of that distance consisting of narrow, rutted, overgrown fire-fighting trails. That has given rise to speculation that Fisher must have had an accomplice who whisked him away.

The continuing saga of Robert Fisher has given rise to a wealth of speculation. Conspiracy types filled the Arizona radio airwaves with theories that Fisher was actually kidnapped and framed by the Mafia because of gambling debts, prescription drug connections, or similar problems. Others claim it was the government itself that set him up because he "knew too much" about insidious experiments going on inside the Mayo Clinic involving cloning, germ warfare, alien autop-sies, or other *X-Files*-like clandestine medical science. Police and FBI agents have found no evidence of any of that being the case—as if they would say if it were.

Widespread rumors of the more believable nature that Fisher ran off with a girlfriend he met at the Mayo Clinic—the alleged accomplice—have also not been verified. Investigators found no other employees miss-ing, leaving love-triangle buffs to shift their attention to an unknown patient, or the mysterious "massage therapist" who gave him more than a rubdown. Lost in such conjecture is the fact that even the most desperate mistress wouldn't want to come out of the shadows and gain respectability through the brutal murders of her boyfriend's entire family.

Another fanciful theory, especially among the New

Age set that has flocked to places like Sedona in the lower Arizona mountains, is that Fisher accounted for every aspect of his escape except for one. Hiding in the cold, dark, spooky caves, he didn't figure in the possibility of being haunted by the angry or confused spirits of his wife and children. "He might be able to escape everything else, but he can never escape the visions of his children," says Donna Theisen, author of *Childlight—How Children Reach Out to Their Parents from the Beyond.* "Night or day, asleep or awake, he won't know when they'll appear or reappear.

"These children and their mother died in their sleep, so they don't know what happened to them," Theisen continues. "One minute, they're going to bed like normal, and the next they're trapped in a whole new dimension. The children could be lost and disoriented, and need answers. If their father is deep within a cave, isolated and in the dark, it would be that much easier for them to break through the dimensional barriers and contact him."

Theisen, a former paramedic herself who also wrote the highly respected *Angels of Emergency* about that profession, has had more pleasant After Death Contacts (ADCs) with her own son, Michael. In *Childlight* she detailed the stories of fifty other parents who have had mostly comforting ADCs with their deceased children. However, some of the children, particularly those who were murdered or committed suicide, returned angry, with their spirits in turmoil. Because of this, Theisen suspects that Fisher may have been driven to kill himself to escape the haunting visions of Brittney and Bobby. "For those of us who have experienced them, these appearances are very real and powerful," she says. "I can only imagine how terrifying they would be to a disturbed man hiding in a cave under those circumstances."

Seattle pediatrician Dr. Melvin Morse cautions those who might scoff at such sentiments. Morse has studied death and dying for nearly two decades, and is the author of the popular books *Closer to the Light* and *Parting Visions*. Mike Gossie of Arizona's Tribune Newspapers tracked Dr. Morse down for a story he wrote about Fisher and the haunted-into-suicide angle.

"Research shows that fifty to seventy-five percent of grieving spouses or parents have some sort of visitation," Dr. Morse told Gossie. "Unfortunately, most people trivialize or dismiss the experiences as grief-induced hallucinations, and cut themselves off from their potential to heal. Research indicates that we are all born with a sixth sense, localized in our right temporal lobe, which allows us to perceive spiritual realities. Furthermore, electromagnetic sensing devices of unknown use have also been discovered in our brains. My theory is that humans are genetically programmed to see and interact with other realities using our right temporal lobe."

Neil Websdale, author of *Understanding Domestic Homicide* and a criminal justice professor at Northern Arizona University, points out that familicide perpetrators usually kill themselves on-site instead of making elaborate escapes only to do it somewhere else. "If he did indeed kill himself away from the scene, that's unusual."

Sticking to less metaphysical reasoning, different branches of law enforcement are nevertheless at odds over the believed fate of Fisher. One group, the Gila

County Sheriff's Department, argues that he's indeed dead by his own hands, probably by shooting himself deep inside a limestone cave shortly after arriving at Hell's Gate. Another group, which includes the Scottsdale detectives and FBI, think he's alive and well, most likely living in a small town under a new identity.

Outlining their theory, the Gila County sheriffs and deputies emphasize that Fisher was reported to have been depressed and suicidal during his previous post-separation camping trip. To them, his return was merely the next step in the familicide chain. "Suicide is a highly likely possibility," Chief Deputy Bill Fogle told Tom Zoellner of the *Arizona Republic* in June 2001. "And if he did it a few miles from where we searched the first time, our dogs never would have picked up a scent."

The rural cops also point out that Blue's tussle with the porcupine and subsequent antisocial conduct is the classic behavior of a domestic dog suddenly having to fend for itself after the death of his master and provider. "If he was going after a porcupine, he was out hunting food," noted Gila County deputy Andy Brunson. Blue hanging around the Toyota in a fearful and aggravated state was similarly viewed as another example of a dog trying to cope with the death of a nearby master. (Blue eventually recovered and was given a new home.)

Additionally, for all his outdoor skills, Gila County investigators are quick to remind everyone that Fisher was a disabled former firefighter who injured his back severely on the job and was dependent upon powerful, sometimes addictive prescription painkillers like Percocet to function. It's doubtful that a man with such a weak back coupled with a strong dependency could travel great distances over the rough terrain, hoisting a backpack loaded with the gear and supplies necessary to survive.

To prove their theory, the Gila County Sheriff's Department planned an extensive, volunteer-powered search for Fisher's body in July 2001. They were forced to back off because of a cornucopia of legal liabilities involved in hunting an armed and dangerous felon inside hazardous caves and over rough terrain.

Scottsdale detectives counter that the murders and escape were too well-orchestrated to be anything but the act of a man with a plan. Aside from the elaborate camping preparations, Fisher had suspiciously added a clause to his auto insurance that covered trips to Mexico. "I believe he is still alive," lead Scottsdale detective John Kirkham has commented to various media outlets. "I don't believe that he committed suicide . . . He was not intent on taking his own life. His intent was to take care of his problem and move on with his life, no remorse, no regret." If Kirkham sounds a bit angry, that's understandable. He was one of the officers who took the bodies of Mary Fisher, Brittney, and Robert, Jr. from the home.

Even some of the more rurally knowledgeable Gila County deputies admit that the northern Arizona forests are far more hospitable than the western North Carolina wilderness where Olympic bomber Eric Rudolph has allegedly hid for nearly a decade now. "There's food, shelter, and water out there," Gila County deputy Tom Rasmussen told Dennis Wagner of the *Arizona Republic*. "Who knows, he might be able to stay out there forever."

Specifically, the area is heavy with deer, elk, turkey, trout, crayfish, javelina, and other game. Tiny towns and stores dot the rolling countryside, as do the well-stocked cabins of Phoenix residents seeking to escape the "Death Valley" type 100-plus degree summer heat. It wouldn't be difficult to break into these cabins and stock up.

The caves, while cold, muddy, and so damp you can see your breath, weave underground for miles and make excellent hiding places. Nagging ghosts aside, Fisher was said to be a skilled spelunker who may have been prepared for the dismal conditions.

"You've got fairly thick vegetation, a lot of caves, and if a person knows what they're doing, it's very easy to hide," observed Tom Lister, a captain with the U.S. Forest Service.

"If he gets into the backcountry, it will be very difficult to find him," longtime friend Paul Mueller told the *Arizona Republic*. "Arizona is full of mineshafts and caves. He's a good hunter, and he's got a water purifier. Food and water, that's everything he needs. He's not a car camper."

Scott Seckel of Tribune Newspapers noted in a story he wrote that previous fugitives using the Arizona wilderness as their refuge have fooled trackers by riding cows, walking backward, smearing themselves in elk and deer feces, and hiding underwater in ponds or cattle tanks using reeds to breathe. They've traveled through storm drains, creeks, and irrigation canals, ducked into caves and mining shafts, and climbed trees. Most of those activities were done to throw off the bloodhounds, which are seen by escapees as being more of a threat than humans.

In 1992 a convict named Danny Ray Horning escaped from an Arizona prison with little more than the shirt on his back. A "weekend warrior" outdoorsman adapting on the fly, Horning led an army of law enforcement agents on a fifty-four-day chase through the Grand Canyon area using many of the techniques mentioned above to avoid capture. For nourishment he ate cactus scraped of their needles by broken glass, burrowing owls caught with his bare hands, and foraged through campgrounds and waste baskets. The most fascinating aspect of Horning's adventure was how close he stayed to his pursuers, often keeping himself just out of reach in the dense forests. He even attempted once to crawl up on an idling police car in the dark and steal an officer's radio, shotgun, and bagged lunch. The unexpected appearance of a second patrol car thwarted the effort.

Horning hitchhiked to New Mexico and seemingly was home free. Then, missing the familiar surroundings of Arizona, he inexplicably returned and renewed the fox and hounds game, eventually being caught near a house in Sedona where he'd stopped to take a drink from a garden hose.

So far, if he's alive, Fisher has avoided giving in to homesickness and making such a mistake. His bank balances have not been altered, meaning he has successfully fought the urge to hit a teller machine for some needed cash. Similarly, the FBI has found no evidence of credit card use. Of course, by now he could very well have new bank accounts and cards. If the Scottsdale detectives are correct, Fisher has merely joined a growing list of an estimated 200,000 U.S. citizens who have changed their names and locations to escape the law.

Most eventually are caught, according to Edmund

Pankau, author of *Hide Your Assets and Disappear: A Step-by-Step Guide for Vanishing Without a Trace.* Fugitives seeking a new identity find the easiest route by making a trip to a local graveyard and searching for a gravestone of a child. The closer that child would have been to the fugitive's own age, the better. The criminal then writes to that state for a birth certificate. Once the certificate is obtained, the new identity falls into place with driver's license, passport, and credit cards.

Pankau told *Arizona Republic* reporters Zoellner and Bob Golfen that outdoorsmen like Fisher have the best chance of staying free by leaving the country for Central America or Canada. "Panama, Honduras, Costa Rica, Belize, these are great countries because they ask no questions," Pankau explained.

Phoenix private investigator Jim Humphrey told the reporters that he starts looking for the missing in familiar places. "People are creatures of habit, basically. You have to find out as much as possible about a person to figure out where he might go. So, if you're originally from Philadelphia, I'd start looking there."

Under this theory, that would place Fisher in southern California, Arizona, Florida, or New Mexico, based upon his past travels.

Pankau agrees with Humphrey's "familiarity" sentiments, adding that old hobbies and habits are another place to look because they are rarely erased with the former identities. Hunters, fishermen, baseball fans, gamblers, dart players, golfers, and so on generally can be found doing the same things in a new version of their old haunts.

Ken Hodgeson, pastor of the Paradise Springs Community Church in Phoenix and a close, twenty-six-year

friend of Fisher, believes his camping buddy is somewhere doing precisely that. Hodgeson said he watched
Fisher's mental state erode over the years to the point
where he wasn't surprised when he heard the news that
he killed his wife. "He just got weirder and weirder
and weirder. The kids, that surprised me."

Zoellner, the *Arizona Republic* reporter who has
covered the Fisher story from the moment the house
ignited, has written front page articles proclaiming
both the "he's dead" and "he's alive" theories. On June
26, 2001, the headline was FISHER NOW BELIEVED
DEAD. Almost a year later a similar banner headline
resurrected the fugitive by saying, ROBERT FISHER
LIKELY ALIVE WITH NEW IDENTITY. Asked to step
away from his usual journalistic objectivity, Zoellner
offered his own personal insights:

> I need to say up front that Robert Fisher could have
> successfully fled the state and may be flipping burgers
> or digging ditches somewhere and hoping his neigh-
> bors don't read true crime books. But I think there's
> also some credibility to the theory that Fisher has been
> lying dead in the woods all this time. He didn't seem
> to have the money, the time, the criminal experience,
> or the creativity to disappear himself. He didn't have
> much more than $280 in his wallet when he fled the
> crime scene. And they found his wife's SUV in a spot
> where he had been known to camp before. His friends
> said that when she had kicked him out of their house
> two years previously for his alleged extramarital activ-
> ity, he went off to the woods and seriously contem-
> plated killing himself. Divorce had torn his life apart
> when he was in high school and he didn't want to sub-
> ject his kids to that. You can't forget—that whatever

else he may have been—Fisher saw himself as a devoted family man with sincere religious convictions. But his bifurcated life was coming apart. His reputed massage parlor habit must have been causing him tremendous guilt and creating tremendous internal pressure.

So there's a fairly credible scenario that goes like this: in the midst of a screaming fight on the night of April 9, Fisher snaps beyond all control and does something he had only been fantasizing about. He gets his gun and shoots his wife in the back of the head. In the midst of his rage, he finishes the job by cutting her throat so deeply that he almost decapitates her. He orders the children to bed, and they comply, terrified. What he then does is an act that psychologists call "suicide by proxy," that is to say, he loved his kids to the point that he couldn't stand to see them live through all the pain he had brought upon the family. Killing them was like a surrogate for killing himself. But when the time came to turn the weapon on himself, he chickened out. Couldn't do it. So he concocts a plan on the spur of the moment, thinking that he'll conceal his crime and run away—he's not sure where. So he pulls the gas line off the furnace, lights a candle on the dining room table and roars off in his wife's truck, intending to blow up the house, but probably not realizing that burning a body is an extremely difficult thing to do and that any experienced medical examiner will be able to quickly recognize a knife wound or especially a bullet wound through charred skin. He flees to his spot in the woods and spends the next few days camped out, trying to forget the unspeakable images that have been burned into his mind—his children's throats cut by his own hands. And then at some point, the mental hell grows too terrible to bear, he walks deep inside the forest where he always felt most at peace, puts his gun under his chin and ends everything. His dog Blue finds his way back to the truck.

When the police came upon the vehicle and the dog on April 20, they apparently searched the area for only a one-and-a-half mile radius. There are lots of deep ravines in that country and they were never checked. That area still has not been properly canvassed.

Finding such a body can indeed be difficult, even in far less remote regions.

Robert Fisher could be Arizona's version of Chandra Levy—a sought-after person who has been squirreled away in the brush. But this homicide is not nearly as high-profile, the police search was much more cursory, and the Tonto National Forrest, or the Fort Apache Indian Reservation—take your pick, he could be in either one—is not an urban park in the middle of the nation's capital. There is virtually no foot traffic there. This is some of the loneliest country in Arizona, in the middle of one of the biggest continuous stands of ponderosa pine trees in the world. Assuming this theory is true, Robert Fisher may never be found.

The body of Levy, the dark-haired Washington, D.C., intern who vanished in May 2001, slowly decomposed for more than a year in Rock Creek Park a few miles from her apartment. An intensive police search of the 2,820 acre park, fueled by sensational media reports that she was the secret lover of married California congressman Gary Condit, proved unfruitful. Her remains were discovered May 22, 2002, by a man hunting for turtles with his dog.

If Zoellner's conjecture is correct, it would take even greater happenstance to find Fisher's bones.

Clean escape or guilty suicide, as time passes, even Fisher's strongest supporters have begun to lose their faith in his possible innocence. "If he did this, there must have been some imbalance or rage or something," his mother, Jan Howell, told reporters. "If Robert is found dead, that will be a rejoicing for me. If he's found alive, he's going to need help."

After defending their son-in-law for eight months, Mary Fisher's parents filed a wrongful death suit against him in late November 2001. If past history is any guide, it might take a long time before either the Coopers or the FBI are able to drag Fisher into a courtroom—civil or criminal. In 1971 a man named John List similarly killed his family in New Jersey and escaped. He moved to Colorado, changed his name to Robert Clark, remarried, and worked as a cook. He wasn't found until 1989, when the new television show *America's Most Wanted* made him one of their early targets.

Fisher's story has already appeared on *America's Most Wanted* at least four times and is now in the heavily rotated syndicated updates of the highly popular *Unsolved Mysteries*. So far, none of the airings have produced any solid leads. What it did produce was a mysterious call from Virginia. "This is Robert Fisher," the man announced. "You will never catch me, and I'm glad I killed the bitch." The call, on August 18, 2001, was traced to a public pay phone on the front outside wall of a pizza parlor in Chester, a city just south of Richmond. The speaker may have also made a quick reference to something that led the police to believe that it might be genuine. They aren't saying what specifically, and the brief call wasn't taped. Usually, this involves details of the murders that were never released to the media, which only the killer and the police would know. Detectives like to hold some information back for this precise reason, to weed out cranks from the real thing.

Chester County sheriffs set up surveillance around the establishment, Pietro's Pizza and Italian Restaurant, 2601 Osborn Road, but there was no sign of Fisher. Employees were interviewed and shown photos. None recognized him. No further contacts were reported.

As with any notorious felon on the run, there has been an avalanche of tips and possible sightings, placing Fisher in bars, drugstores, fast-food joints, restaurants, supermarkets, and construction sites. A bartender at the Rye Creek Bar and Restaurant in northern Arizona said that on the night of April 10—the same day Fisher's home exploded—a man fitting Fisher's description came in with a dark-haired woman and ordered a shot of scotch. The woman, feeling ill or anxious, vomited in the rest room, while the man drank and nervously paced. Police were unable to confirm the report, and reiterated that they've found no evidence that Fisher is or was traveling with a female companion. (Friends add that Fisher rarely drank.)

"I think that we probably will find him," Detective Kirkham says. "Will it be something that I can predict when? Probably not. It may be tomorrow. It may be years down the road. It depends on us finding the mistake that he made that we haven't picked up on yet, or on him making a mistake."

Scottsdale police sergeant Douglas Bartosh agrees. "Obviously, he's a very intelligent guy. He's capable of surviving, whether it's in the wilderness or another urban environment . . . This [hunt] has become international. The world has six to seven billion people. With the FBI's help, we intend to have everybody out there looking for him. We will check out every tip we get. This is the epitome of community-based policing."

Scottsdale police sergeant Douglas Dirren was struck by the overwhelming success the FBI has had with tracking down Top Ten felons. "There have been 475 people put on the list, and 445 of them have been captured. The odds are in our favor that at some point Robert Fisher will be apprehended."

Robert William Fisher was born April 13, 1961. He's six feet tall, 190 pounds, with brown hair and blue eyes. He walks erect and stiff, with his chest out because of an old back injury, and can't turn his neck well. He has surgical scars on his lower back, and a gold crown on his upper left first bicuspid tooth. He's dependant upon painkillers, generally Percocet. Fisher is a skilled outdoorsman who is good with rifles, pistols, or bows, and likes to camp in the roughest conditions. His favorite spot is said to be at the base of the Mazatzal Mountains near Sunflower, Arizona. He also enjoys campsites and wilderness areas in California and New Mexico. He may be working in a hospital as a respiratory therapist or catheter technician, or riding under the lights as a paramedic.

The Reward

Chances of the average Joe spotting Fisher and collecting the $50,000 reward? Excellent. With his back injury, stiff posture, need for medications, glib, confessional manner, gold tooth, medical skills, and outdoor nature, Fisher has a lot of traits that should make him easy to identify. Look for a new resident of a smallish rural town in the West, possibly working in the medical field as a paramedic or hospital technician, but more likely laboring in an unrelated, blue-collar job where licenses, degrees, and background checks aren't a primary concern. He would come across as a seemingly devout, churchgoing hunter who talks in riddles about his past, hinting of something dark but never quite spelling it out. A man with a bad back and a mysterious background who may have quickly replaced what he lost, possibly marrying a widow or divorcée with children that he met at his new church.

If he's dead and his body has been decomposing in the northern Arizona pine forests near Cherry Creek and Young, you can still claim the reward by locating his remains.

A poem by Brittney Fisher:

Creed

I would be true, for there are those who trust me;
I would be pure, for there are those who care.
I would be strong, for there is much to suffer,
I would be brave, for there is much to dare.
I would be friend to all—the foe, the friendless;
I would be giving, and forget the gift.

I would be humble, for I know my weakness;
I would look up—and laugh—and love—and lift.

· My Dog Blue
By Brittney Fisher

Dogs come in many different shapes and sizes. They all have their own unique personalities. There are no two dogs alike. My dog, Blue, demonstrates many different personalities at times which make him special to me. My dog is very playful. He loves balls and toys to chase, to catch or to chew. Blue is very energetic. He loves to go on walks. He'll come up to you and set a ball at your feet. It's like he's saying in his own special language, "Play with me! Play with me!" You'll end up playing with him because you can't say "no" to such a cute face.

Blue is also very cuddly. When you sit on the couch or on the chair, he'll walk up and climb up into your lap even though he's really too big to sit on your lap. Sometimes, he'll just come sit down by you and gaze at you curiously. By the way he is acting all calm and quiet, you know he wants to be scratched. Somehow, when you scratch him, it just makes you feel kindhearted since you know you are pleasing him. Even though he's very energetic at times, he is also lazy at other times. After he finishes playing, taking a walk, or gulping down his food, Blue will just lie around. His favorite spot to lay is in this cabinet in our entertainment center. He could lay there for hours. Blue also likes to lie in a spot in the backyard.

As you can see, my dog has many different personalities. Every dog has his unique personality which makes him different. These differences make each dog special in his own way in his owner's eyes. Just as Blue is to me.

Chapter 11

Osama bin Laden—
Terrorist

· ·

Reward: $27 million

We anticipate a black future for America. Instead of remaining United States, it shall end up sepa-rated states and shall have to carry the bodies of its sons back to America.

—Osama bin Laden, May 1998.

As society changes, so has the FBI's Ten Most Wanted list. Looking back over the past half century, what was once designed as a way to use the burgeoning mass media to help capture criminals has grown into some-thing far more important from an anthropological per-spective. Studying our worst criminals, or more specifically, whom we view to be our worst criminals at any given moment, reveals how we've grown, and unfortunately, regressed, as a society.

Politics have always played a big part in the FBI's fight against crime. Some say it's played too big a part. While that's debatable, there's no denying that conser-vative administrations coincided with extra attention being paid to liberal militants in the 1960s and 1970s. In turn, a liberal administration brought increased attention to conservative militants in the 1990s.

The 1990s also ushered in the beginning of a new wave of criminals-with-a-cause that obliterated ideological distinctions—the international terrorist. This group has quickly proven to be the most vicious and frightening Most Wanteds of all.

For the past quarter century, America was warned that the terrorists plaguing Europe and the Middle East would eventually land on our shores. As with the alarm over the African killer bees, we cringed a bit reading the stories, then mostly ignored it, hoping the problem would remain safely confined to those faraway countries. It didn't. Initially, American interests, companies, embassies, consulates, military bases, soldiers, and equipment were targeted overseas. While upsetting, it was still happening in distant lands most Americans couldn't find on a map. Even when strange-sounding names like Mir Aimal Kansi, Ramzi Ahmed Yousef, Abdel Bassett Ali Al-Megrahi, Lamen Khalifa Fhimah, and Usama bin Laden began popping up on the FBI's Ten Most Wanted list throughout the 1990s, they were revolutionaries from abroad with confusing causes who committed their crimes somewhere else. Kansi shot up a CIA building in Afghanistan in 1993, killing two and wounding three. Al-Megrahi and Fhimah bombed Pan Am Flight 103 over Lockerbie, Scotland, killing 259 passengers and crew members, and eleven Lockerbie villagers on the ground. Bin Laden was wanted for the 1998 bombings of U.S. Embassies in Dar es Salaam, Tanzania, and Nairobi, Kenya, which killed more than two hundred. Terrible crimes by terrible men, but far, far away.

Yousef bombed the World Trade Center in New York in 1993, bringing it closer to home, but the six deaths were minimal by comparison to what was happening overseas—and what was to come.

All but one of the men mentioned above were eventually hunted down and brought to justice, which sent a message to the world that America wasn't to be messed with. That helped ease our collective minds.

Emphasize the "all but one." That one, already residing big as life on the FBI's Most Wanted list since June 7, 1999, proceeded to orchestrate the still unbelievable horrors of the date that has gone down in infamy, 9/11/01. Under the training, financing, and inspiration of Saudi Arabian master terrorist Usama bin Laden, FBI Most Wanted Number 456, a scattered band of nineteen fanatical Muslim suicide bombers hijacked four American passenger airliners and used them as bombs to destroy both towers of the World Trade Center in New York and a section of the Pentagon in Washington, D.C. The fourth and last jet, United Airlines Flight 93, took off from Newark forty minutes late at 8:42 due to routine delays. It was believed to be targeting the White House or Capitol, but instead crashed in an unpopulated area eighty miles east of Pittsburgh, Pennsylvania—and about fifteen minutes from Washington, D.C. It is theorized that the passengers on the behind-schedule airliner, aware of what had happened in New York and Washington through cell phone conversations with relatives, attempted to overpower the hijackers and caused the jet to plummet far from its intended target. Other, more hushed reports whisper that it was surgically disabled by a U.S. fighter jet. If true, the government would naturally be loath to admit taking such drastic but understandable action for myriad political and legal reasons. (At 9:40 A.M. that morning, President Bush ordered that any aircraft threatening Washington was to be shot down. Flight 93 crashed at 10:06. Witnesses reported seeing a small white jet tailing the 757 prior to the crash, and air traffic controllers initially mentioned seeing an F-16 around it as well. While acknowledging it could have come to that, the government has steadfastly denied that it ordered the 757 shot down.)

Bin Laden, who would soon be known by the now more common translation of his first name, Osama, was unfortunately not aboard any of the suicide airliners.

If America had been the proverbial "sleeping giant" before 9/11, that shocking assault woke the nation up. Suddenly, the "killer bees" had arrived in our most well-known cities and were stinging everybody in sight. The crazed foreign terrorists with their strange religion, centuries old land squabbles, and fanatical devotion to causes most Americans are clueless about had accomplished their goal of opening our eyes.

Virtually every aspect of 9/11 has long since been relayed, replayed, dissected, and analyzed, and will continue to be for years to come. One small factor may sum it up best—the timing. In any given twenty-four-hour period, the targeted buildings would have been relatively empty for fourteen of those hours. The eight-hour period from 10:00 P.M. to 6:00 A.M. would have been the least populated, with even the twenty-four-hour Pentagon working with a skeleton crew. The same shock, outrage, and eye-opening result could have been accomplished by targeting the buildings during those dark, quiet hours, an unspoken rule that had been followed by domestic radicals, militants, and protest groups for decades. Destroying property in such a manner sends a message that the groups responsible are crying out to be heard. Although nobody likes to admit it, such displays can be successful negotiating tactics. Throughout history, they have forced differing sides to the bargaining table and acted to loosen stubborn resolve.

Killing people, on the other hand, only inspires hurt, rage, and a desire for revenge.

By hitting the World Trade Center buildings and Pentagon moments before and after 9:00 A.M. on a weekday, Bin Laden was going after the maximum human death toll. A few hours later, thousands of people would be heading out for lunch, staggering the shifts from late morning to early afternoon. The late afternoons would have seen additional thousands attending meetings outside the office, leaving early for child care commitments, or attempting to beat rush hour. But at 9:00 A.M., most people are dutifully at their desks, punching literal or symbolic clocks, checking assignment sheets and organizing schedules in order to get a handle on the rest of the day.

Which is why, when the twin, 110-story, ten million square foot World Trade Center towers first collapsed, the death toll in the heavily populated skyscrapers was predicted to be as high as 25,000 by some grim estimates. Thankfully, the buildings didn't immediately collapse. It took more than an hour for the blazing jet fuel flooding the upper level crash points to melt or weaken the steel trusses and structure braces enough to cause the buildings to implode upon themselves, one after the other, at 10:05 and 10:29 A.M. (The north tower, hit first at 8:48 A.M. between floors 94 and 98, was actually the second to collapse, taking thirty-nine minutes longer than the south tower, hit a bit lower between floors 78 and 84.) The delay enabled the majority of the buildings' occupants to escape. The precious minutes also allowed heroic policemen and firefighters to reach the scene and assist in the rescue of thousands of dazed, confused, and injured workers. More than four hundred policemen and firefighters subsequently died in the process, including one who was hit on the ground by a desperate worker who leaped from a burning upper floor.

The only good news, if it could be called that, was that the body count kept going down, until the final New York numbers were determined to be less than 3,000. That's still a lot, but it's a far cry from the 25,000 to 58,000 (full capacity) Bin Laden may have been striving for.

The Pentagon fatalities were also much lower than initially feared. The carnage there totaled 189, including the sixty-four passengers and crew members inside American Airlines Flight 77. The expansive, 3,705,793 square foot military complex, which houses 23,000 employees, is spread out over five, wedge-shaped, five-story sections set on twenty-nine acres, making it a more difficult target. The entire compound, including lawn area, parking, and support structures, covers 583 acres.

A second factor that stands out is the population of the two prime civilian targets. By attacking New York in general, and the World Trade Center in particular, Bin Laden may have destroyed a quarter-square-mile section of the planet that, aside from the United Nations, harbored the most diverse concentration of cultures from around the world. Nearly five hundred people from ninety-one different countries perished, including Arabs and Muslims. That figure doesn't include immigrants, new citizens, or first generation Americans. (According to the *New York Times*, close to half of the teenagers attending public high schools in New York City were born somewhere else.) The vast array of nationalities made America's pain personal for dozens of nations watching in shock from afar. Bin Laden's logic there is mind boggling.

When this project was started, it was hoped that by Chapter 11, Osama bid Laden, like his terrorist cohorts before him, would have long been caught and replaced on the list by a more familiar and less frightening domestic bad guy, maybe another flashy drug dealer, a colorful mobster, or a home-grown liberal or conservative radical who bombed an empty building or mailbox here and there. The odds were promising that would be the case. Bin Laden's atrocity ignited a war in Afghanistan, as America chose to extinguish the entire Taliban party that ruled the country with stone-age iron fists while harboring and sheltering terrorist factions such as Bin Laden's al Qaeda. The unprecedented effort was, and sadly remains, by far the most massive manhunt in world history, making the dragnet to catch Olympic bomber Eric Rudolph in North Carolina pale by comparison. Despite the intense motivation of the United States military machine, its state-of-the-art equipment and training, combined with the unprecedented $27 million price tag on Bin Laden's head, he has yet to turn up—dead or alive.

And so the search continues.

And so we must once again delve into the questions of who is this man, Osama bin Laden, what does he want, why is he so angry, and why does he hate Americans and Jews with such fervor?

The award-winning PBS news program *Frontline*

did one of the best jobs in providing these answers, producing a series of programs and reports that have been broadcast and published on the Internet since before 9/11. Tapping sources close to the expansive Bin Laden family, *Frontline* provided a penetrating glimpse into what makes Osama bin Laden tick. Toss in the efforts of *Time* and *Newsweek* magazines, the television networks, and hundreds of newspapers working independently around the world, and a clearer and even more disturbing portrait emerges.

Right from the beginning, Bin Laden's story starts off sounding absurd to American sensibilities. He is the seventh son and seventeenth child in a family of fifty-plus brothers and sisters, the result of the polygamous nature of many Arab cultures. Osama's mother was Syrian (other reports say she was Palestinian). The King Lion ruling the pride, Mohammed Awad bin Laden, moved to Saudi Arabia from South Yemen in the 1930s. A humble, hardworking, devout Muslim, Bin Laden senior produced a capitalistic success story of Horatio Alger proportions. His rise mirrored that of the giants of industry who were creating dynasties in America around the same time. A poor bricklayer with big dreams, he ingratiated himself with the Saudi Royal family through the simple process of underbidding on the design to build King Saud's palaces. Mohammed bin Laden produced what he promised, further impressing the immensely wealthy Saudi rulers. He became so valuable as a builder that he was respected by the rival factions of the royals, a position that helped him act as a negotiator and liaison between King Saud and future King Faisal when a squabble arose between them. When King Faisal emerged victorious and took the throne in 1953, he found the treasury barren. Mohammed bin Laden stepped in and paid the salaries of Saudi government workers for six months out of his pocket. That so impressed King Faisal that he issued a billion-dollar proclamation that all government building projects should go to Bin Laden.

Included among the lucrative contracts was the construction or renovation of major mosques in Al-Aqsa, Mecca, and Medina. Through these and myriad other projects in the oil rich desert nation, Mohammed bin Laden became as wealthy as a king himself. Yet, the gracious man never forgot his roots, nor did he try to hide from them. According to *Frontline*, he kept a porter bag he used from a long ago job on display in the main reception room of his palace.

As the head of such a large clan, he was by necessity a dominant and firm father. He preferred to keep the army of children (twenty-four sons) in one location as opposed to scattering them and their sometimes jealous, backbiting mothers in different residences, as other wealthy Saudi men frequently do to maintain their sanity. Under his direct tutelage, his kids were infused with a strict religious conscience and deep moral and social code. The boys were encouraged to act strong, like men, from an early age. Again, unlike others in his polygamous society, Mohammed bin Laden was said to play no favorites among his children, cherishing all equally while avoiding the urge to give special attention or privileges to those sired by his favorite wives.

How growing up as an equal but possibly lost and insignificant member of such a large family affected young Osama's psyche is not well-known, but neither is it difficult to imagine. It brings to mind Woody

Allen's lament in the animated movie *Ants* regarding the psychological trauma of being the "middle child in a family of two million."

Not only was Osama overrun with antlike rival brothers and sisters, but he didn't have his singular father very long. Despite being one of the older brothers in the clan, his father nonetheless died in a plane crash when Osama was only thirteen. Pushed into an early adulthood, he did the dutiful Muslim thing and married a Syrian relative at seventeen. He is reported to have seven sons of his own from that marriage, and has since filled his legal Muslim quota by adding an additional three wives and a dozen or more children.

As devout as his father, Osama was said to take special interest in the pilgrimages his father hosted, and his older brothers continued, that welcomed scores of Islamic scholars and Muslim leaders from around the world to their home in Jeddah. Many of these leaders were radical in belief and nature, and no doubt inspired young Osama with their fervor. He was quick to join a relatively radical group known as the "Muslim Brotherhood," but did not distinguish himself among them.

Educated K-1 through K-16 in Jeddah, he earned a degree in public administration from King Abdul-Aziz University in 1979. Unlike so many wealthy and even middle-class Arabs, including some of his brothers and nephews, he never spent a day at an American university, not even for a brief exchange program. Instead, he remained isolated at home, studying under such teachers as Mohammed Quttub, a well-known Islamic writer and philosopher, and Abdullah Azzam, a radical Palestinian who pushed for a one billion strong New World Order of sorts created by uniting all the earth's myriad Muslims, presumably under one whip. According to *Frontline*'s sources, Bin Laden is not nearly as well-traveled as it is believed, numbering Syria, Pakistan, Afghanistan, and Sudan as the only places he's ever been outside his home. That is quizzical for a man whose terrorist reach spans the globe.

As a young businessman, Bin Laden was governed by his religion, refusing to invest in non-Muslim countries. He didn't trust banks or stock markets, feeling they were operated by the hated Jews. Still, the company built by his father was such a goldmine that his personal fortune, even split fifty-two ways with his horde of brothers and sisters, was at one time said to be as much as $300 million.

Despite his provincial ways, there was enough happening in his small corner of the world to direct his destiny and make him widely known. The event that turned his life around was the Soviet invasion of Afghanistan at the end of 1979. Following in the footsteps of his former professor, Adbullah Azzam, the twenty-two-year-old Bin Laden traveled to Pakistan in the early weeks of the war. There, he was sold on the "mujahedeen" (Afghan resistance) against the hated Soviets and began hitting up his brothers, relatives, and friends to provide financial support for the Afghan freedom fighters. He was said to have raised an enormous amount of money for their cause, and began making frequent trips to provide the needed weapons and supplies. In 1992 his devotion to the war against the atheistic invaders was such that he left the safety of Pakistan and began entering the war zone inside Afghanistan, bringing millions of dollars of construction machinery, weapons, and other supplies. Soon, he was not only backing the Afghans financially, but was jumping on bulldozers, digging trenches under fire, and fighting alongside them.

By 1986, Osama had promoted himself to general and began building and operating his own military training camps, six in all. That wasn't as difficult or expensive as might be imagined. Weapons and explosives are cheap and readily available in the Middle East, and Muslim soldiers fight for next-life rewards rather than money. An ambitious leader far less wealthy than bin Laden can build and maintain a considerable army in that region of the world. Bin Laden did dip into his riches, however, to bring in veteran soldiers from Syria and Egypt to help with the training and battlefield strategy. Eventually, Osama had not only established a respectable army, he had created his own front against the Soviet flanks.

The news of Osama's religious-based resistance spread. Gung-ho recruits began pouring in from around the Middle East. His forces engaged the Soviets in a half-dozen major battles and scores of smaller skirmishes, including fierce confrontations in Jaji and Jalalabad. To keep everything organized and documented, Bin Laden and Azzam established a point of demarcation, a guest house, records center, and starting-off point for recruits known as "al Qaeda," or "the base." It was an upgrade of a similar nerve center Azzam had previously established that was called Maktab al Khidmat.

Osama was a "people's general," humble by nature and respectful of his men. He fought beside them, and sometimes even cooked for the troops and served their meals. He lived among them in small shacks or sheds, never retreating to more comfortable lodgings that he could well afford. Although an admitted killer and terrorist, he is reported to be unwilling or unable to lie, possibly due to his intense religious beliefs. Those who know him say he can be alternately shy and dominating. He seldom laughs or smiles, taking on a serious, dedicated tone. He's not much of an orator, preferring to read, research, and monitor world news reports.

In battle, he was said to be fearless and totally unafraid of dying. He was under intense fire dozens of times in Afghanistan, and watched many comrades get blown apart all around him. He was injured numerous times and returned to the fray as soon as he was well. He's also extremely cautious, wary of having electronic devices around that might pinpoint his location.

The Soviet withdrawal in 1989, following a brutal defeat to Bin Laden's wild-eyed forces in Jalalabad, made Osama a legendary figure in Afghanistan and neighboring regions. The small country's victory over the huge world power was seen as an endorsement of their religion, deity, and cause. Lost in the celebration were the billions of dollars in U.S. aid that helped fund the triumph. Also lost was the fact that his rabble-rousing mentor, Azzam, and two of Azzam's sons, had been killed by an assassin in Pakistan who detonated a remote control bomb underneath Azzam's moving car as he was on his way to a mosque to pray. Unconfirmed reports say Bin Laden himself ordered the hit following a dispute over the postwar direction of al Qaeda.

While Osama was gaining fame and almost godlike status in Afghanistan, he wasn't nearly the hero back home in Saudi Arabia. Wary of his growing power and antigovernment mind-set, the royal family sought to curb his activities by limiting his travel. He accepted it

at first, banking on the pending crisis in Iraq and
Kuwait to position him to do for his home what he did
for Afghanistan. As he predicted, Saddam Hussein unleashed his massive army and attempted to take over
his neighbors, starting with oil rich Kuwait in August
1990. Osama eagerly volunteered his military skills
and battled-honed army to his hometown royal family.
While waiting for their response, a bomb dropped
from which he is said to have never recovered. Instead
of turning to him, the Saudi royal family accepted a
similar offer from U.S. President George Bush.

For the Saudis, it made perfect sense. Why depend
upon the unstable Osama and his dedicated but rag-
tag band of soldiers financed by a single man's personal fortune when they could instead have a highly
skilled, technologically advanced military unit from
the wealthiest, most powerful nation on the planet?
Osama didn't share that logic, viewing the agreement
as a literal deal with the "Great Satan." He attempted to
rally others to his cause, tapping into the easily manip-
ulated religious groups and radical Muslim activists,
reminding them that the American army was comprised of rock and roll loving Christians, despised Jews,
and uppity women who wore pants, drove cars, didn't
veil their faces, and, more horrifically, sometimes even
gave men orders! Soon, a *fatwah* was declared sup-
porting Bin Laden's original desire to keep the nation
pure of such shameful practices, even in a time of crisis. Based upon this sacred Islamic "religious decree,"
Bin Laden reopened the training camps in Afghanistan
and waited to be summoned like the proverbial cavalry.
Banking on his Soviet-busting hero's status, he quickly
attracted 4,000 fresh new recruits to further pump up
his eager army.

A trigger-happy black sheep like Bin Laden was a distraction the harried Saudi leaders didn't need. They already had enough to worry about with Iraq's 500,000 strong infantry breathing down their necks. Instead of using Bin Laden as a fallback in case things became desperate, the Saudi government made it crystal clear they wanted no part of him or his uncontrollable private army. Osama's movements were curtailed again, and he was given numerous cease and desist warnings. Furious, Osama used his family connections to get the travel ban lifted in 1991, convincing officials that he needed to handle some business interests in Pakistan. Once there, he discovered that Pakistan had become too cozy with the Saudi government for his suspicious blood, so he quickly hopscotched back to Afghanistan.

His suspicions were on the mark. It's been reported that Saudi and Pakistani agents tried to capture or even assassinate him during this turbulent period. Bin Laden's friends and relatives in both Saudi Arabia and Pakistan warned him of such plots.

Unfortunately for Osama, Afghanistan wasn't the Mecca he imagined either. The Russian withdrawal created a vacuum that plunged the newly liberated nation into an internal power struggle over which faction would take control. It was yet another example of the civil discord resurrected in so many of the former Soviet bloc nations once they gained their autonomy. Centuries old grudges, border disputes, political differences, and religious sect rivalries bubbled to the surface in liberated Afghanistan. Osama stayed neutral and even tried to arbitrate, but there was nothing even a beloved war hero could do to end the bickering. He eventually had to flee Afghanistan.

Ever resilient, Osama hopped back on his money-powered sleigh and hit Khartoum, Sudan, like a turbaned, black-bearded Santa Claus. He showered the poor sister Muslim nation with construction equipment and millions of dollars worth of needed supplies. He established a road-building company, a goat tannery, and two massive sunflower seed farms, financing the operations at huge losses. Such generosity naturally pleased Sudan's radical Muslim cleric leaders, as did Bin Laden's efforts to convince his brothers and other Saudis to invest substantial sums in the developing country. Although still wanted by his own nation, and stifled by the freezing of his cash and assets in Jeddah, the same bloated family that may have diminished him as a child was now his strongest asset. Having fifty-one filthy rich brothers and sisters can come in handy. The relentless tide of his family's $5 billion construction fortune continued to flow his way, as did donations from scores of immensely wealthy secret admirers and devoted Muslims. That helped him overcome the squeeze in Saudi Arabia and the costly benevolences in Sudan.

It was a fortunate hereditary break because things weren't about to thaw back home anytime soon. It took the American forces less than four months to crush Saddam Hussein's uninspired army in Desert Storm, putting an end to matters by April 1991. That also ended any lingering pipe dreams Bin Laden had of riding in on a white steed, saving the day, and regaining favor in Jeddah. The quick and decisive American victory only served to throw gasoline on the smoldering flames of Bin Laden's growing anti-American hatred. He would soon satiate his gnawing angst by taking action.

A few days before the end of 1992, a small bomb exploded inside a hotel in Aden, Yemen, where U.S. soldiers had stayed while in the process of a humanitarian aid mission to war-ravaged Somalia. Two Yemeni Muslims traced to Bin Laden's training camps in Afghanistan were arrested. This is believed to be the first direct terrorist act committed under Bin Laden's command. Like so many violent acts that would follow, it was cold-blooded not so much in its stated intent as in its chilling ineptness and miscalculation. The America soldiers left before the bomb exploded. The only causalities were two Austrian tourists. The deeply religious al Qaeda offered no apologies for the tragic error. In fact, the innocent civilians caught in this inaugural crossfire would be a sign of things to come.

Undaunted by the fiasco in Yemen, and secure in his continued financial standing, Osama intensified his campaign against his own government. He formed a rival political party known as the "Advice and Reform Committee," and dispatched a string of antigovernment, antiroyal family communiqués. He made no secret of his boiling hatred and violent intentions toward Saudi Arabia's American allies, and he gave his blessing to continued efforts by his eager underlings to make some noise through hit-and-run acts of violence.

Reverting back to their more successful military operations, a group of guerrillas suspected of having al Qaeda ties pinned down and killed eighteen U.S. soldiers and injured seventy-three in Mogadishu, Somalia, on October 3 and 4, 1993. The battle, chillingly retold in the recent book and movie *Black Hawk Down*, was Bin Laden's most successful anti-American operation to date. The U.S. Special Forces

unit, attempting to bring food and aid to the famine-
and warlord-ravished country, killed more than three
hundred guerrillas in return, a factor that is often overlooked. It was their eventual retreat from the mercy
mission, however, that inspired Bin Laden and al
Qaeda fighters worldwide.

In 1994, Bin Laden had one of his lieutenants, Al
Fawwaz, establish a media information office in London to better publicize the statements, decrees, and
successes of al Qaeda. The office, according to the
FBI, doubled as a front for terrorist activities. The "be-
nign" information center functioned as a recruitment
base for anti-American trainees, acted to procure
equipment, and established telephone links using both
satellites and land lines. The London headquarters also
served as a central communications outpost for al
Qaeda cells around the world. The Saudi government
countered the move by revoking Bin Laden's citizenship and seizing additional assets.

By this time, the homeless Bin Laden had become
the Pied Piper of Middle Eastern rebels with or without
a cause. Bands of devoted ex-mujahedeen, still itching
for someone to fight, followed him from hideout to
hideout. Islamic terrorists of every stripe knew they
could find respite in his secret camps and work at his
public companies. Bin Laden let it be known that even
former Saudi enemies like the Shiite Muslim terrorists
and Iran's Hezbollah were welcomed to join al Qaeda
and unite against a greater common evil—the United
States. That evil became even more pronounced in Bin
Laden's eyes when the United States stubbornly refused to withdraw its Christian, Jewish and women
soldiers from Saudi Arabia following the Desert Storm

victory. Instead, to Bin Laden's red-faced horror, America set about establishing permanent military bases in the area to maintain order.

Having "Great Satan" outposts so close to Islam's "two most holy places," Mecca and Medina, was an affront that had fundamentalist Muslims fuming with robe-renting rage. It thus came as no surprise that one of al Qaeda's first official decrees from their newly established London media center was to demand the immediate withdrawal of U.S. forces in Saudi Arabia, Yemen, and the Horn of Africa (Somalia). If America refused, the decree continued, then they could expect to be attacked until they—like the Russians before them—turned bloody tail and ran. Bin Laden sealed the proclamation with an open letter to Saudi Arabian King Fahd, seeking his support in driving the Americans out of the oil-rich kingdom.

Rebuffed at every point, Bin Laden's minions committed their first overt act of violence against his home country. A bomb planted in a truck exploded at a U.S.-operated Saudi National Guard facility in Riyadh, killing five Americans along with the by now requisite number of innocent civilians—this time two workers from India. Bin Laden, desperately clinging to the deceit that he could still sway his countrymen and regain favor, denied culpability but supported the actions. The rebels were promptly caught and beheaded in Riyadh's main square by the no-nonsense Saudis. Before being executed, they credited Bin Laden's communiqués for their inspiration.

Still stinging over America's continued presence in Saudi Arabia, Bin Laden presented his veteran Afghan trained soldiers with a newly declared war, this one a campaign of terrorism against America. At the same

time, Sudan, realizing that their Santa Claus was rife
with darker agendas, was growing increasingly un-
comfortable with their wealthy guest. He had showered them with material blessings, but had also gotten
them blacklisted worldwide as a country that spon-
sored terrorist activities. Widespread reports that Bin
Laden was not only laying down roads, but was operating multinational terrorist training camps, chemical
warfare laboratories, and was attempting to create nuclear weapons, further unsettled his hosts. Sensing
their dismay, Bin Laden returned to Afghanistan in
1996. The country, now overrun with warlords, was as
unsettled as ever, but he was still revered by virtually
all the rival factions and was protected and given sanc-
tion wherever he went.

When the fanatical, fundamentalist Muslim Taliban
party finally gained control of Afghanistan in late
1996, Bin Laden was locked in even tighter. The se-
vere rulers, intent on jerking Afghanistan back into
the rigid religious past, assured Bin Laden that protecting him was an honor. The Taliban viewed the
tall, slender Arab as a saint from the Holy Land of
Saudi Arabia who used his wealth and standing to assist his fellow Muslims in their jihad against Russia.
In turn, Bin Laden helped them establish a government and taught them how to handle foreign trade
and business relations without being snookered by
savvy middlemen. In numerous cases, he advised
them against doing deals—particularly regarding oil
and gas interests—that he felt gave them the short
end of the stick.

Subsequent attempts by Saudi and Pakistani espionage agents to smoke Bin Laden out of his Afghani
hole were repeatedly thwarted. Each time, he would

get wind of the operation and retreat deeper into Taliban strongholds.

Sensing a growing problem, President Bill Clinton signed a secret order giving the CIA carte blanche to destroy Bin Laden and his organization by whatever means necessary. Plans were literally on the drawing board when the next attack came on June 25, 1996. A bomb-laden truck crashed into Khobar Towers, a U.S. military residence in Dhahran, killing nineteen American soldiers. A debate ensued inside U.S. intelligence circles whether to again pin the blame on Bin Laden or view it as the work of a separate Saudi Shiite group. For once, Bin Laden's London mouthpieces didn't leap in to clear the mystery by taking credit, possibly because the heinous nature of the assault made them rethink their public giddiness.

Still, it was apparent that al Qaeda and Bin Laden were, at the least, inspired by the event. Bin Laden took the opportunity on August 23 to issue a twelve-page, full-scale declaration of war against America. The London press office eagerly spread the news of this latest "jihad" (holy or religious war). The objectives of Bin Laden's thriving al Qaeda and sister al Jihad groups were boldly proclaimed: to kill American soldiers stationed in Saudi Arabia and Somalia and drive them out; to murder Americans working in embassies; to liberate the Muslim holy sites; to cloak their activities through the establishment of front companies, false identification, fabricated travel documents, and coded correspondences; and to deceive disapproving local authorities regarding their activities.

"There is no more important duty than pushing the American enemy out of the holy land . . ." Bin Laden wrote. "Due to the imbalance of power between our armed forces and the enemy forces, a suitable means of fighting must be adopted, i.e., using fast-moving, light forces that work under complete secrecy. In other words, to initiate a guerrilla war, where the sons of the nation, and not the military forces, take part in it."

As almost an aside, the declaration also called for the ouster by force of the Saudi government. Infuriated by this little tidbit, the Saudi royal family attempted once again to drag their wayward son home for a proper beheading. To their dismay, they discovered that no amount of effort or bribes could get any of the Afghan warlords to cough him up.

Newly sheltered, Bin Laden began training and exporting al Qaeda operatives to other Muslim hot spots, spreading them around like a deadly bacteria to Egypt, Algeria, the Palestinian territories, Kashmir, the Philippines, Eritrea, Libya, and Jordan. Skilled al Qaeda officers and trainers were dispatched to Tajikistan, Bosnia, Chechnya, Somalia, Sudan, and Yemen to build forces on-site. The al Qaeda curriculum? Sabotage, urban warfare, explosives, and assault operations against power grids, airports, railroads, hotels, and military bases. Detailed maps of U.S. cities were used to pinpoint future target areas, and undercover agents waiting for assignment in America were taught how to blend in by shaving their beards, wearing Levi's jeans, humming American Top forty tunes, splashing on department store cologne, going to strip joints and nightclubs, and settling into newly constructed neighborhoods where everyone was a stranger.

The assignments given these human time bombs were generally nonspecific. They were told to simply "improvise" by attacking, killing, and destroying targets of their own design and choosing, while Father Bin Laden nodded approvingly from afar.

As if to taunt the Saudi and American forces hunting him, Bin Laden's busy publicists set up an interview with a female British documentary reporter. The exiled Muslim launched new threats against America and rambled on about the unleashing of his cherished Islamic holy war. He followed that up by giving an interview to an Islamic magazine reporter that revealed another of his growing list of beefs.

"The evidence overwhelmingly shows America and Israel killing the weaker men, women, and children in the Muslim world and elsewhere ... Also their withholding of arms from the Muslims of Bosnia-Herzegovina leaving them prey to the Christian Serbians who massacred and raped in a manner not seen in contemporary history."

Seeking a wider audience, Bin Laden sat down with Ted Turner's CNN network in March 1997 and let fly more hate rhetoric.

"We declared jihad against the U.S. government because the U.S. government is unjust, criminal, and tyrannical. It has committed acts that are extremely unjust, hideous, and criminal whether directly or through its support of the Israeli occupation ... In our religion, it is not permissible for any non-Muslim to stay in our country ... We are a society of more than a billion Muslims."

Weary of Bin Laden's anti-American threats, the United States joined with the Saudis in a plot to locate and extract the exiled Saudi in 1997. Word of the operation leaked and was blasted in the Muslim media. Like so many attempts before it, the compromised mission had to be scrapped.

After laying low for a while at the Taliban's request, Bin Laden was soon up to his old tricks. He worked the Taliban's malleable religious leaders into the proper frenzy and got them to endorse their own "fatwah" against the Americans. Emboldened by this success, and encouraged by a continued flow of followers and recruits from Muslim nations around the world, he began emerging from the shadows. In early 1998, Bin Laden proclaimed still another holy war against Jews and Americans under the guise of the "International Islamic Front for Jihad on the Jews and Crusaders." This fatwah implored Muslims worldwide to kill Americans—men, women, and children—anywhere they could be found.

"We . . . call on every Muslim who believes in Allah and wishes to be rewarded to comply with Allah's order to kill the Americans and plunder their money wherever and whenever they find it. We also call on Muslim ulema, leaders, youths, and soldiers to launch the raid on Satan's U.S. troops and the devil's supporters allying with them, and to displace those who are behind them so that they may learn a lesson. The ruling to kill the Americans and their allies—civilians and military—is an individual duty for every Muslim who can do it in any country in which it is possible to do it . . ."

Increasing both his arrogance and public profile, he agreed to sit down with one of "Satan's" leading town criers, American television journalist John Miller of ABC news. The May 1998 interview, conducted at a remote mountaintop camp in southern Afghanistan, was aired on *Nightline* on June 10. A group of Bin Laden's supporters were also present, and were allowed to ask fawning questions as a warm-up.

Bin Laden preached to this choir of sycophants:

"The call to wage war against America was made because America has spear-headed the crusade against the Islamic nation, sending tens of thousands of its troops to the land of the two Holy Mosques over and above its meddling in its affairs and its politics, and in support of the oppressive, corrupt, and tyrannical regime that is in control. These are the reasons behind the singling out of America as a target . . . Their presence has no meaning save one, and that is to offer support to the Jews in Palestine who are in need of their Christian brothers to achieve full control over the Arab peninsula . . . Terrorizing oppressors and criminals and thieves and robbers is necessary for the safety of people and the protection of their property. There is no doubt in this. The terrorism we practice is of the commendable kind for it is directed at the tyrants and the aggressors and the enemies of Allah . . . Terrorizing those and punishing them are necessary measures to straighten things and to make them right . . . In today's wars there are no morals, and it is clear that mankind has descended to the lowest degrees of decadence and oppression. They rip us of our wealth and of our resources and of our oil . . . We fight the governments that are bent on attacking our religion and on stealing our wealth and on hurting our feelings . . ."

Bin Laden didn't elaborate on how his feelings were hurt. Instead, he powered on with the threats.

"The hostility that America continues to express against the Muslim people has given rise to feelings of animosity . . . Instead of fighting the Americans inside the Muslim countries, [they] went on to fight them inside the United States of America itself . . . The enmity between us and the Jews goes far back in time and is deep rooted. There is no question that a war between the two of us is inevitable . . . The leaders in America and in other countries as well have fallen victim to Jewish Zionist blackmail . . . Any effort directed against America and the Jews yields positive and direct results . . . It is far better for anyone to kill a single American soldier than to squander his efforts on other activities."

When it came to Miller's turn, the questions were naturally tougher, and the answers were in turn more defiant.

"We do not care what the Americans believe . . . It does not scare us that they have put a price on my head. If the whole world gets together to kill us . . . they will not succeed."

Queried about his propensity to kill innocent civilians, Bin Laden had a ready answer:

"The Americans started it, and retaliation and punishment should be carried out following the principle of reciprocity, especially when women and children are involved . . . Those who threw atomic bombs . . . against Nagasaki and Hiroshima were the Americans. Can the bombs differentiate between military and women and infants and children? . . . America has no shame . . . We believe that the worst thieves in the world today and the worst terrorists are the Americans . . . We do not have to differentiate between military or civilian. As far as we are concerned, they are all targets, and this is what the fatwah says . . . I am one of the servants of Allah and I obey his orders. Among those is the order to fight for the word of Allah . . . and to fight until the Americans are driven out of all the Islamic countries . . ."

Bin Laden additionally confirmed suspicions that his victory over the Russians created the monster he became:

"[The Soviet Union] were defeated by Allah and were wiped out. There is a lesson here . . . We are certain that we shall . . . prevail over the Americans and over the Jews . . . Today, however, our battle against the Americans is far greater than our battle was against the Russians. Americans have committed unprecedented stupidity . . . After our victory in Afghanistan . . . the legend about the invincibility of the superpowers vanished. Our boys no longer viewed America as a superpower . . . Our boys were shocked by the low morale of the American soldier [in Somalia] and they realized that the American soldier was just a paper tiger . . . America had to stop all its bragging and all that noise it was making in the press after the Gulf War . . . After a few blows, it forgot about all those titles and rushed out of Somalia in shame and disgrace, dragging the bodies of its soldiers . . . I was very happy to learn of that great defeat that America suffered . . . While America blocks the entry of weapons into Islamic countries, it provides the Israelis with a continuous supply of arms, allowing them to kill and massacre more Muslims . . . The American government is leading the country towards hell . . . We say to the Americans as people . . . elect an American patriotic government that caters to their interest and not the interests of the Jews. If the present injustice continues . . . it will inevitably move the battle to American soil . . ."

That move would come later. On August 6, 1998, the Egyptian Jihad warned of a pending "message" to Americans "which we hope they read with care, because we will write it, with Allah's help, in a language they will understand."

The following day, the message was delivered. Bin Laden dramatically upped the ante of his terrorist campaign with the August 7, 1998, bombing of the United States Embassy in Nairobi, Kenya. An al Qaeda trained terrorist tossed flash grenades at the security guards in order to maneuver a truck carrying a bomb as close to the building as possible. It was supposed to be a suicide mission, but the operative, later identified as Mohamed Rashed Daoud Al-Owali, panicked at the last minute, leaped from the vehicle and ran.

As before, it didn't seem to bother Bin Laden and his deadly gang that of the 212 people slaughtered, only twelve were actually Americans. Less than a handful of the 4,650 people injured in the densely populated downtown area were Americans. Within minutes another bomb exploded near the United States Embassy in Dar es Salaam, Tanzania. That one killed four Americans and seven foreign service nationals while wounding seventy-two. Only two of the wounded were Americans.

The date was significant. It was the eight-year anniversary of the United Nations sanctions against Iraq, and the eight-year anniversary of American's entry into the Desert Storm war. Iraq had informed the United States that it would not accept the sanctions beyond eight years.

This time, Bin Laden's London press office quickly dispatched releases taking credit for the bombings, going so far as to detail that a Saudi planned the Kenya attack while an Egyptian was responsible for the Tanzania action. The subsequent U.S. FBI investigation involved the largest overseas deployment of personnel in FBI history, bringing in agents from thirty-eight of the fifty-six FBI Field Offices. Bin Laden reacted by again retreating behind the walls of his Taliban protectors. Meanwhile, rumors were swirling anew that the al Qaeda founder was close to assembling a nuclear bomb and had perfected the chemical weapons he first attempted to develop in Sudan. To further fuel the terrifying reports, an Arabic newspaper, *al Hayat*, published a story saying that Bin Laden had already secured a Soviet-made nuclear bomb from a central Asian country.

Two days before Christmas 1998, Bin Laden agreed to be interviewed by *Time* magazine and addressed the issue of just how far he would go.

"If the instigation for jihad against the Jews and the Americans . . . is considered a crime, then let history be a witness that I am a criminal," he said. "Acquiring weapons for the defense of Muslims is a religious duty. If I have indeed acquired these [nuclear] weapons, I am carrying out a duty. It would be a sin for Muslims not to try and possess the weapons that would prevent the infidels from inflicting harm on Muslims."

It took a year for the FBI and United States Attorney's Office to gather evidence, identify the fifteen conspirators in the embassy bombing, and hand down a legal ruling. "Today's indictment underscores our resolve to bring to the bar of justice each and every person who participated in these heinous crimes that resulted in the death of hundreds of innocent people, both American and foreign nationals of all religions," announced Mary Jo White, U.S. Attorney for the Southern District of soon-to-be-targeted New York. "The charges also show the reach of the worldwide terrorist network threatening civilized society today."

Lewis D. Schiliro, assistant director in charge of the New York FBI office, was equally resolute: "We said we would spare no effort to bring to justice all those responsible for the embassy bombings, and we mean it. Indictment is not the culmination of the process, but an important step in the process. While nine of the fifteen defendants remain at large, this office has a good track record in locating and apprehending the international fugitives. That is our objective and our expectation in this case."

White and Schiliro headed a law enforcement group known as the Joint Terrorist Task Force. It was comprised of the FBI, New York Police Department, United States Department of State, the U.S. Secret Service, the U.S. Immigration and Naturalization Service, the Federal Aviation Administration, the U.S. Marshal's Service, the Bureau of Alcohol, Tobacco and Firearms, New York State Police, the Port Authority of New York and New Jersey, along with police and government officials in Kenya and Tanzania.

The indictment, of course, did nothing to slow Bin

Laden down. To the contrary, on October 12, 2000, a small boat eased up to the side of the USS *Cole* while it was docked for refueling in the tranquil waters of the Yemeni port of Aden. The vessel suddenly exploded, killing seventeen U.S. sailors, injuring thirty-seven more, and blowing a gaping hole in the port side of the guided missile destroyer. A videotape filmed during one of Bin Laden's son's wedding not long afterward included a clip of the proud papa gloating over the USS *Cole* tragedy. "The pieces of the bodies of the infidels were flying like dust particles," he said. "If you had seen it with your own eyes, your heart would have been filled with joy."

A year later there would be the ultimate "joy"—the 9/11 atrocity.

While Bin Laden and others remain free, the FBI and crew have helped capture and punish many of his top henchmen. On May 29, 2001, a federal jury in Manhattan convicted four of the men involved in the East African embassy bombings on all 302 counts brought against them. The quartet were sentenced to life in prison without parole. Nine of the twenty-two eventually indicted were captured prior to 9/11, while others may have been killed in the war in Afghanistan that toppled the Taliban regime.

Zacarias Moussaoui, the so-called twentieth highjacker, was busted on immigration charges in Minnesota a month before he could fulfill his alleged mission inside his assigned 9/11 jet. He has been charged with numerous terrorist conspiracy counts. Moussaoui's incarceration has not stilled his tongue. He's accused the FBI and the U.S. government of knowing about the 9/11 plot in advance but choosing to let it play out in order to have an excuse "to destroy

Afghanistan." Government officials deny such an insidious scheme. At a court hearing in July 2002, the diminutive, French-Moroccan admitted he was part of al Qaeda, pledged his loyalty to Bin Laden, and indicated that he wanted to plead guilty to the charges against him. His much delayed trial has been set for late 2003 or 2004.

Aside from the now vanquished Taliban, Bin Laden has powerful bands of equally fervent supporters in Saudi Arabia, Yemen, Somalia, Kenya, and most of the Gulf countries. His al Qaeda terrorist camps are still in operation, governed by a *majlis al shura* (consultation council) that may be expanding beyond the need to rely so heavily upon him. The more horrific and outrageous Bin Laden's attacks, the more his legend grows in his supporters' eyes. America's response to 9/11 by invading Afghanistan was seen as overkill by many Muslims sitting in the middle, who have now come over to his side.

Threats of continued terrorist actions have peppered the news pipelines ever since, including some that targeted the media itself. A series of scattered mail attacks using the highly deadly bacterial poison anthrax followed in 9/11's wake, but they never expanded beyond the initial wave sent mostly to media organizations. It's yet to be determined if Bin Laden or a home-grown criminal was connected to this frightful effort. The first media outlet targeted, the Florida headquarters of the celebrity-oriented supermarket tabloid *The National Enquirer*, received the initial poisoned letter in early October 2001. Staff member Bob Stevens, a photo editor at the *Enquirer*'s sister publication, *The Sun*, died.

It's hard to imagine why a terrorist would target the

entertainment-oriented publication—unless one travels around America with the eyes of a foreigner. The *Enquirer*, *Star*, *Globe*, *Examiner*, and *Sun* could very well be the newspapers a newcomer is most aware of, seeing their blaring headlines in every supermarket, newsstand, and convenience store. That, combined with the patriotic tone of the papers and a series of highly insulting anti–Bin Laden stories, including some that pictured the Muslim leader in women's clothing and reported that he had an underdeveloped sex organ, could have made it a target. It was only after other newspapers, television news programs, and radio commentators questioned the logic of targeting the seemingly insignificant tabloid that follow-up anthrax letters, both real and hoaxes, began showing up at NBC News, CBS, Fox News, the *New York Times*, and the *New York Post*, in addition to congressional offices in Washington. It could be that an unsophisticated foreigner was listening and quickly coming up to speed on the true nature of America's media pecking order.

Suspicions of a more overt, 9/11-like terrorist offensive reached a crescendo in May 2002 when new FBI chief Robert Mueller, speaking before a convention of district attorneys, termed another assault on America as "inevitable."

"There will be another terrorist attack. We will not be able to stop it," Mueller candidly admitted, to the discomfort of many in the audience. "It's something we all live with . . . I think we will see that in the future. I wish I could be more optimistic." He added that it was nearly impossible to plant informants inside al Qaeda because the degree of fanaticism required is hard to fake. Similarly, the FBI and CIA have discovered that it's extremely difficult to "turn" somebody already on the inside because those displaying that degree of fanaticism for real are not going to be swayed. Mueller's disquieting statements followed earlier remarks by Vice President Dick Cheney and other top officials conceding the very same inevitability.

"We need to keep reminding the American people of our vulnerabilities," added National Security Advisor Condoleezza Rice.

Members of the Senate intelligence panel, who are routinely briefed by the White House, said they also believe future terrorist attacks are inevitable—though not necessarily soon. "I believe it's going to come," agreed Senator Richard Shelby (R-Ala). "Now, whether you mean by imminent, is it going to happen today, tomorrow, or two years? We're not sure."

A day later, both Secretary of State Colin Powell and Defense Secretary Donald Rumsfeld echoed similar warnings. Powell acknowledged that the terrorists were "trying every way they can" to get their hands on biological, chemical, and nuclear weapons from places like Iran, Iraq, and North Korea. Rumsfeld agreed, telling the Senate Appropriations Committee that "we have to recognize that terrorist networks have relationships with states that have weapons of mass destruction and that they inevitably are going to get their hands on them, and they would not hesitate one minute to use them."

President George W. Bush, as is his style, cut right to the chase. "The al Qaeda still exists, they still hate Americans and any other country which loves freedom, and they want to hurt us."

Capturing Bin Laden would do wonders to alter

those dark predictions. That is, if he's still alive. Some FBI, government, and military officials believe he was killed in late 2001 or early 2002 during one of the many missile and artillery attacks launched by American forces against al Qaeda strongholds, and that he's been sealed inside a cave where he was suspected of hiding, most likely in the Tora Bora region. A second theory, however, unfortunately seems to be more plausible. The last images seen of the terrorist leader, shortly after the war began in Afghanistan, showed a frail, rapidly aging man whose hair and beard were turning white. It appeared that the once courageous warrior who had so boldly taken on the Russians was being almost literally eaten to the bone by the oppressive stress of the massive military effort to bring him to justice. Bin Laden's advisers implored him to stop releasing any further interview tapes because his deteriorating condition was demoralizing his followers worldwide. He has not been heard from since.

His supporters certainly have. A harrowing wave of suicide bombings in Israel and Tunisia during 2002 and 2003 took nearly a hundred lives and wounded hundreds more. The Tunisia bombing in April 2002 occurred at a synagogue on the island of Djerba and killed seventeen people, including eleven German tourists—more collateral damage that al Qaeda couldn't care less about. Bin Laden's son, Saad, twenty-two, is suspected of being one of the masterminds. American terrorist experts fear that Saad bin Laden may be carrying his father's torch.

"There are three, four, five, six, seven people who . . . know where the bank accounts are, who know the key players, the key planners, and are perfectly capable of running that operation," Defense Secretary Donald Rumsfeld said. "Whether the son ends up being one of them, one never knows until . . . that takes place."

On June 23 a man believed to be al Qaeda spokesman Sulaiman Abu Ghaith released a creepy audiotape taking credit for the latest bombings, threatening to attack America again, and assuring the world that their esteemed leader Osama bin Laden was alive, well, and preparing to unleash more 9/11s.

"Our martyrs are ready for operations against American and Jewish targets inside and outside," the voice coldly announced. "America should be prepared. It should be ready. They should fasten the seat belts. We are coming to them where they never expected. The current American administration every once in a while releases terrorist attack warnings. I say 'yes, yes, yes' we are going to launch attacks against America!"

Abu Ghaith is a Kuwaiti religious teacher who was stripped of his citizenship after rejoicing as a Bin Laden spokesman following 9/11. The tape was sent to the Qatar-based al-Jazeera satellite television network. There was no indication where Abu Ghaith was when he recorded it. The tape further stated that Bin Laden himself was preparing to make a television address to bolster his forces and assure the Muslim world that the terrorist war against America and Israel will continue unabated.

Florida Senator Bob Graham, chairman of the Senate Intelligence Committee, said he believed Abu Ghaith's tape was authentic, and speculated that Bin Laden is hiding in Pakistan's western tribal lands.

As if on cue, a heavily armed Egyptian immigrant named Hesham Mohammed Hadayet, forty-one, went to the El Al ticket counter at Los Angeles International Airport less than a month later, July 4, 2002, and randomly gunned down two Israeli immigrants and injured three others. Hadayet, a Muslim limousine driver, was packing a .45 Glock semiautomatic pistol, a 9mm handgun, and a six-inch knife. He was promptly killed by the no-nonsense Israeli security agents that guard Israel's national airline all over the world. One of the victims, Yaakov Amnov, forty-six, was the father of nine young children. He was at the El Al counter that morning dropping off a friend. The second victim, Victoria Hen, twenty-five, was an attractive ticket agent engaged to be married. Government officials and media commentators who were quick to downplay the incident as "isolated" and not part of an organized terrorist cell seem to have forgotten Bin Laden and al Qaeda's repeated call for Muslims to individually commit whatever acts of violence and destruction they are capable of, large or small.

Two weeks later the FBI's executive assistant director, Dale Watson, speaking before the National Conference of Community Oriented Policing Services, stated that he believed Bin Laden was dead. FBI and White House officials were quick to counter that Watson was just giving his opinion and there was no evidence to support it. Intelligence sources told Kevin Johnson of *USA Today* that if Bin Laden were dead, they would have surely picked up the news through wiretaps and listening devices focused on known al Qaeda operatives. Nothing of that nature has been heard.

Watson additionally referred to al Qaeda as "the

fleas of the world" who still have active cells operating inside America planning future attacks. He warned the police officials in the audience to be on the lookout for them in their communities.

The same day, U.S. Customs announced that since 9/11/02, they've intercepted $22.8 million in 369 separate seizures that were being sent out of America to support terrorist organizations. That included $9 million to Middle Eastern countries designated as terrorist strongholds. An undisclosed percentage of the overall total was specifically intended for al Qaeda.

Another example of what this finances occurred on July 31, 2002. A remote-control bomb hidden inside a bag under a dining room table blew apart the packed cafeteria of the Frank Sinatra International Student Center at the Mount Scopus campus of Hebrew University in Jerusalem. This time, the terrorist hit a bonanza. Of the seven people killed, five were Americans, including three students studying overseas, a librarian, and a graduate program administrator visiting from New York. The remaining two were Israelis. More than eighty others of various nationalities were injured. The Islamic terrorist group Hamas quickly took credit and vowed that such violence would continue until Israel turns over their nation to the Palestinians.

"We have grieved with all the people of Israel as they have faced Palestinian terrorism," said U.S. Ambassador Daniel Kurtzer, a former student of the school. "Now that five American citizens have been killed, our grief is even deeper."

"I'm just as angry as Israel is right now," President Bush added, growing weary of the unending battle against Arab terrorists. A few months later Bush would be moved to anger again when al Qaeda operatives bombed a resort in Bali, killing more than 200, mostly Australian tourists.

"They [al Qaeda] are a defeated force," Afghan President Hamid Karzai told CNN's *Late Edition*, providing a ray of optimism amid the relentless string of bad news. "They are on the run. They're criminals in hiding."

If the first half century of FBI's Top Ten list proves anything, it's that "criminals in hiding" can be the most dangerous kind.

Osama bin Laden was born in 1957. He's tall, six-four to six-six, with brown eyes and brown, salt-and-pepper, or snow-white hair and beard. He is left-handed and walks with a cane. He may have various scars from war injuries on his lean body. He usually wears a turban and Arabian robes. *America's Most Wanted* sometimes has a display on their Web page that shows how Bin Laden would look using various disguises (www2.amw.com/amw.html).

The Reward

Chances of the average Joe spotting Bin Laden and collecting $27 million? Improbable. Despite his long reach, Bin Laden has not traveled much in his life, preferring to remain in a shrinking list of friendly Muslim countries in the Middle East. If he's still alive, he's most likely hiding in a remote area of Afghanistan or Pakistan, frequently changing his location and hauling what few belongings he has in a Japanese pickup truck. He is wanted in his own home country of Saudi

Arabia and can't return there. His followers, however, remain devoted and fanatical, and will do anything to shield, shelter, and protect their hero, who has become a symbol of radical Muslim, anti-American activism. If needed, he still has access to an unlimited family fortune.

"I don't know if he is dead or alive . . ." President Bush said on July 8, 2002. "If he is [alive], we'll get him. If he's not, we got him."

Captures and Replacements

· ·

On November 5, 2002—election day in America—
FBI's Most Wanted Number 471, James Spencer
Springette, was captured near Caracas, Venezuela.
Springette, a major drug smuggler who operated out of
Atlanta and Augusta, Georgia (see Chapter 8) was
tracked down through a joint effort of the FBI, U.S.
Customs, DEA, and the Richmond County Sheriff's
Office.

Springette was captured by Venezuelan military intelligence officers who boxed him in after he was spotted driving a car just outside Caracas. He attempted to
flee on foot, but was quickly rounded up without incident. Springette was in Venezuela for a vacation, and
was traveling alone without weapons or armed body-
guards. "He's been free for a long time, since 1999, so
I guess he felt safe," said Pat Clayton of the U.S. Drug
Enforcement Administration.

The Virgin Islands native was carrying the usual
false identification, but was recognized from his photo-

graphs. His identity was later confirmed by the FBI via his fingerprints.

The immensely wealthy cocaine smuggler, who is also wanted for the attempted murder of a British Virgin Islands police officer, was placed on the FBI's Ten Most Wanted list on April 25, 2002. He is the 446th Top Ten Fugitive to be arrested since 1950, and the sixth to be taken down in 2002. He's also the thirty-second top-tenner to be caught in a foreign country.

This, however, might not be the last we hear of the globe-trotting Springette. He was arrested in Medellín, Colombia in January 1999 but managed to escape from a prison in Bogota a month later. Fifteen prison employees were disciplined after the multimillionaire drug dealer was ferreted out of the facility inside a mattress.

Fearing a similar escape, U.S. officials made sure Springette was immediately extradited to Augusta. He appeared before U.S. Magistrate Judge W. Leon Barfield, a lightning-quick twenty-six hours after his arrest. He stood before Barfield in a wrinkled yellow shirt and jeans and confirmed that he was indeed James Spencer Springette. He was brought to the federal courthouse in a convoy of twelve marked and unmarked vehicles packed with FBI, DEA, and U.S. Customs agents, along with Richmond County Sheriff's deputies. U.S. Attorney Rick Thompson and Assistant U.S. Attorney J. Michael Faulker asked Judge Barfield to hold Springette without bail until his trial. The request was granted.

Springette's spot on the Top Ten List was taken three months later by Michael Alfonso, a.k.a. Michael Alfonso Johnson, a Spanish-speaking Illinois day laborer and sex offender accused of murdering two ex-girlfriends in the Wheaton area, a suburb of Chicago.

On June 6, 2001, police say Alfonso was lurking in the shadows when Genoveva Velasquez, twenty-eight, arrived for the breakfast shift at a McDonald's restaurant where she worked. Before she could enter the familiar restaurant, Alfonso approached, pulled a .38-caliber revolver from a duffle bag, and shot her five times, including the last few while she lay dying on the ground. Velasquez, a twelve-year McDonald's veteran who was twice named assistant manager of the year, died at the scene. The Glendale Heights resident was the mother of one child, an eight-year-old daughter, and worked two jobs to support both the girl and her own parents. She met Alfonso at her second job, a Pampered Chef's distribution center in Carol Stream, another Chicago satellite city. She worked there on the packing line while he operated a forklift.

Velasquez had called police about Alfonso hassling and threatening her the day before while they were both at Pampered Chef's. She had recently reconciled with her estranged husband, Abel, and that apparently set Alfonso off. Abel Velasquez worked at the same McDonald's as his wife and was there the morning she was gunned down.

Officers had patrolled the Velasquez home the previous night after the fireworks at Pampered Chef's, but found no sign of Alfonso. His threats caused alarm because he was both a criminal and former mental hospital patient who had been convicted of repeatedly raping a seventeen-year-old teenager in an apartment house lobby in 1990. He was sentenced to six years in prison for that offense, earning an early parole after serving a third of his term. He was arrested and convicted again upon his release for aggravated battery and possession of a weapon by a felon.

Despite the Wheaton McDonald's location in a typi-cally heavily trafficked spot near the Danada West Shopping Center, Alfonso was able to flee on foot after the shooting, vanishing into a residential area to the west. Police swarmed the area with trained dogs, but the trail quickly went cold—ironically enough behind a neighborhood Catholic church. Police believe he stashed his car there, a black, 1994 Pontiac Firebird, and made his getaway. The vehicle was found August 16, 2001, abandoned inside a long-term parking lot at the Indianapolis International Airport. It sat collecting dust for seven weeks before it was discovered during a routine check of license plates. There has been no sign of Alfonso since.

This wasn't the first time that the volatile misogynist responded with deadly rage after being rejected. Nine years before, in 1992, police believe the recently paroled Alfonso stalked and murdered another ex-girlfriend, Sumanear Yang, twenty-three, also of Wheaton. Alfonso exacted his vengeance upon Yang, a hairdresser, in early September of that year after she put an end to their brief relationship due to his disturb-ing behavior. After shooting her in the head, Alfonso dumped her body in a wooded area inside Silver Springs State Park located in Yorkville, Illinois. Her skeletal remains weren't discovered until November 9. Police had previously found Yang's car, set ablaze, in Chicago on September 18. Alfonso was the major sus-pect, but prosecutors were never able to build a strong enough case against him until the Velasquez murder. He thus skated—and lived to kill again.

Although the police and FBI have not charged him with any other deaths, it's possible, considering his track record, that Alfonso may have beaten, raped, and killed other women as well. His jacket is littered with domestic abuse reports and restraining orders filed against him by various women.

Michael Alfonso, of African/Spanish descent, was born June 26, 1969. He's short and wiry, five-feet-five, 150 pounds, has a scar on his chest under his left arm, and has a tattoo of the woman's name, "Blanca," burned into his shoulder blade. As far as investigators know, the mysterious Blanca remains alive.

The Wheaton-born killer is known to sport earrings in both ears and often can be found working out in area gyms. Aside from the Wheaton, Illinois area, he's wandered to Phoenix, Arizona; Columbus, Georgia; Memphis, Tennessee; Alabama, Mississippi and Puerto Vallarta, Mexico. He may be working as a forklift operator, a chef, or as a construction worker.

Alfonso is the 476th person to make the Top Ten Most Wanted Fugitives list. There's a $50,000 federal reward for his capture, plus another $10,000 offered by county and state law enforcement organizations, along with McDonald's Restaurants. He's considered armed and extremely dangerous, and has been featured on *America's Most Wanted* numerous times since July 2001.

On the rewards front, in March 2003, an Egyptian collected a cool $27 million for providing the information that led to the capture of Khalid Shaikh Mohammed, a top al Qaeda leader. Mohammed, said to be the terrorist organization's Operations Chief, helped plan and orchestrate the 9/11 attacks. He was nabbed in Pakistan, and had been on the FBI's Most Wanted terrorists list. The Egyptian, a former terrorist himself, moved out of the region after collecting the money.

On May 31, 2003, Olympic bombing suspect Eric Robert Rudolph was caught by a lone rookie police officer in Murphy, North Carolina, as Rudolph rummaged behind the Vally Village Shopping Center. It was 4 a.m., and the officer, J.S. Postell, thought Rudolph may have been either a burglar or a homeless person stealing late-night food deliveries. Rudolph gave up without resisting. After initially giving a phony name, he confessed his true identity at the police station.

Rudolph had been the object of an intense, five-year manhunt in and around the same area where he was finally found. He apparently had been living in a cave or caves in the Appalachian Mountains, not far from his boyhood home near Topton. (See Chapter 4.)

Since Rudolph was taken by a police officer, and was not apprehended as a result of a citizen tip, the $1 million bounty on his head was left on the table.

Rudolph's arrest came with a new theory as to why he went on his bombing spree: anger over the Food and Drug Administration's refusal to approve a cancer-fighting drug, laetrile, that he felt might have been able to save the life of his stricken father.

Epilogue

Future Top Tenners
. . . .

With the space program pretty much on hold, it doesn't appear that the Hans Solos and Boba Fetts of the world will be showing up on the FBI's Ten Most Wanted list any time soon. You can bet there's a big sigh of relief coming out of Washington over that. It's bad enough that the FBI now has to essentially police the entire world, much less expanding to the universe.

What kind of criminals can we expect to see listed over the next half century? More of the same, no doubt. Drug dealers, gangsters, serial killers, child molesters, cop killers, bank robbers, and prison escapees aren't going to fade away like the typewriter. They're certain to be represented well into Y2K.

There is one new breed of lawbreaker that is causing much concern. As the world becomes more and more dependent upon the Internet, the first cyber criminal is bound to pop up on the list any day now. It could be a computer hacker who brings a major government agency or corporation to its knees, someone who finds a way to shift money on a massive scale, an identity thief who ruins the credit ratings and lives of hundreds or thousands of unsuspecting people, or a scam artist who uses new technology to run the same old con games. More likely, however, it will be that strange creature who is to the virtual world what bombers, serial killers, and terrorists are to the real world—the virus creator.

The Internet was barely in its toddler stage before evil computer genius types with baffling motivations began sending out destructive viruses and "worms" with pleasant-sounding names like Melissa, Jerusalem, Tequila, Michelangelo, StrangeBrew, ILOVEYOU, Stages, Anna Kournikova, Code Red, and Klez. These malicious, predatory programs travel from machine to machine at the speed of light, eat through the critical operational software, and obliterate data stored on the hard drives and disks of business and home computers from one end of the world to the other. Already, dozens have infected the World Wide Web, causing billions of dollars in damages—all for nothing more than the sick amusement of their maniacal creators.

On May 29, 2002, the FBI announced that it was creating a new cybercrime division as part of a sweeping, overall reorganization of the historic agency. The beefed-up computer crime-fighting squad will expand upon the bureau's already established National Infrastructure Protection Center, the Feds charged with guarding the most critical computer networks from viruses and other attacks. Once this intensified cybercrime division gets on its feet, say around mid- to late 2004, expect to see the first cyber criminal's mug on the Most Wanted list.

Meanwhile, the main focus of the FBI for the immediate future will continue to be terrorists. The FBI is strengthening that division as well, increasing the number of agents and support staff assigned to terrorism from 2,178 to 3,718, and working closer with their brother agents at the CIA. The FBI is also creating a new central Office of Intelligence at their headquarters in Washington that will oversee domestic terrorism investigations and act as a link to the scattered Field Offices. The aim of the new division is to avoid the past problems associated with headquarters not being quick or insightful enough to heed and connect related warnings coming from agents outside Washington. The issue came to a head in May 2002, when it was revealed that two months before 9/11, an agent in the Phoenix FBI office, Kenneth Williams, sent a memo to Washington expressing concern that a rash of Arab nationals, Muslims, and potential terrorists, many with strongly stated anti-American beliefs, were training at flight schools in Arizona and other states. Some of these same Arabs ended up being part of the group that hijacked the 9/11 jets. This included Hani Hanjour, the man believed to have piloted the airliner that crashed into the Pentagon. Hanjour received his training at the JetTech flight school in Phoenix, a branch of the Pan Am International Flight Academy.

Similar concern had been expressed in Oklahoma and Minnesota. In addition, there were reports of flight school instructors being suspicious of Arab students wanting to learn how to steer and guide jets while being totally disinterested in how to land such aircraft.

"The events of September 11 marked a turning point for the FBI," Director Robert S. Mueller said in announcing the reorganization. "After 9/11 it was clear that we needed to fundamentally change the way we do business . . . Responding to post 9/11 realities requires a redesigned and refocused FBI. New technologies are required to support new and different operational practices. We have to do a better job recruiting, managing and training our work force; collaborating with others; and, critically important, managing, analyzing, and sharing information. In essence, we need a different approach that puts prevention above all else. Simply put, we need to change and we are changing."

Mueller, who was sworn in as director only a week before 9/11, specifically pointed to the Phoenix memo as a loophole that needed to be closed:

> . . . In the end, two things have come to symbolize that which we must change. First, what did not happen with the memo from Phoenix points squarely at our analytical capacity. Our analytical capability is not where it should be, but I believe that this plan addresses this . . . From new priorities, to new resources, to a new structure applying a new approach, I believe we are on the way to changing the FBI. And while we believe these changes to be a dramatic departure from the past, in the end our culture must change with them. Long before me, the bureau had years of major successes based on the efforts of the talented men and women who make up the FBI. It is a history we should not forget as we evolve to an agency centered on prevention.

> . . . It is a work in progress. We must continuously reevaluate where we are and how things are working. And, far more than in the past, we must be open to new ideas, to criticism from within and without, and to admitting and learning from our mistakes. As recent

events have made all too clear, the world is a dangerous place. Never before has this country depended so
heavily on the FBI to protect it at home. I am confi-
dent that the talented men and women of the FBI are
up to the task, and I believe that these changes will
help them achieve it.

Mueller meant business, because it didn't take long
for examples of a toughened-up and less restrained
FBI to emerge. On June 25, 2002, it was reported that
agents were squeezing librarians to gather information
on the reading habits of suspected terrorists. This particular crime prevention investigation technique was
called off in the 1970s after civil libertarians and other
activists called it an invasive abuse of power. It was
resurrected as part of the sweeping antiterrorism laws
enacted after 9/11.

The agents scouring library records were not only
seeking information on what books and magazines the
suspects were studying, but their computer terminal
use as well. In either case, they were obviously taking
note of flight manuals, bomb construction guides, military operation journals, biographies of revolutionaries
or anti-American foreign leaders, maps, and building
blueprints, to name a few. As expected, library direc-
tors and civil rights groups protested anew, but their
voices were muted by the still lingering horror of 9/11.

On the general crime front, the FBI also announced
in late June that preliminary figures showed that the
overall crime rate had risen for the first time in a decade. Based upon the turbulent year 2001, crime was
up two percent over 2000, the first time since 1991 that
the rate had increased. The figures held true for all the
individual areas except aggravated assaults, with car

thefts leading the way at a disturbing 5.9 percent increase, followed by robberies jumping 3.9 percent and murders 3.1 percent. Burglary (2.6), arson (2.0), larceny (1.4), and rape (0.2), were up as well. The only good news was that aggravated assaults were down 1.4 percent. The largest increases geographically were in the West, South, and Midwest.

Hang on. The second half century of the FBI's Most Wanted list promises to be an even wilder ride than the first.

Victim's Corner

• •

Below is a speech given by Emily Lyons, a former nurse at the New Women All Women clinic in Birmingham, Alabama. Lyons survived a bombing at the clinic that the FBI says was set off by Eric Rudolph, the same man they believe is responsible for a deadly explosion at Atlanta's Centennial Olympic Park in 1996 (see Chapter 4). Eric Rudolph is currently on the FBI's Ten Most Wanted list.

Hawaii, April 30, 2000

Thank you for allowing me this opportunity to tell my story. I was recently the speaker at the National Council of Jewish Women's conference in Dallas. Their theme for the evening was storytelling.

I believe that storytelling is how we learn about history. Stories (good or bad) have been passed down from generations to generations. If that process is stopped, people will forget the history that is needed to shape our future. For the next few minutes I want to give you a brief historical story of hatred and violence. After hearing it, I hope you will be able to pass this on to someone else.

As Steven Spielberg so eloquently put it in his documentary film regarding the Holocaust and some of its survivors—"We have to recognize that people are not born with hatred, they acquire it. We must listen to the voices of history so that future generations will never forget what so few have lived to tell."

Two and a half years ago this person who cared for people became a person who had to be cared for. January 29, 1998, was the turning point in my life. At 7:33 A.M. a bomb exploded outside the clinic where I worked. A Birmingham police officer was murdered and I was seriously injured. It is amazing how a few microseconds can change your life forever.

As you listen to this story caused by hatred and violence, I would like for you to try and imagine yourself in my shoes or my husband's, one of my children or parents, family member, or close friend. I want you to be able to feel how one event of extreme violence can be so devastating to your life or to someone you love.

On that fateful day, I went to work like any other day. A stranger attempted to kill me, using a pipe bomb, because he disagreed with my beliefs. We all have different opinions, values, and beliefs. They can be religious, cultural, ethnic, sexual, political, etc. Does this sound like a reason to kill someone?

I woke up two weeks later. Two weeks of my life passed away that I knew nothing about. As I began to come out of my long sleep, I realized something was very wrong. I couldn't talk because there was a tube in my throat to keep me breathing. I wasn't eating either, because there was a tube in my nose for that. My eyes would not open. Everything from head to toe was in tremendous pain. My extremities felt like large dead weights that wouldn't move unless someone moved them for me.

Once I was able to comprehend, they told me a bomb had been placed outside the clinic where I worked. It exploded about twelve feet from where I was standing. The pipe bomb contained dynamite and nails. It was aimed at the front door. If any of you believe that the person accused of this crime didn't intend to hurt anyone, THINK AGAIN!

The force of the blast was so strong that I was blown out of my shoes and my clothes were shredded. The fireball from a bomb reaches about 3,000 degrees centigrade. That's over 5,400 degrees Fahrenheit! I had first-, second-, and third-degree burns over most of the front of my body.

The bomb was packed with one- and half-inch nails. The FBI drove a crowbar into the ground where the bomb was placed. From there, they tied bright pink string to each nail stuck in the brick of the building. Just to the left of the center of the cone, the missing strings formed the outline of a person. There were no strings there because the nails were in me instead of the building. Several intact nails and dozens of fragments still remain inside me because it would do too much damage to remove them.

Officer Sanderson was bent over the bomb when it exploded. His body was literally torn apart. Because he was to the side, there were only a couple of nails in his body. The bomb was aimed at the front door, which is where most of the nails went. This device was not meant to close the clinic or to do property damage. The bomb was intended to murder.

To make sure that the bomber killed someone, he stood across the street and watched. When he decided that the two of us were as good as any to murder, he pressed the button and detonated the bomb by remote control. This was no less premeditated murder than someone walking up to a stranger with a shotgun and pulling the trigger.

Think about the odds of someone surviving a point-blank shotgun blast. A shotgun shell has a few grams of powder and some round pellets. I faced a stick of dynamite and dozens of nails.

According to a recent Discovery Channel show on bombs, the force kills a person within fifteen feet of the explosion. The shrapnel kills people for several feet beyond that. I was twelve feet from the bomb.

People heard and felt the explosion for miles around. It is amazing that I can hear at all. My left eardrum ruptured, which accounted for one of my eighteen operations.

The first thing the surgeon told my husband that day was that I had a hole about the size of a fist in my abdomen and that my intestines were exposed. Both my small and large intestines had to be resectioned, as there were areas that could not be repaired. When people say that I am a gutsy lady, they don't know how literal they are.

My right hand was mangled. The broken little finger did not heal correctly, so the bone is bowed. The middle finger had an open joint injury, meaning that it was torn apart at the joint. I will never be able to play the piano or write like I used to. That part of my life is gone.

The slogan for Timex used to be, "It takes a licking and keeps on ticking." The commercials would show watches that had been run over, dropped out of airplanes, etc. I had a twenty-year-old Timex. Guess it won't be featured on a Timex commercial, as it will forever display 7:33.

The force of the blast tore the flesh off both lower legs. Both bones were shattered in my left lower leg. Amazingly, my right leg did not break, but it did sustain more muscle loss and nerve damage than the left. My left leg had an external fixator, which is four screws drilled into the bone, connected by a metal rod on the outside of my leg. It took months to get my other leg out of a brace, but the day finally came. Due to nerve damage caused by an operation last December, I am back in the brace that I fought so hard to overcome. This time, it looks like it will be a permanent attachment.

For several days my legs were covered with pigskin. That slowed the blood loss down some, but I still had to be given several pints of blood over the first couple of weeks. As far as blood loss goes, you could say that I had a complete oil change the first day. Even though the emergency room was about four blocks away, I was down to one-third of my blood volume by the time I got to the hospital.

Skin will only grow over muscle, not bone. So, they split both of my calf muscles and wrapped part around to form what is called a muscle flap. They disconnect the motor nerves from that section, but leave the sensory nerves. When someone touches my leg, I feel it in a different place. They were able to find an undamaged section of my left thigh to be used as a donor site for the skin grafts that followed. The skin grafts took months to finally heal.

My legs sure don't look like they used to, but they are beautiful to my husband and I, considering they thought they might have to amputate. The vascular system was destroyed in my left leg, so they had to take the femoral vein of my right leg and turn it around to make it into an artery for my left.

Both knees have long scars where they were opened. There was so much shrapnel that the joints would not bend, so they had to be cleaned out. They were nailed into position.

I was in the hospital for eight weeks and two days, but who's counting. It took that long to go through the twelve-step program that was required before I could go home. The twelve-step program is not something where I get up and say, "My name is Emily. I am a bombing survivor." And the crowd says, "Hi Emily." It just so happened that there were twelve steps between the second and third floor of rehab. Learning to walk took me from requiring two people to set me up on the side of the bed, to them setting me in a chair, to a walker, to finally those steps. The day I finally made it to the top of those twelve steps, I was soaked with sweat, but you don't know how happy I was.

My right eye orbit and other facial bones were broken. The shear force of the blast was so strong that it tore my eyelids, which had to be sewn back on.

My left eye was torn apart by a stiff piece of wire approximately one inch long. Apparently, the wire was spinning when it hit, so it was torn into pieces and the remains had to be removed. My right eye was badly damaged, but some limited sight has been restored through a series of operations.

If you get a chance to look at the pictures that I brought, please look closely. I hope that you will not take for granted the everyday physical abilities you have. I also hope that the threat of being shot, beaten, stabbed, or bombed will make you think about how valuable your freedom of choice is. What happened to me could have happened to any of you.

Being blind is "interesting," for lack of a better word. It is so much more than not being aware of light. Even though I am a college graduate, I was suddenly illiterate. People sometimes think about being young again. Be careful what you wish for. Someone had to cook for me. Someone had to hold my hand if I wanted to walk a few feet, much less cross a street. Others described things to me that a normal adult would have recognized. Being a forty-two-year-old child is not what it is cracked up to be. I had committed no crime, but I was a prisoner. No bars were needed to hold me; I dared not venture beyond the confines of my room without sight.

Many women are imprisoned in this country without the use of bars. They are prisoners within their own bodies. They are unable to access the reproductive health care that they need. This is often due to misinformation, lack of resources, and ever-increasing restrictions placed on them by those who wish to control them.

Sight is such an important thing. The fact that I only have one eye and it has been damaged has made me treasure vision. There are varying degrees of blindness. In another way, I was blind before the bombing. I was blind to the facts involving the right to reproductive health. I didn't see that there were people out there who were willing to kill to take away our freedom of choice. Sure, they were always there. Yes, I knew in the back of my mind that it could happen. But I never, ever thought that it would involve me. Well, I guess you could say that I had a real "eye opener" on January 29 of 1998.

You should be outraged at the nationwide violence waged against reproductive health care providers. No one should tolerate this. No one in this country should have to endure harassment, scare tactics, intimidation, or bodily harm in order to seek, provide, or endorse reproductive health care.

We talk about "equal access." Here is a sober thought for you: In this day and time, the only thing equal about access to reproductive health care is that everyone has an equal opportunity of being injured or killed. I urge you to get involved so that our children will not face the same situation.

Our best means of fighting back is to passionately speak out. Are you truly passionate about your involvement regarding women's rights and access to all areas of reproductive health care?

If you are, then let people know it! Why would you want to be silent? Fear? Intimidation? It might ruin your career? If that is the case, then your silence is yet another victory for those who wish to control you.

If you're not passionate, what are you waiting for? What will it take? If you are not willing, then are you deserving of these freedoms and rights?

Our freedoms, especially freedom of choice, are in danger each and every day. Yes, I said our freedoms. What happened to me could have happened to any of you. This threat is not only from bombers, but also through the political system. Yes, America currently enjoys a political environment that allows choice. This could easily change. If people become complacent about our freedoms and rights, it will change. You have heard the phrase "Use it or lose it." I hope that you remember a slightly different phrase, "Defend it or lose it."

People in high and low places are attempting each day to erode away at our freedoms, by using whatever means possible. My injuries have taught me not to underestimate these people. They cannot be ignored.

Our freedom has been fought for by generations before us, just as we do today. Countless people have died in other countries for our freedom. Many have paid for our freedom with their lives here in the United States. Few things of such value come cheap. Our rights must be protected at all costs. I am here to tell you that it is worth the price.

People frequently ask, "Why do you do what you do? You were almost killed. Aren't you afraid? Why speak out and risk being hurt worse?" Part of the answer to the question is simple—I have a slight stubborn streak. The bigger answer is to let the suspect know that he failed. He did not silence me. He did not shut the clinic down. He did not create the silence he longed for. He did not instill the fear in me he had hoped for. If we allow fear to control us, then the opposing groups win. Instead of killing me, he made me a mentally stronger person, capable of reaching and educating more people than I could have ever imagined.

My husband's father was a prisoner in Germany in World War II. He talked about listening to the screams of someone who had been bombed during the war. We think of such things as only happening in a land far away, in a time long ago. It certainly should not be a story of our generation, and certainly not in America. His stories of the hate, the disregard for human life, the suffering, and the violence belong in the past. They should be part of a previous generation's life. Actually, they should not be a part of any generation, but we should have at least learned not to repeat the injustices.

A line of a song goes, "Teach your children well." We should have learned from past generations. We should not allow history to repeat. Yet, the violence continues. Make sure that our children do not follow in the footsteps of those like the person who tried to murder me.

I do not want this destructive event to happen to someone else. I want people to know that violence is not and never will be the answer to any situation in this country. If showing the world what my injuries are will avoid even one act of violence, then it is a worthwhile cause. For me, the story must be told.

It has been over twenty-seven years since *Roe* v. *Wade*. Who would have thought that twenty-seven years later we would still be fighting the same battle. At that time, we thought legalizing abortions was all that would be necessary. We were WRONG! We have to continually protect that right, day after day.

This may be the last year we will be able to celebrate the *Roe* v. *Wade* victory. As we all know, this year is politically crucial for men and women in this country regarding reproductive health care. Several Supreme Court justices will be leaving during the next presidential term. George Bush has already said that he will appoint their replacements based on their willingness to overturn *Roe* v. *Wade*. His stance has been that abortion at any stage is "unconstitutional," except in cases of rape, incest, or when the woman's life is in danger. He has given no legal basis as to why it is unconstitutional, only stating that America's heart has not been right in the past. Steve Forbes has said that Bush's position on abortion is too soft and said Bush [quote] "seems at heart to be pro-choice." Bush changed his stance on abortion after that statement. Now, he says that he will push for a constitutional amendment banning abortion without exception. If Bush wins, we lose. All that I, and others, have endured will be for nothing.

If those rights are taken away, history will repeat itself. I have said it before and will continue to say it. Women will control their bodies—even when faced with the possibility of death. Is that what we want for our future generations? I don't think so. It is so important that groups like this continue to fight to maintain those freedoms that we hold so dear to us.

Over twenty-seven years ago, the tide turned. Instead of the government deciding whether or not a pregnant woman should be forced into being a parent, now people who claim to be antigovernment feel that they should decide parental status for others. If someone disagrees with their views, then they feel that it is their God given duty to murder the person with the opposing opinion.

Officer Robert Sanderson was not the first to die at a clinic which provides reproductive services. Because of Dr. Slepian, Sandy's death was not the last associated with reproductive rights. The clinic bombing where I was injured and Sandy was murdered gained nationwide, if not worldwide, attention. It should. People must be told that the high price of violence is not the answer.

The clinic was closed for a week. None of the employees quit, patients either rescheduled or went to another clinic, a nurse was taken from another health field to fill my place, and an officer was taken from other law enforcement duties to provide security. If there is one thing that I would like to get across to people, it is that violence did not work.

What the violence did do was to make Officer Sanderson's wife a widow, who has to raise her two children alone. It mangled my body and cost Worker's Compensation Insurance around $750,000.00. Another $13.4 million have been spent in the search of the person accused of the crime. Violence not only fails, it is also expensive.

Perhaps some feel that laws to protect us are not needed because what happened to me was such a rare event. Indeed, this was the first time that a bomb was used to murder at a clinic. However, this type of terrorism is far from being an isolated event. The Army of God's handbook goes into great detail of how to illegally impede a woman's access to health care. The tactics range from Super Glue in the locks, concrete in the sewer system, where to put butyric acid in a building to get the best effect, and how to make a bomb. They even suggest that people with a terminal disease should wire their body with dynamite, go into a clinic and detonate themselves. They say, "Since you are going to die anyhow, you might as well take others with you."

You should have a blue handout of a map. This map gives some indication of how often these illegal tactics are used. The map was part of an article in the November '98 issue of the *Village Voice* entitled "The Terrorist Campaign Against Abortion." As you can see, the violence is spread from one end of the nation to the other. Please take the time to look at this map. This is a map of your country, which is under attack.

As you view the bombings, arson, and acid attacks, please keep in mind that things are actually worse. This map does not show any attempted offenses, just completed ones. No detail is given of activities less serious than an acid attack. Murders of doctors and other clinic staff that could not be directly linked to reproductive health are not listed.

You should also have another handout with numbers provided by NAF that tells the true story of how bad things really are. The handout even tells you that the actual number of incidents is most likely higher.

We all know that they use bombs, guns, knives, snipers, and chemical warfare. These are the weapons of war. However, their most important weapon is fear. The good news is that we decide how effective their primary weapon is. We decide if we are going to allow fear to keep us from doing our jobs. Bullies will control you for as long as you let them. Please keep this simple fact in mind: If you allow fear to hold you back, then they win.

Sadly, we know that violence is not only tolerated, it is encouraged. Each year, a dinner is held called the White Rose Banquet. This banquet honors criminals who have been sent to prison for murder of reproductive health care providers. The person suspected of the bombing in my case is a hero to them.

Someone has asked me what type of law I thought would have prevented the bombing. No law can stop someone who is willing to face the punishment for murder. However, there are things that must be done to alter the environment that created the bomber.

A brief victory was won last year against the clinic worker's hit list placed on the Internet. The so-called "Nuremburg Files" was a list of providers, including the names, addresses, and sometimes photographs of their spouses and children. When a provider was murdered, their name had a line drawn through it. Those who were injured, including myself, were grayed out. This site, which glorified and encouraged murder, was temporarily taken off the Internet, only to return a few months later. Even though it has returned, at least it was removed for a while.

Other sites remain unchallenged, like the one maintained by Reverend Trosch at www.trosch.org. There is even a section devoted to my injury and the glorification of the person accused. This type of violence worship creates the environment that yields hate, which leads to violence, which often results in murder.

There are plenty of opportunities for change. Not only do we need more laws to deter the violence, we must also fight to keep the tools we have. You can make a difference. The fact that you are here says a lot. You are here to support our freedom. We all know that your support and your work, through various means, are to protect a woman's right to an abortion and adequate reproductive health care. However, it is far more outreaching than that. Your work helps to ensure that women and providers at clinics are not maimed, mutilated, or killed.

We have a government for the people, by the people. Well, you are "the people." Vote for those who will help protect your freedoms. Begin and/or continue talking with those in political office. Educate everyone who will listen. Encourage tolerance—not just in this matter, but other areas as well. Continue your support of Reproductive Rights. Get involved in change for the better.

If there is not a continued change for the good, then there will be more fatalities like:

Dr. Barnett Slepian

Robert Sanderson

Leanne Nichols

Sharron Lowney

James Barrett

Dr. John Britton

Dr. David Gunn

and others who felt it was important for women to have that freedom of choice. Why do I list these people? They died for our freedom. The least we can do is to remember them. I can only hope that the next President will not make their sacrifice meaningless.

My husband and I often joke about B. B. and A. B., "Before Bomb" and "After Bomb." It seems that one event separates two lifetimes.

Before the bomb, I was not very outspoken. I went to work, I did my job, I went home. At one point in my career, I tried to teach. However, the idea of getting up in front of twenty to thirty people was terrifying to me. You would never have found me speaking to a crowd such as today. Things have changed. One of my "after bomb" sayings is that "not much intimidates you after you have been blown up."

The former governor of Oregon was the M.C. at a NARAL event last year where I spoke. She became outspoken when the school system would not allow her autistic child to attend public school. She said, "The average person is one injustice away from being an activist." How true. The blast only lasted a few microseconds, but has changed my life forever. I now know how easy choice can be taken away from us, especially by the antiabortion extremists. I hope that you will not wait for an injustice to happen to you like mine. Go into action NOW!

In 1998 the journey seemed endless. There were so many days during my rehabilitation that I had no idea how I was going to find the strength to continue. I was able to find my strength by the realization of one very simple fact—I had to. If I wanted to walk again, I had to find a way to endure the hydrotherapy. I had to find the strength to take a few steps each day. If I was to free myself of that hospital room, I had to find the strength to go forward. If we want to continue to be free, then we have to find the strength to fight those who would take our freedoms away from us.

I have always been pro-choice, but the threat of losing that choice never seemed real. Somewhere in the back of my mind, I knew that there were people out there who threatened our freedom. The protesters were always present, just like the thought of a bomb or a shooting. It was easy to ignore the protesters, and a bomb was just something that might happen in some other town.

No threat seems real until it happens to you. I never thought that I would be here today talking with you about surviving a bombing.

I have had my wake-up call. I can tell you, the threat is so very real.

During a visit to New York, I saw a pro-choice ad. It

read, "Of all the things from the '70s to make a come-back, there's one we really hate to see." It showed a Volkswagen and a Lava lamp. Then it showed a coat hanger. Let us do our part to make sure that stays a clever advertisement instead of our reality.

I have two teenage daughters, ages fifteen and nine-teen. Reproductive choices have been legal their entire lives. I hope they will understand—the fact that people won their rights before they were born does not make their freedom of choice any less valuable. Their rights are still in danger, and we must all do everything we can to protect them.

Sometimes I search for the strength to keep going. I am reminded of a line in a song, "How do you pick up the pieces and go on?" I found the answer from a line in another song: "I get by with a little help from my friends."

Women have a friend in each of you. Your presence here shows that you believe in women's freedoms and you are willing to be involved in protecting those free-doms. You do so at the risk of your own lives. I have said it before, and I will say it again. Freedom, like most things of value, has a very high price.

The determination that you show in protecting re-productive rights for all women and men across this country is not only essential to them, but also ex-tremely important to me. Your work is a constant re-minder for me that people are indeed dedicated to standing up for women's rights and freedom of choice. Your commitment lets me know that what I have endured for the past two years has not been in vain.

Without your continued support of reproductive rights, there may not be adequate resources available for the ever-increasing demand for reproductive health care in the twenty-first century.

I would like to leave you with a question to think about: What is reproductive freedom worth to you and are you willing to pay that price?

Thank you for allowing me to share my story with you today.

Emily Lyons, R.N.
Clinic Bombing Survivor

To contact Emily Lyons to have her appear before your group:

Emily Lyons
267 W. Valley Avenue #365
Homewood, AL 35209
emily@emilylyons.com